THE BRIGHTER SIDE OF A DEATH THREAT

Reflections, opinions & recollections of an ordinary bloke on an extraordinary journey through life, with all its challenges & rewards.

by **LANCE SMITH**
AKA SIR CUMFERENCE

The Brighter Side of a Death Threat

ISBN: 978-0-9945307-4-5
© 2020 Lance Colbert Smith
All rights reserved.

No part of this book may be used or reproduced in any manner whatsoever without the written permission of the author, except in the case of brief quotations embodied in critical articles or reviews.

Published in Australia by Rainbow Works Pty Ltd. Pottsville, NSW.
Cover design by Marney Atkins-Smith
First Edition: March 2020

DISCLAIMER

Rainbow Works Pty Ltd is committed to publishing works of quality and integrity. In that spirit, we are proud to offer this book to readers; however, the story, the experiences, and the words are the author's alone. The author claims everything written here is true, but it may not be entirely factual. Events and characters are portrayed to the best of the author's memory, but memory is not always entirely reliable and is always coloured by opinion and perception. As in all memoirs, events may be compressed, some details altered, and some stories slightly embroidered to better entertain. The writing style is the author's, preserved in editing regardless of technical correctness, in order to accurately convey the author's inimitable, fun and irreverent personality and manner.

The author, editor and publisher acknowledge trademark rights relating to any and all companies and products referenced herein.

DEDICATION

I dedicate this tome to my long suffering, beautiful love: Helen, and our wonderful outback angels, Rob and Deb.

CONTENTS

Dedication	3
Introduction	7
From the city to Broken Hill	9
Coffs Harbour	15
Bathurst	19
Coota-Bloody-Mundra	23
Lakemba and Punchbowl High School	31
London Fire Brigade / Europe—and the U.K.	37
Homeward bound and Jolly Roger	43
Discovering Australia—from Kings Cross to Daydream Island	47
Daydream Island and the Whitsundays	53
Sale and Lakes Entrance to Batemans Bay	67
Beautiful Batemans Bay	75
'A Fabulous Reid'!	105
The George Bass Surfboat Marathon	111
Country Comfort and Thredbo	117
The brighter side of a death threat	135
Bear Cottage and the Celebrity Cavalcades	147
The magical Hills and centre stage	157
Tamworth Country Music Festival	175
Queensland Here We Come Again	181
The Outback Trailblazer and Angel Flight	201
Hummingbird House Children's Hospice	227
It's farewell from me	231
About the Author	236

INTRODUCTION

"Write the book, Dad."

"Tell us another story, Pa."

I've been hearing it for years. Well, the time has come.

In the process of writing and recording those memories, I am even more mindful of the wonderful journey I have been fortunate enough to travel. Now, away from all the hustle and bustle, I can reflect on the laughs, the joy, the experiences of life's challenges and be very grateful to so many for such an incredible innings.

I hope these pages bring a smile to those I really cherish, and I thank all my family and mates for enriching my world. Without you, these pages would be blank. The wisdom of those past and present is my inspiration. I just hope these recollections cause you to keep dreaming.

I have long believed those who say, "In life you only need three bones":

- a wish bone
- a backbone and
- a funny bone

To wish is a positive—nothing happens unless we first dream.

The drive to turn it into reality and do it is a bonus, and

A sense of humour is a must.

Many of you know I have taken many leaps of faith without a safety net—hence all the broken bones. Failure is not falling down; it is staying down. When you get to my age, you have made heaps of mistakes if you have lived your life properly.

Over eight decades, and in many countries, I've had countless highs, lots of pot holes and a wealth of wonderful and character-building experiences. Through it all, an amazing assortment of friends, family and colleagues have kept this lucky bloke reasonably on the straight and narrow.

Yes—I've been blessed! And then some.

From a father who was one of the lowest forms of life and a beautiful mum who left us far too early, my three siblings and I have survived the many challenges of life and, each in our own different ways, have arrived at the peak of a majestic mountain and been able to soak in the pleasure of those spectacular views.

But it hasn't been easy. No way.

As the sun is setting on this old fellas memories, I must pen some of those great experiences, the millions of belly laughs, the many failures, the challenges, some fabulous outcomes and some hair raising moments.

Along the way, one thing stood out: a lesson I was grateful to learn; something that threw the word 'petty' out of my dictionary. For almost 20 years we ran the 'Children's Hospital Express'. The unbelievable Sister Chrissy, Doctor Michael and the doctors and nurses from the Camperdown Children's Hospital Oncology Clinic (later Westmead) and those brave young kids on our annual Ten Day Queensland Extravaganza, all staring death in the face: their ability to laugh, their zest for life, and their amazingly positive resilience taught me the 'Brighter Side of a Death Threat'.

They will feature prominently in the following pages—and will fare much better than some others.

It takes a cast of thousands to complete one of life's greatest-ever tales of comedies and tragedies—and some will be miffed. Many will laugh as they remember. Some may even applaud.

Yes, there will be the odd exaggeration and 'filling' in the gaps, but by and large my memories—good and bad—of a wonderful journey deserve airing. They show a rich tapestry of life.

To those who don't fare too well—forget legal action. There is nothing left. I spent it all having fun and loving life.

Now read on…

CHAPTER ONE
FROM THE CITY TO BROKEN HILL

Imagination is the highest kite you can fly.
...Lauren Bacall

In the beginning—10th January 1943—Sydney.

A son, Lance Colbert Smith, to Albert Smith, Architect, and Jean Langham Smith (nee Dawson), bookkeeper.

My wonderful mum, Jean, was born in Molong, N.S.W., 26th May 1920. She was a 'premie' baby as my Grandmother, Constance Haldane Ann Dawson, (nee Croft) had fallen out of a carriage and brought on the birth. (That might explain things!).

As a child, Jean was apparently a tomboy: broken arms twice, falling out of high trees and the like. She was a great girl.

The family had a large farm in Molong and Mum remembers, sadly, standing on the balcony of their homestead after a drought, watching the bank auction their property and then evict them.

When a student at NEGS, Armidale, Mum had her left hand fingers broken in winter, by teachers, to make her write right handed.

After losing the farm, Grandfather Lance took on a teaching role at Tudor House, Moss Vale, and later they shifted to Sydney.

LANCE SMITH

Funny story: Grandfather Lance's family were very wealthy and owned a shipping company. Connie's mother was a servant in their household. Grandfather Lance fell in love with Connie. The family disapproved—a commoner. Lance stood his ground, and the family refused to go to the wedding.

On the wedding day, Grandfather thought it proper to call in and say goodbye to his mother and younger siblings before catching the train to their honeymoon destination—Wallacia, south of Sydney. His mother and the two children offered to walk with him and Connie to the ferry. Then they decided to catch the ferry to Circular Quay with them, and finally the bus to Central—very strange. Even stranger when mother and children produced train tickets to Wallacia. Grandfather's mother had steamed open the envelope of the letter sent to the Wallacia accommodation and then booked the room next to them.

Grandfather was very annoyed. He then extended his and Connie's stay on the proviso they did not allow his mother and siblings to stay as well.

Mum often told us the story about Sheila and herself at school. Dorothea McKellar, in those days, lived on Scotland Island, Pittwater. Apparently a real snob, she thought Jean and Sheila were well above 'the pack', and often waited outside their school in her latest model Rolls Royce and gave them a lift home—our early brush with fame.

Grandfather Lance died of pancreatic cancer, aged 50. Grandmother Connie died at Manly, aged 98, and Mum died in Canterbury Hospital in 1972, aged 52, with her sister Sheila and my brother and sisters by her side. Sheila died recently aged 96.

Mum was a very beautiful, loving and caring soul. She and sister, Sheila, were really close.

I remember Mum's funeral at St. Clements Church, Mosman, well, and her mum, Connie, crying and sobbing very loudly and for ages. It was a horrible day.

Perfect segway—talking of horrible: my father Albert. Mum met my father at Newport Surf Life Saving Club. The less said the better: a gambler, drunk and born loser. The only good I can say is that he had three siblings—

THE BRIGHTER SIDE OF A DEATH THREAT

Stan, Isabelle (sis) and Harry. All top people. He died at 84, and seven people attended his funeral. I didn't.

Albert was a government architect and was regularly moved, hence our living in Sydney, Broken Hill, Coffs Harbour, Cootamundra and back to Sydney in those early years.

Early Memories

Where do I start?

My pre-teens at All Saints College in Bathurst? A 17-year-old alone in Egypt and the Suez Canal? An 18-year-old in the London Fire Brigade? All escaping one thing... a spiteful father. Or do I start with driving tow trucks at great speed in Sydney as a teenager—or as an entertainer on Daydream Island? Many choices.

I guess it should start way back.

I am told my first memory should have been the night in Mosman when the Japanese midget submarine torpedoed the nearby HMAS Kuttabul. My parents thought we were being bombed and put me in a box under our heavy dining room table—but no. I do not remember. I was only one year old.

I do remember getting my tonsils out at Mena House, Mosman, at age 3, and all the ice cream and jelly I could eat. But I also remember the stench of the ether mask they shoved over my face to knock me out.

We lived, for two years, with our relatives in Condamine Street, Balgowlah. We had no money. I can still smell the delicious aroma of the cakes from the Sydney Road bakery—but we were rarely able to afford them. Mum's sister, Sheila, talks of my father's horrific and brutal treatment of me: a sign of things to come. I was four.

My first clear memory is in Broken Hill. We were living in a Government house and Mum took me to my first ever theatre—a pantomime—*Dick Wittington and His Cat*. It was in a small hall, and I vividly remember booing at the villain and cheering on the hero. It had a lasting impression on a four-year-old. It sure set my imagination on fire!

LANCE SMITH

My first attempt to escape my father was when I was four. I came home from school, couldn't find Mum in the house so asked him where she was. He advised, "She has gone to live with the Aborigines in the hills." Later that afternoon, Mum returned home and asked where I was. Father told her I was 'playing with friends', so the alarm was not raised until after dark.

I was spotted by a driver in his headlights on the side of a dirt road out of town, heading to the hills and the Aboriginal settlement. He took me back to town and the police.

Then—Christmas 1948, aged five—the second time I 'left home'. I recall I took brother Barry—then three—for a walk, before our parents woke up. Along Thomas Street were two buses lined up to take the families of the Broken Hill Mines to their annual picnic, a few hours away, at Silverton. Somehow I convinced the driver of the last bus that our parents had left on the bus in front, so he took us.

Some five hours later we heard the siren as the Broken Hill police arrived to take Barry and I back to Broken Hill and our parents. We were well fed, looked after, and watered by the miners. We even got a present from Santa and the police gave us ice creams. I guess we were the 'unstolen' generation.

My third attempt to run away was more successful—in Coffs Harbour—but that's a later story.

I also remember sister Franny being born in January 1949 in Broken Hill hospital—those big brown eyes—and then 'bubby Joe'. Marcia completed the quartet in January '50, again in Broken Hill Hospital. The four musketeers began their journey, and, yes, I do remember stealing the goldfish from our neighbour's fish pond, and fracturing Barry's skull with a rock for telling on me… but he got even. He stabbed me. But I lived—the start of many survivals. And I also remember the magnificent Sturt Desert Peas—still my favourite flower, along with the Coffs Christmas Bells.

The four musketeers are still great mates—seventy years on.

I must point out our parents never had a car or a licence, (Mum's early lessons in the Braithwaite's Ford Anglia were an absolute disaster) and we never had a penny—so we never went anywhere.

When we shifted to Broken Hill, my father told Mum he had paid the removal insurance. A lie. Lots of their wedding presents were smashed…

THE BRIGHTER SIDE OF A DEATH THREAT

and no insurance.

Albert was a gambler (very unsuccessful), a drunk, and forged Mum's signature to get her meagre savings to pay his gambling debts—in between belting me to prove his manliness and power.

Mum was allowed to go to the movies once a week. He would give her ninepence: threepence for the bus and sixpence for the ticket. Nothing to eat or drink.

The one skeleton from Broken Hill is that we are told Mum finally found love, in the form of one John Francis, a local mine worker who lived three doors up. I only found out years later, and I wish we had got to know him. I am just thankful Jean may have had some love/joy in her life. Ancestry DNA tests have now confirmed all the rumours. Great story.

I was eight when we left 'the Hill' to go to my fathers next posting—Coffs Harbour. After Broken Hill, the sand, the ocean, the fishing off the jetty—a new world! Imagine that.

CHAPTER 2.

COFFS HARBOUR

There are no mistakes, only lessons.
...Chinese Proverb

We lived between Top Town and the jetty, in the last house in Barry Street (no longer there), on the edge of the bush. A track led to the Coffs racetrack, the aerodrome and all the creeks and caves in between, and lots of bush trails.

I remember all this because it was my 'territory'—where I could escape to. I loved creek fishing. First up, a bent pin tied with cotton and 'dough' to catch Gudgeons. Then the Gudgeons as bait to catch eels. Finally the fire to roast the eels. My trusty shanghai felled many a pigeon—also roasted on my fire and eaten, along with yams I used to dig up and fry. It was just me, my beautiful Christmas Bells and my imaginary friends. Butterflies were all fairies in my private garden… they still are.

I well recall Albert tying my wrists together with a rope looped over the long clothesline in our backyard and whipping me with a jug chord every time he could catch me. There was no escape, and no one ever came to my rescue.

One day, following a hell of a whipping, I decided to leave home. My third attempt. I was ten. I convinced my trusted school friend, Duncan

Brown, to leave with me. We took a loaf of fresh bread, butter and jam from his place and headed into the bush with my shanghai and fishing 'tackle' to live. Barry tells me the police were summoned next day, and he took them to all my known haunts. They did not find us, though they came close at the WW2 bunkers.

One night, when we were light on tucker, I decided to make a raid on our house—a stupid decision. I fell asleep in a suitcase under the house and slept in. They were waiting, and I was caught and returned to my 'hell' with a very stern warning from the police. I was kept apart from Duncan as a punishment. Another lesson.

Duncan died a few months later of Leukaemia—aged 11. My first brush with a loss. I think that was one of the few times I questioned the purpose of life.

Coffs did produce some great memories. My first brush with fame: I met (separately) famous wartime pilot Douglas 'tin legs' Bader, and 'The Lithgow Flash'—Marjorie Jackson. Both arrived at Coffs Airport… on a Butler Airlines DC3.

I taught little brother Barry, then aged seven, to ride a bicycle. I took him to the top of Hospital Hill, sat him on the bike and let go the seat. I now realise I should have checked the brakes first. His broken fingers pointed in some odd directions and the bones stuck out. Oops… more whippings.

Wirth's Circus came to town. There was a train crash—one of them was the Circus train. One elephant and, I think, five lions escaped. Instant radio broadcasts and police with megaphones up and down all streets 'stay indoors—do not go outside'.

Our mum saw absolutely no reason why we should be deprived of one second of education and I remember her opening the front door, checking left and right and told me to 'look after your little brother and watch out for lions' as she shut the door behind us. I remember us being the only students to arrive at school that day from the entire district and Headmaster, Mr. Bloomfield, was bewildered. Brother Barry reckons there were a few others.

I well remember going to sea in Harry Fanning's trawler many times, to deliver supplies to the Lighthouse Keepers family on Solitary Island. There

THE BRIGHTER SIDE OF A DEATH THREAT

were no beaches—just cliffs. Supplies and people were winched off the trawler by crane in a huge cane basket and hauled high up to the cliff-top to a small landing platform. Then we trawled a fishing line for hours on the return cruise to the mainland.

I was taught to swim. I remember my first rip at Park Beach. Frightening.

The night we were fishing off the mile-long Coffs jetty, Barry hooked a trevally—and in he went. Yes, the trevally dislodged the seven-year-old from the jetty, and he fell a long way into the shark-infested harbour waters.

Years later, I realised the jetty was only 200 metres long and—even at low tide—only about three metres from the water. But through young eyes, it was a mile long and 50 feet above water. Oh—and I don't think anyone has ever been taken by a shark in the harbour itself.

I do remember over twenty inches of rain in one day. Bucketing down.

But I can also remember the first time I ever saw sharks attacking bait fish. We were standing atop the southern headland at Coffs, looking down at a massive black ball of bait fish and the sharks peeling through the waves to attack—fascinating. I was to vividly remember this later in life when I was caught up in a similar situation when surfacing from a dive—but that comes later.

I remember the awesome sight of sugar cane night fires in the Dorrigo mountains.

I learnt to drive in Coffs—aged nine. Tom Davis, the aircraft refueller, often drove us along the airstrip at the 'drome. He taught Duncan and I how to drive. Wow. Along the airstrip in his old Riley. Short gear stick. We felt so grown up!

Aged 10, the news broke—my good life was about to begin. Jean had a bright idea of how to save me from Albert. She had been hiding money—enough to send me off as a boarder to All Saints Boys College at Bathurst. I will be forever grateful for my two-years-reprieve as I was packed off from Coffs— to re-appear at Cootamundra in 1955.

The only thing I would really miss was my bush 'territory' and those magnificent Christmas Bells that grew wild. Sadly, I think they are now extinct.

CHAPTER 3

BATHURST

If your ship doesn't come in—swim out to it.

All Saints College Bathurst, in 1953, introduced me to many things. One was the fairer sex. Marsden Girls College was on the other side of the Macquarie River—and Bathurst was freezing. But the only way I was able to impress Marion Whitley, aged 12, was to swim across the Macquarie River in the winter dark, to Marsden, and sneak in.

One of my college tasks was to feed the pigs in the lower paddock. I would make it late afternoon and sneak to the riverbank and swim like mad. I got pneumonia three times in two years—and then Marion left!

Years after leaving All Saints, they combined with Marsden to be a co-ed college. Story of my life—a man before his time!

Being a poor kid, a rich school had its challenges—the 'shop' supplied all necessities—toothpaste, brushes, boot polish—even snacks. There were only three kids barred from the shop. You guessed it! I was one. The items were charged back to parents and Albert never paid his bills—so I was on the banned list. However Albert still managed to pay for his many affairs and one night stands and his mounting gambling debts.

One of the rich kids—from Dubbo—gave me a penny once a month, and I would walk into Bathurst the next Saturday morning and buy one penny's worth of broken biscuits from a lovely old lady at Moran and Cato's. She always filled a huge brown paper bag. I was in heaven.

I still remember the Fijian Rugby Union team playing a match on our school oval—wow! And most of them were bare footed in the winter.

The coldest I can ever remember was playing under 12's rugby in Blayney. The ice in the puddles on the field cracked as we ran through the grass in minus two degrees, and the morning mist was eerie. It was freezing.

One of my school tasks was to stoke the hot water boilers—so I used to put my school shoes in the furnace and heat them up. Paradise.

And I fondly remember the 8.30 p.m. cocoa—after night prep. Delicious and steaming hot! Then I would go to sleep in our dormitory—illegally listening to my crystal set. Life was good in Barton House.

In 1954, All Saints staged the biggest and best Coronation Ball in Bathurst. 11-year-old primary kids we were only allowed to look in the windows, but I can still see the decorations and the **huge** crown on the stage. The only photo I ever kept of my first eleven years on earth… and when I sent it back to the college, forty years later, I was awarded Life Membership of the 'Old Bathurstians' and they put it on the front cover of the 'VIM Magazine'—very posh.

Probably the first man I ever looked up to was our headmaster, Mr. Ted Evans. He knew I had no money, no privileges, and he looked after my interests and saw to it that I didn't miss much. Years later, I realised it may well have come out of his pocket.

I remember him telling me, "Be yourself—every one else is taken!"

I kept in touch with Mr. Evans for some forty years. He remained stern and wise right up to his death and I last spoke face-to-face with him in Sydney, 1992. Long retired, he was still working on college projects, and I remember being very proud when he came to see 'Fiddler' at the Hills Centre, along with 40 other All Saints 'Old Boys & partners', in 1990.

THE BRIGHTER SIDE OF A DEATH THREAT

Backstage, he said to me, "It isn't where you come from, it's where you're going that counts." Wise words.

I also remember collecting sugar cane with my classmates and drying it. Straight after we sang in the school church choir on Sunday, we would sneak down to the riverbank and smoke dead cane. I ended up with 'Yellow Jaundice' and stayed in the sick bay over school holidays whilst the other kids all went home. C'est La Vie…

And, once, just once, we were taken by bus to drive around the famous Mt. Panorama race track. Awesome. Sixty-four years later, I had my 75th birthday party at Rydges Resort on Conrod Straight. Memories.

But all good things come to an end. Albert lost all our money and I was taken out of All Saints to do my first year of High School at Cootamundra.

CHAPTER 4

COOTA-BLOODY-MUNDRA

The very least you can do in your life is to figure out what you hope for. And the most you can do is to live inside that hope, not admiring it from a distance, but live right in it— under its roof.

…Barbara Kingsolver,
American novelist.

Coota may not be everyone's first choice for a bonzer holiday—but it was a great place to start my teenage years. I hated the thought of living back with Albert—but Bathurst taught me there was an outside world, and I just needed to figure out how to escape and explore. I soon had high hopes and plans to do this.

Coota has many memories—good and bad—I became a teenager there! It was a town divided by religion. We were not supposed to talk to our neighbours, the Hukins and the Pigrams. They were Catholics. I forgot and paid the price.

My first 'job' was washing bottles at Beddies Pharmacy, then working in Cohens store school hols and Saturdays. My favourite part was making milkshakes and drinking the leftovers. I then got the two paper runs with Pinkstones at the 'Coota Herald', which Les Drane and I had for two years plus. I started collecting old newspapers and reselling to the butcher in Parker Street and collecting bottles for refunds. The Coota footy matches were a gold mine. I was rich!

I saved up and bought a real football. Three pounds four shillings and sixpence—a fortune. I couldn't wait to get to the park and my first kick was on the footpath in front of our house—under a truck and exploded, flattened, caput!

Talking of footy, Coota was in Group 9 and the Maher Cup era. The night we beat Gundagai and won the cup is forever etched in the brain. Coota had the only Railway Station in N.S.W. where the lines went north, south, east and west—even Central only went three ways then. The first we knew was when all the steam train whistles started when the team came home. Then the two truck/trailers—one with the Town Band, the other with the team and the cup—going up and down Wallendoon and Parker Streets for hours and the whole town lining the streets, singing, waving and dancing. Boy—what a celebration.

Talking of dancing, John Lord (who lived opposite us and was in my class) and I fancied ourselves as top swimmers, and our coach suggested we take up tap dancing to strengthen our leg muscles. We signed up for the Molly Windred School of Dance, and when the famous 'Sorlies' stage show came to town in 1957, over 60 years ago, John and I opened the show tapping and singing *California Here I Come*— played on the piano by Stan Bourne—my first stage appearance.

Talking of swimming—Coota did have a pretty strong team, but we had a stand out champion, Julie Lake. Julie's dad, 'Horrie', was our barber (yep—I did have hair at 13).

One weekend we were heading to the championships at West Wyalong and stopped for a break in Temora. Some bought a fruit juice drink. In the middle of her race, Julie doubled up in the pool and sank. Everyone dived in. Ptomaine poisoning. It was a 'Pharlap' reaction. Our champion had been nobbled. The orange juice in Temora! Julie later became Julie Ceeney and John, Julie and I ended up in Batemans Bay and still close 60 years later.

THE BRIGHTER SIDE OF A DEATH THREAT

They are both gems.

Les Drane and I managed to get into a fair bit of trouble. We started catching goannas for pets. Didn't go over too well when we let one of them loose in his dad's paint shed.

Then we would cycle south of town to 'the gap' where the steam trains roared over the highway viaduct. We used to climb up onto the rail bridge, crawl along the lines, and hide in the concrete hole underneath as the trains went over us. Got scalded a couple of times.

Les's dad was a fox hunter, and we used to go out predawn and climb mountains to get downwind and lie in wait. Mr. D. had a fox whistle, and the three of us had .22 rifles.

I remember the awesome sight one morning when the sun came up and we were above the clouds, with just a few hills poking through—spectacular and silent…

At school, Spencer George was the teacher in charge of assembly, and Les and I were regularly sent to Mr. Whenholzes office (Deputy Head) to be caned for some made up misdemeanour.

The worst thing about school was the mandatory milk. **Yuk**! We would watch it sitting in the sun till playtime and be made to drink it hot! Then, as soon as I rode home, Mum would make us drink Scotts Emulsion—every day—to ward off the milk germs.

But one thing I remember well at school was the kids from the Aboriginal girls home: the so-called 'stolen generation'. Those girls were impeccably presented every day. They really liked their stern old Matron Hiscock and did well in all areas of school and sport. Great kids. I don't get too caught up in the rights and wrongs, but I am sure they got it wrong sometimes and right at other times. That is bureaucracy, still today. But I am also sure each of those girls got a great education and pathway to adulthood.

The movie *Jedda* came out. Our first colour movie and our first with Indigenous leads. Awesome.

Where I do get angry is for the 130,000—yes, one-hundred-and thirty-thousand—little kids taken from England, Scotland, Wales and Ireland—many under false pretences—and brought out here as 'fodder' for despicable so called 'carers'. No one seems to stand up for them.

LANCE SMITH

It was also in Coota when I was 'got at'. Mum sent us to Church and Sunday School every Sunday, and everyone thought it was wonderful that my Sunday School teacher took such an interest in me. They didn't see the raping, the threats and the hurt and dirt I carried for many years. I totally get it when I see oldies today still scarred. Fortunately, I was given a great coping mechanism.

That was life for me. A paedophile at church, caned regularly at school and belted continuously at home. I just presumed that was life's normal.

I remember Coota had a visiting 'Reverend', and it was expected that each family feed him one night. His name was Reverend Proudman.

Our eyes opened when we saw the feast. It was very special—a midweek roast lamb instead of rabbit. We kids had been drilled, in the lead up days, on how to say 'Amen' at the end of the Grace.

The Reverend would have thought us very 'normal', until sweets. We never had sweets except on those rare occasions, and our youngest, Marcia, —or Bubby Jo to us—gave us up. She asked, "Do we have to say prayers for the pudding too?"

In those days our bread, milk and ice all arrived by horse and cart and I have wonderful memories of Sunday nights—lights out, fire crackling and the radio on, listening to *Sunday Night At The Movies*. Every week my imagination took me far away to beautiful places. I always knew there was such a world. I just had to escape and find it. I remember *Night Beat, Randy Stone, Bob Dyer, Jack Davey* and the *Adventures Of Smoky Dawson*.

I sure blotted my copy book when Grandma Connie came from Sydney on a big steam train to look after us kids while Mum and my father went on a rare trip away—to go to a wedding. I decided to get square with Icky (Barry) for dobbing me in, just because I made Fran and Marcia pretend to be ghosts with sheets over their heads and run in front of cars at night. They took my threepence pocket money, so I couldn't go to the Globe Theatre!

So—we had one very dark room which was a short cut from the hall to the kitchen. I tied a rope taut about a foot off the ground and screamed out to Barry for help. Old Connie got there first, tripped over the rope and broke her arm. Alas, no wedding trip for Mum, and me in the sin bin—again!

THE BRIGHTER SIDE OF A DEATH THREAT

I also spent weeks digging a huge hole behind the old Tasma Theatre and covering the trap up to catch Barry. Beautiful. Instead, I caught Mum. I heard the scream. More punishment. Well deserved.

Oh, yes. On another occasion I was at the pool when the fire brigade station siren wailed—calling all volunteers. Us kids raced to our bikes to follow the fire engine. We were very excited when it headed towards our street but amazed when we saw it was ***our house***!

Yes, Barry was heading out to burn our paper rubbish when he passed our dead old pine Christmas tree, just inside our garage, lined with tar paper. He wondered if dead pine leaves burn—and set it alight. They do!

After the fire brigade left, it took an hour to find Barry. He had climbed in behind a big wooden chest of drawers (in the same room I tripped Connie up) and—guess what? Albert felt sorry for him so belted me for not teaching Barry it was wrong to play with matches. Nothing unusual there.

Coota was a classic whenever the fire siren went. The town had a manual-plug switchboard, so everyone wound the handle furiously to be told by the telephonist where the blaze was—gossip personified. I remember Mum's sister, Sheila, visiting her poor relos. Siren went. We phoned. Fire engine passed our house, followed by firemen on push bikes, (some wearing pyjamas). Sheila was amazed.

As a sign of things to come, I did very poorly at school. My lack of concentration was legendary and it was more than the dogs' tail wagging in Coota. It was Les and I—and occasionally Ray Sutton—wagging school… Swimming in dams and catching and cooking yabbies and goannas was our classroom. We left the Dux of the class to be fought out by Alan Mc Neil, Daryl Arkinstall and our Julie Lake.

But I must have shown promise because I was 'appointed' teller by the School Bank. Every Monday I collected the pennies—sometimes two shillings—and faithfully added them to the Commonwealth Bank passbooks. My own 'fortune' grew to a massive 70 quid because of my various jobs. One day I got my passbook and the balance was five shillings. My father had struck again.

LANCE SMITH

I always found it funny that Don Bradman never admitted to being born in Coota. Even funnier, because I was a bit wayward, my folks thought it best I join Scouts. I ended up Leader of the Tasmanian Devils. Our Scoutmaster was local Chamber Magistrate Murray Farquhar—he ended up a famous politician and in gaol for years for fraud, I think. I was led by the best crims money can buy. My father and my scoutmaster.

Mum joined the local Drama group 'The Cootamundra Players'. She starred in *The Admirable Chrichton* and *Ten Little Niggers*. I remember loving those shows, and years later I played the killer judge in *Ten Little Niggers* in Batemans Bay.

My own second time on stage was big time. Our church choir, under Mrs. Manwaring, took a bus to Wagga Wagga for the annual much-hyped regional Eisteddfod. We were in the unaccompanied (no conductor) section. **We won**, and sang all the way back to Coota.

In 1954—aged 11—we hit the big time. Mum was taking us to Sydney on the big steam train to wave to the Queen as she drove through Sydney's Macquarie Street. I am sure she saw me. Those big buildings and streetcars. The highlight of the trip was a visit to Cahill's Cafeteria and a meat pie. Wow! I remember every mouthful. Delicious… and posh. We came back on the Southern Aurora that night.

Some thirty years later, John Lord and Ray Sutton convinced me to go with them to 'The Class of 55' reunion. We walked into the R.S.L. and were surrounded by the oldest people I had ever seen. Never again—and that was 30 years ago. I'm a dinosaur.

In 1957, the word came though we were bound for the big city. We had nowhere to live and no money.

The decision was made. Mum, Franny and Bubby Jo were to stay with Sheila at Balgowlah and Icky and I were to live with Albert's sister, Isobel, whom we had never met—at Cronulla. I don't remember where Albert went.

I remember our train pulled into the country platform at Central and Mum took us to another part of the station and handed me a piece of paper

THE BRIGHTER SIDE OF A DEATH THREAT

with 'Cronulla' written on it. She told me when the train pulled up at that station, Barry and I were to get out and be met by 'Aunty Sis' who, apparently, had a photo of the two of us.

It was a long ride and eventually we made it. We got out and waited and waited and waited. Just on dark this lady came running up the road sobbing how sorry she was that she was late. It was Aunt Sis, mother of cousins Malcolm and Ian—both keen surfers.

And here we were… our new life in the big smoke.

CHAPTER 5

LAKEMBA AND PUNCHBOWL HIGH SCHOOL— THE TOW TRUCK ERA AND FINALLY, THE GREAT ESCAPE!

However much I am at the mercy of the world I never let myself get lost by brooding over its misery . I hold firmly to the thought that each one of us can do a little to bring some portion of that misery to an end.

...A. Schwietzer.
French Philosopher and Physician

It is 1958. I am 15—nearly a man! We have found a place to live: two bedrooms for the six of us, in Lakemba, and a school, Punchbowl High, for me to finish my intermediate.

I envisaged an escape. I was excited about the prospects of leaving school, getting a job and as far away from Albert as I could. I hatched a twelve-month plan.

Mum and Albert's first decision was the sleeping arrangements. Them in one bedroom; Fran and Bubby Jo in the other. Ikky and I were assigned a mattress on the open back verandah.

Boy, do I remember 2.30 a.m. on the first Thursday night! I heard the burglar coming down the side path. I cowered as he lurched past my mattress and loaded the can from our outside dunny onto his shoulders to take it away. We had regular 2.30 a.m. chats once a week, until the verandah was enclosed a year later.

I continued my hate for all things school. The only good thing at Punchbowl High was meeting my classmate, Viv Hanley. We have remained good mates for the past 60 years.

'Chemical Cook', the science master, was in charge of the assembly and, once again, I was regularly sent to the Headmaster to be caned for 'disturbing the assembly'. One day, Viv tells me, I was called to go to the office for a caning—and I wasn't even at school. I was wagging that day.

For some reason, Mum sent us all to four different schools: me to Punchbowl. Barry to Canterbury, Franny to Wiley Park and Marci to Beverly Hills.

The only good memory was that my swimming improved out of sight and Punchbowl won many carnivals. One day, Viv Hanley and I were swimming in the School Senior Relay at the State titles at North Sydney Olympic Pool. I had made it to the top! We made it to the 100-yard relay finals and were up against world champion, Jon Konrads. Konrads and I were the final swimmers in our respective teams and I won—by a touch. What I hadn't said was that I started with a lead of some eighteen yards and he nearly caught me.

I took a while to figure out how we were the first people in Hilton Avenue to have a black and white TV—on day one even! The whole street used to come in relays to watch it. Turns out Albert was on the N.S.W. Government tenders board and it was a 'present' from a successful tenderer.

A year of misery, then school was over. Yeah! 1958. I was 15 and got the first job I applied for—a junior in the Bank of New South Wales at Bankstown. Nine quid a fortnight for a 5½ day working week—a fortune.

I was sent to the local hardware store to buy a can of striped paint.

THE BRIGHTER SIDE OF A DEATH THREAT

Duh! I went.

I was sent to the post office to pick up a verbal agreement form. Duh! I went.

Yep, I was the office clown… and still as gullible today.

My workmate, John Griffith, and I started playing guitar. Even though I was saving like mad, I spent two-and-six a week on guitar lessons at Palings.

We called ourselves 'The Colbert Brothers' (my middle name) and entered the Australia-wide *Terry Dear Amateur Hour* in the early 60's. We won the duets/trio section, beating a number of well known acts that went on to fame and fortune.

Also in 1960, big things were happening. By March, I was working at night driving a tow truck, and saving well. I got my licence in November 1959, aged 16 years and 10 months.

As my savings grew, I was able to plan my escape. A fellow bank worker, Geoff Howarth, wanted to explore England and Europe. Sounded like a good idea to me. Mum was not so sure. She thought 17 was too young. In the end, she agreed if I saved my ships' passage plus a return ticket, and 250 pounds spending money, I could go—nearly 1000 pounds. Big money.

Driving tow trucks was a baptism into another world. I rolled two of them: one outside my old school trying to impress the students how fast I could turn a corner. I failed. The other was not my fault. Driving to an accident on the Hume Highway at Yagoona, the front wheel of the Ford 250 buckled and I rolled. I hit five cars (four parked). No one was hurt; just damaged pride and a telling off from the boss at Marland's Smash Repairs.

I was taught the tricks by a real pro—John Moriarty, a colourful character and larrikin of the first order. He did some crazy things, but saved my bacon a few times in disagreements with other towies. J.M. survived, somehow; loved a bet and a cricket tragic. He is now a retired mechanic on the Central Coast with a long-suffering beautiful wife, Ros. We all have some horrible memories of crashes.

As if driving tow trucks wasn't enough excitement, I then became a repossession agent. Davey (Crocket) Howlett and John Kerin were two very well known repo agents, and I used to do their towing. They introduced me to another side of life.

Everyone hates repo agents: those who have given false addresses and are caught out and those who have never been caught by one. I did learn some valuable lessons—the hard way: like, never repossess a car in a hotel carpark when the owner and his mates are watching from the bar. Four days in Bankstown hospital!

The law says we were not allowed to take vehicles from private property. It was truly amazing the hundreds of times someone else must have stolen a wanted car and I just happened to 'find' it abandoned in the street. We had to report all repossessions to police, so they knew if someone reported it stolen.

A couple of highlights during this time: Crockett and I repossessed a hearse from Campbelltown and drove it back to Bankstown. We thought we'd have some fun. Crockett was under a sheet in the body of the hearse. I drove, and John Kerin was in the front. We pulled up in Chapel Street, Bankstown. Crockett became 'alive' under the sheet and jumped out the back. I had a starting pistol and 'shot' him. He fell. We loaded him back in and drove off. We thought it was hilarious. The police had a very different view and we were all thoroughly reprimanded.

Another time, near Katoomba, we knew where a 'missing hirer' had a sports car stashed and locked in a garage, and we had to take the doors off in the dark. The only time we could make a noise was when the nearby trains went past. It took five trains and two hours, but we did it. We later 'found' the car in the main street of Leura. Lucky us. Missing hirers were top money.

Talking of money—three jobs and working 7 days and nights meant my bank balance was soaring.

There were a couple of downsides, like the time one of our police associates was visiting at our Hilton Ave home and fired his revolver in our lounge room. Not good. The less said about our special arrangements with some police, the better. But if you lived on a notorious corner like Noble and Boronia at Greenacre, or King Georges and Canterbury at Wiley Park, the spotters fees were very lucrative. Trouble was, the four houses on four corners all rang different tow truck companies and you had to be first there. Hmmm. A police 'association' helped!

THE BRIGHTER SIDE OF A DEATH THREAT

I took up diving/spearfishing and joined the 'Liberty Plains' spearfishing club. We spent a lot of time underwater over the years. One day I was teaching a fellow Hilton Ave mate, Ron Bessell, to dive—at Boat Harbour Kurnell—when I saw a very large Wobbegong Shark. I knew they were okay if you gave them a wide berth and were not carrying fish in a bag. I pointed it out to Ron, who promptly walked on water some 200 yards into shore. I have never seen anyone so fast in the water. Ron and Robyn Anne are still mates today.

Despite all this, hard work paid off and I was able to book passage on the Sitmar Lines *Castel Felice* and we sailed out of Sydney Harbour, bands playing, streamers fluttering—and I could still hear my grandmother 'Connie' calling 'Lancipop' when we sailed past Pittwater and across the Equator into the northern hemisphere. A totally new life.

I had finally escaped!

CHAPTER 6

LONDON FIRE BRIGADE / EUROPE— AND THE U.K.

Learn from yesterday. Live for today. Hope for tomorrow.
                                             ...Albert Einstein

Seven weeks on the high seas, Italian Bands, cheap 'Spumante', dancing—calling in at many ports, The Suez Canal—those remarkable Arabs on the bum boats that spoke so many languages—riots, gunshots and deaths in Aden, Naples and Pompei. All very exciting for a 17 year old… and finally, Southampton, the old dart and a new life.

Like most Aussies, Kiwis and yarpies, I headed for Earls Court, full of 'Aussie' pubs and meeting places. I only lasted seven days before heading off to Europe with my bank workmate, Geoff Howarth, and a Kiwi—Gordon. Gordon was a tight fisted, scheming miserable bloke **but**—he had a car! I am sure Geoff and I paid way more than our share.

After six weeks of hair raising driving on 'the wrong side' in Europe and many near misses, we had a bad head on smash in Southern France. Gordon ended up in hospital, so Geoff and I took off by train for Greece, where I found work in a Piraeus Café.

LANCE SMITH

During that six weeks with the Kiwi, I remember one night in Berlin. We had been on the 'other side' of the wall all day, in East Berlin, and came back. Gordon and I had a disagreement, and I stepped out of the car to have it out man-to-man. Gordon drove off, taking my coat, wallet and passport!

We were staying in tents in a suburb called Wannsee, in Berlin, on the Konigstrasse, and my challenge was to find a cabbie prepared to take me back there—with no money, no I.D. and no idea of the address. The cabbie spoke no English. I spoke no German, so we conversed in very poor French. When we found the place, the cabbie was very relieved to get the Deutchmarks… and I was 'relieved' of a lot of my savings.

I was amazed at the American jukebox influence wherever we went in Europe. If I didn't know every Elvis song beforehand, I did now. Plus the Dean Martins, Frank Sinatra and Tony Bennett crooners were keenly played.

I ended up stopping in Delft, Holland, for nearly six months: a fabulous town famous for it's pottery and universities. I got a job as a hospital 'orderly'. I remember one patient, an old lady, very impressed that the hired help spoke such good English. Luckily she didn't try me in Dutch. I also saw Jack Brabham win the Dutch Grand Prix at Zandvoort in 1960. A spectacular race track, but a spectator was killed just along from us when a car went into the crowd.

Geoff had headed back to England, so I went to Paris for many months. I had lodgings at the 'Hotel D'Amerique' in Cadet, not far from the Moulin Rouge and the Sacre Coeur Basilica, in the Montmartre quarter. I spoke reasonable schoolboy-French and dined every night with the concierge and family. I found plenty of work and loved life in 'Gay Paree', and got to speak almost as 'a local', until one day I was escorting a sporting team to a rugby match and had a real challenge.

I then crossed the Channel and met up with Geoff, and we headed north through The Lakes District and Yorkshire to Scotland. I really loved the north of England… and still do. With Melinda, Lyth, Angus and Isla living in Yorkshire, we visit there often at The Manor House, Barmby Moor.

On returning to London early 1961, I found digs in Blenheim Crescent, Ladbroke Grove, (Notting Hill). I desperately wanted to live alone and found a cupboard—loosely described as 'a small bed sitter'—not too far from the

THE BRIGHTER SIDE OF A DEATH THREAT

toilet and bathroom. It was three pounds per week, so needed a job very soon. The coin-fed electricity meter was outside my door!

I had met a bloke named Dave Cracknell, and we hit it off. Dave was applying to join the London Fire Brigade, so I went with him. I spun a yarn about parents having a 10-year posting to London, and got in!

Wow! Nine pounds eleven shillings for a forty-eight-hour week, four twelve-hour day shifts followed by four twelve-hour night shifts and then four days off. Heaven! I joined in March 1961. First up, four months training in the London Fire Brigade, Lambeth College. Sub Officer Rose was the O.I.C., a loud mouthed former army RSM who lived for bullying and punishment… and I was well practised in both, thanks to my father.

Dave and I went in daily on his Vespa motor scooter. One day, we came off in the rain and slid under a moving double-decker bus. Missed both of us but mangled the scooter.

Nearing the end of the course, we were the senior class, and I came up with a great idea to 'haunt' Sub Officer Rose. We had been doing First Aid and working with a full, genuine, skeleton. I hatched a plan, and late at night Dave and I scootered into London and scaled the ten foot wall at the college. I had taken the keys to the main block and skeleton closet. We climbed the five-storey fire drill tower and hung the skeleton from the top deck with the placard 'Sub Officer Rose' hanging from the skeleton's feet.

It caused a ruckus. We were all paraded next day and threatened with everything—including instant dismissal. They brought in the police. Unfortunately, Rose remembered he had seen me do a hangman's noose in our rope work classes and I was extensively grilled but never charged. This is the first time I have ever admitted to the crime!

Dave and I both graduated and I was posted to Blue Watch at Kentish Town. Rose's farewell comment was, "I know it was you."

I loved it. Proper meals—dinner and breakfast on the nigh shift, breakfast and lunch on the day shift. Daily volleyball in the exercise yard, fabulous fire drills—particularly the hook ladders.

Joe Banks was an 'old' fireman (probably 45) who had joined the fire brigade in 1939 to avoid being sent to the battlefront. He then survived the horrific Blitz of London, the nightly bombings and fires—certainly as dangerous as any battlefront. Joe and I were a great team with hook ladders.

The wooden hook ladder was ten feet long. Very light with pianoforte wire for strength. At the top was an 18-inch metal hook with teeth. The idea was a two-man team with two ladders. The first man put the hook either on the first floor window sill (if open) or through the glass window if closed. He then climbed the ladder and 'hooked' onto an 'eye' with a huge pear-shaped belt clip. Then, with left leg on ladder and right leg extended out for balance, the second person passed his ladder up to the first who kept it going and locked it into the second-storey window uncoupled, then climbed to the second floor and repeated the process. The highest building Joe and I ever scaled up the outside was twenty-one stories high.

We were chosen to be the London Fire Brigade demo team and did many a display for V.I.P's at headquarters, scaling the ten-storey drill tower in under three minutes.

One of these was for Lord Mountbatten, and I remember the day well. Something went wrong when they lit the oil fire during our hook ladder display and the engine for the crew to put out the fire didn't start. By the end of the drill, Lord Mountbatten could have sung any Al Jolson song. He and all the V.I.P's were black from the oil smoke. Embarrassing for the Fire Brigade chiefs.

One night—right on pub closing time—the bells went and we all raced to the engines. The watch room guy, 'Spud' Murphy, I thought was yelling 'plane crash'. Turned out to be a train crash at nearby Islington. We were the first to arrive—carnage. There were carriages hanging from the railway bridge, fires everywhere you looked. A night to remember.

Another night we were called to a chimney fire in Holloway—a common occurrence. Our Station Officer, Busty Whitmarsh, and second in charge, Sub Officer Witham, bound up the stairs to open the front door as we could see sparks belching out of the chimney. Everything normal, until Busty put his hand on the door knob and yelped. The whole house was on fire.

As we moved into the house, hoses gushing, Harry Margiotta and I made our way into the kitchen. There was a three-year-old kiddie strapped into a stroller—dead. Mum and dad were at the nearby pub. Heart breaking. The drying clothes were too close to the kerosene heater.

We had many a challenging obstacle—turning out on ice covered roads, rescuing people trapped in flooded basements—even a gaol fire. Exciting days.

THE BRIGHTER SIDE OF A DEATH THREAT

I played rugby union for the London Fire Brigade and also the Old Tottonians. I toured England, France and Wales playing. Even a curtain-raiser at Cardiff Arms Park, the holy grail of Welsh Rugby and that singing.

I read what is still my favourite book, *The Duffer of Danby*. It taught me how to find more of life's opportunities if you chase them. But remember: if you don't look you won't find them. I agree with George Bernard Shaw—"Life is not about finding ourselves, it is about creating ourselves."

My 'omen' to return to Oz came at the Friday night Clapham Dog races. A group of us went from work and I knew nothing about the 'sport', but there was a dog called 'Holden Great' coming out of box four. Because it reminded me of home, and because I was winning, I stupidly put ten quid on it (a week's wages) at ten to one. A local then devastated me, advising 'Holden Great' turns somersaults in the box and mostly comes out backwards and loses. The others thought this hilarious—at my expense. This night, the dog came out the right way and won by seven lengths. One hundred quid. Enough, combined with my original reserve savings, to get me home.

The following week, I booked my passage, resigned from the Brigade, had many great farewell parties, went to Ireland for a few weeks, then headed for the ship, the Greek liner, the SS *Bretagne* (which sank after a fire on the next voyage). We called in to Madiera (Portugal), Cape Town, Durban, Freemantle and Melbourne.

The only downer at this point was a boozy weekend with a group of Aussie sailors on R. and R. I woke up on a Sunday with both arms wrapped up—tattoos. It took a few weeks for the scabs to reveal the 'masterpieces' on both arms. I've been kicking myself ever since.

On returning home, I was mindful of the fact Mum's only advice before heading overseas was, "Don't get married or tattooed." So for the first six months after I got back, I wore long sleeves to hide them. Mum was not impressed when I finally did 'the reveal'.

In 1963, I came home. My twice yearly phone calls to Mum—her birthday in May and Christmas Day—cost three pounds for three minutes—a fortune; over one third of my wage. Also, we were paid monthly, so I lived like a prince for the first week, a normal person for the next two then a homeless person for the last week. Thank goodness for meals at work and baked beans. I sometimes had no money for the electricity meter. I used to read by candlelight.

On my days off I had worked many part time jobs—labourer for Wimpeys Road Construction, a battery factory at Hammersmith, and delivering wines in a van. It was here I found Poms don't venture too far in one day and thought we Aussies were mad with the distances we were prepared to drive.

I remember going to Paris for a party one Saturday night. They thought I was bonkers.

On my days off, I worked as a road layer for 'Wimpeys' (not the hamburger chain—unfortunately).

I was very good at cards… particularly 'Nap'. One day we were in the van, on a rain delay, playing cards. I had counted the hearts and knew I had won the huge 'pot'—over three weeks wages. Wow! I laid down my cards and, somehow, an Irish workmate palmed a card that had been previously laid back into his own hand… and I lost. A valuable lesson indeed, but it hurt.

CHAPTER 7

HOMEWARD BOUND AND JOLLY ROGER

Life is change. Growth is optional. Choose wisely.
...Karen Clark

I boarded the *Bretagne* at Southhampton and set out for Oz. With my limited funds, I was sharing a cabin with seven others way down near the engine room. Luckily for me, a young lass from Hurstville, Vicky Hayes, whose folks owned a chain of butcher shops, took pity on me on Day 1 and offered to share her Stateroom on the top deck. How good was that!

Vicky introduced me to the ships barber, one Roger Thorby, a youngster on his maiden voyage. We hit it off and spent a lot of time together.

One night, a group of surfing guys from Sydney's North Shore took exception to my new stateroom status and we decided to sort out our differences. The good news is I was not one of those taken to the ships infirmary, but the bad news is I did end up in the brig with a fellow I didn't know, named Bruce Walters, who later became a good friend in Batemans Bay.

Between Vicky and Roger, I was 'bailed' back to the stateroom a few days later. Jolly Roger fell in love with a fellow passenger, Carol, who left the ship at Freemantle, and he was broken-hearted. He stayed on the ship back to England, then the next sailing to the colonies he jumped ship in Perth and chased Carol. He was rejected on the grounds that (i) he was an illegal immigrant and (ii) jobless.

The only other person he knew in Australia was me, so he landed on our doorstep in Lakemba for 'a couple of nights'. He stayed eighteen months on a couch in the dining room and became 'Roger the Lodger'.

Roger continued to chase Carol, and finally she agreed to wedding bells, so Prince Charming took off to find love. Jolly and Carol returned to England, had two daughters, and eventually brought a house built in 1634 in Ilminster, Somerset, and ran a barber shop from the front room.

Some 20 years had elapsed and we lost touch. My brother Barry was in England and did some detective work. He turned up unannounced at the barber shop and was told by Roger (who had not recognised him), "I'll be busy for a while… come back in an hour."

Barry said, "Sure Jolly" and walked out. Poor Roger. He knew something was amiss and ran into the house to tell Carol, "Someone just called me Jolly and I don't think it was Lance".

An hour later, Barry re-appeared and, for the only time in his life, Roger shut the shop to go out celebrating.

All four of us, Barry, Franny, Marci and I have since spent many holidays travelling the U.K. with Roger and Carol, and they came out here and spent many months with us.

One trip, we were booked in to the Cotswalds and I had arranged to meet former Tamworth Mayor, Warwick Bennet and wife Margaret, for dinner with the six of us—in a delightful town near Lower Slaughter called Burton On The Water. Because Warwick had been there for a week or so, I suggested he select the restaurant. Mid winter, it was dark by 3 p.m., and raining when we got there at 5 p.m. Warwick took us fifty yards up the road to a split-level Mediterranean restaurant. Great hosts. Very welcoming. They suggested we try some of their own suggested entrees and just order mains. We agreed. Warwick chose the wines and a grand feast began.

By the time the selected entrees were finished, we were full. Warwick ordered more wine to wash it down and we just toyed with our mains. We had really overdone it.

Eventually we called for the bill. Now, Helen is always saying to me, "Don't convert", when we are spending other currencies, **but** $AUS 1600 for

THE BRIGHTER SIDE OF A DEATH THREAT

dinner for six! I was shattered, but nowhere near as gobsmacked as Jolly!

Turns out Warwick had ordered top shelf wines at 80 quid per bottle. We had three. No way out; we had to pay. Out came our three credit cards and, you guessed it, cash only. Ouch. A tiny sign as we came in.

Luckily, Warwick's hotel was nearby. Roger had a cunning kick in his sock and we just scraped it up.

Roger passed away a few years ago, and we are still in touch with Carol.

On many of our trips, we went via the Lakes District and stayed at our mate Annie's Hotel at Kendal, 'Stonecross Manor'. Super. (Annie was a former Country Comfort colleague.) On one last night, we were staying at an old 'Grand' Hotel in Harrogate. That night, I wrote over twenty post cards and put them aside to get stamps next day. Needless to say, I forgot the post cards and cursed my forgetfulness as it had taken me a few hours, and the cards were expensive too!

Imagine my surprise, weeks later, to find the Hotel had found the cards and put their own stamps on and posted them, and everyone received them. There are plenty of good people in this crazy world of ours.

Oops. I'm getting ahead of myself.

CHAPTER 8

DISCOVERING AUSTRALIA—FROM KINGS CROSS TO DAYDREAM ISLAND

Imagination is a preview of life's coming attractions.
...Einstein

It is now 1963. I am almost twenty one.

Travelling the world had given me the desire to see more of our great land, and I started to imagine how I could achieve this. I came to realise happiness is a journey—not a destination.

But first I needed a bank roll, so it was back to what I know: the Fire Brigade.

Nothing is ever as easy as it seems, and I was gobsmacked to find out I was too young. I joined the London Fire Brigade at 18, but N.S.W. was a minimum age 21, eight months away. So—I took on a bread run for Watsons Bakery, Condell Park. My run was some twelve shops and 180 or so private residences, starting at Connells Point, through Sylvania, Sutherland, Engadine and Heathcote, plus I went back to driving tow trucks and repossessing.

On my 21st birthday, in 1964, I graduated from the N.S.W. Fire Brigade training school at Paddington under Jack Nance and 'Bud' Abbott, a former Changi POW. I was assigned 'B' platoon at Headquarters in Castlereagh Street for the first six months, mainly on the 'flyer' (first response) and turntable ladders, but occasionally 'District Officers' or 'Inspectors' driver.

We had a DO (District Officer) named Bill Goodwin, aka Bill the Goose. (He was well named). One night, I was his driver, and we turned out to a fire at Hen and Chicken Bay, Five Dock: a boat, about 100 metres out from the wharf. The DO commandeered a row boat, loaded the extinguishers and pushed off. They only got about ten feet and came to an abrupt halt. Billy the Goose jumped overboard to push them off the sandbank. Trouble was, he had not untied the stern rope and that is what caused the sudden stop. He jumped into twenty feet of water and all I could see was his red helmet drifting away in the tide. We did jump in and pull him out.

Another night and another boat fire, this time in Sydney Harbour. He commandeered a small rowboat on the wharf at Rose Bay. It had holes and we sank about 200 metres out in the harbour.

Another night I was on the salvage and we were turning out to a fire at Circular Quay. We never made it. Our driver was a useless bloke named Ross Smith, and he floored it. Trouble was, he forgot to turn and we went straight across Castlereagh Street and through the shop window on the other side. How embarrassing.

I do remember, another night, turning out to a huge fire at a harbour foreshore, Hunters Hill Oil Refinery. Frightening. Exploding fuel tanks and drums lit up the Sydney night skies like a giant red ball. Police had evacuated everyone within a mile or so. We were fighting it for six hours before any food/water arrived for us from—guess who—*the Salvos*. God bless 'em.

I was transferred to 'B' platoon, Kings Cross, in July '64. Our Station Officer was Bill Baker—or 'Ah Fong', as he was called. I know not why.

This was the start of a few great years. Norm Parker (later to become DO Parker—'Star' of the huge Newcastle earthquake) and I were the two juniors, alongside Larry William (the bat), Barry Morteson, John Sheedy, Ron Brigden from out west, Doug Wallace, John Morrison and Pat McGrath.

In December we were joined by a young bloke from a Nabiac dairy (near Taree). The only night life Dave Holden had ever seen was their porch light on their dairy farm. Why they sent him to Kings Cross, I will never know, but we were merciless. We knew a lot of the local 'girls', many of whom were really top people facing huge challenges of some sort or another. We had them continually offering Dave their 'wares' and he would run a mile and hide out the back of the station. Dave was an easy target.

THE BRIGHTER SIDE OF A DEATH THREAT

Dave was always the best dressed, so one day I hid in the exercise yard and he was 'belled' to the front. As he crossed the yard, I came out from behind the door with a bucket of slops from our cleaning duties and he wore the lot.

A few hours later, I was dressed in the best parade uniform to take over the watch room. I was warned that Dave was hiding with a drill hose. As I crossed the yard, he came out and drowned me. The look of revenge turned to horror when he looked at the brass numbers and realised I had on **his** dress uniform, boots, tie, socks etc. The only thing of mine wet were undies.

Practical jokes were part of the Fire Brigade culture… but not necessarily smart. Our normal shift-change procedure was to assemble between the two fire engines for roll call. Once formalities were completed, one shift went home and the oncoming team immediately headed to the kitchen for a cuppa before starting.

One afternoon shift, about 11 p.m.—just before cracker night, as everyone was assembling—I lit a cigarette, punctured a hole near the filter and pulled through the wick of a giant bunger, the size of a TNT stick. I then taped it under the big kitchen table and went to roll call, then left the station for my part time job at the Darling Harbour fruit and veg markets. When we came in next day, there was baked beans on the kitchen walls and ceiling and reports of pandemonium. I never owned up.

One night, Pat McGrath pointed out an old 'drunk' had fallen asleep on the seat outside the fire station and his bottle of rough port in a paper bag was beside him. We took it and refilled it with some pretty toxic stuff. Years later, I reflected it was not a smart move on our part, but it seemed funny at the time. Anyway, we replaced it and watched. Imagine our delight when another bloke staggered past, saw the old bloke asleep with the bottle, pinched it and ran. He would have got one heck of a shock. I reckon if he broke wind, his shirt tail would be on fire!

Poor Dave Holden, again. We arrived on shift one afternoon to find our fire engine had broken down and the only replacement vehicle available was from the Fire Brigade Museum at Fivedock—an old Garfield, crash gearbox gate—a real relic. 'A' platoon had transferred all the gear and some didn't fit, so things like the 30 kg, four-into-one brass coupling, were lashed on.

A couple of hours into the shift, we had an alarm call to HMAS *Kuttabel*. I was driving, with Bill Baker beside me and the rest of the crew sitting sideways and hanging on. As we turned the corner at the El Alamein Fountain, the huge four-into-one coupling came loose. Dave grabbed it to hold on. All I saw in the rear view mirror was Dave and the coupling flying through the air and crashing through the windscreen of a VW sedan. He never forgave me.

Dave went on to become a very respected Inspector, and we are still very close to he and his beautiful wife, Ros, today, as he enjoys retirement at Padstow Heights.

Some nights, I used to busk outside Kings Cross Fire Station, acoustic guitar—just guitar and vocals. Made a good quid and bought a brand new guitar.

One thing I was very proud of was the night we were called to a multi-storey building, alight in Orwell Lane, Kings Cross. I was driving with Bill Baker on the siren. As we turned into the very narrow street, we saw the building well alight and people hanging out the windows. Somehow, we passed all the parked cars at speed and did not touch any of them. We were able to rescue all those trapped and later—when 'C' platoon went to bring the engine home—they had to shift every parked car as the engine didn't fit! Go figure.

Most fireys 'Quarried', which means part-time jobs on time off. I worked regularly for MSS (Metropolitan Security Services) on special assignments—a great job and some interesting challenges. I also worked at Hook & Beazleys stall at the Sydney markets (midnight to 6 a.m.) and Bedford Cartage, truck driving and general deliveries when there were staff shortages. Kept us busy, but good for the bank balance.

My diving got more serious whilst in the fire brigade. I teamed up with a police diver, Terry Rigby, and we spent our days off down south, spearing sharks and selling them to fish shops. We used mainly shotgun heads and made good money. Had a few hairy encounters, but made it through them all. There were two shark breeding areas under cliffs, one at Kiama and one

THE BRIGHTER SIDE OF A DEATH THREAT

at Jervis Bay that we frequented.

Terry and I won a swag of medals and trophies at State and National spearfishing titles for our club, Liberty Plains.

Another day, I was diving for lobsters in the shallow reefs on the northern beaches out from Long Reef Golf Club, with a fellow firey, Barry Ross, from 76 station, Bondi. We were working in narrow gutters and there was a fair sized swell. I felt Barry knock into me, then heard the scream. It wasn't Barry who knocked me, but a big tiger shark. It also knocked Barry, who let out a holler that should have been heard down to Palm Beach.

I don't know who was the most frightened. As for the tiger shark, it took off at speed—thank goodness—and we got out pronto. Incredibly, Barry went from brunette to 'silver' in just a few weeks. He was then called 'Silver' for the rest of his short life.

He died at Bondi the following year. I have no idea if the cause of death was related to the encounter.

Norm Parker and I met a couple of gorgeous girls from Penshurst way—Robyn Phillips and Penelope Rutledge. We were invited to a weekend beach party up north. We finished our night shift on Friday morning and headed north. I don't think we slept the whole weekend—lots of fun, downing the odd ale or five.

On Monday I was scheduled to drive back to Sydney and was really wiped out. We went to a chemist and bought 'no doze'. Those who know me know I rarely do pills of any sort, so two of these kept me awake for three days. I was a mess.

Norm is still married to the lovely Penny, today living at Port Stephens—a terrific couple.

He was District Officer in Charge of Newcastle the day of the huge earthquake. He still has lots of admirers today who remember his feats and great decisions in the aftermath of that tragedy.

One of their sons, now a policeman, was recently recognised for bravery. Like father like son.

Robyn and I decided we would set the world on fire. I resigned from the Brigade and we shifted to Brisbane. Around two months later she fell in love

LANCE SMITH

with a golf pro and I was out… all over Red Rover.

I shifted into a flat in Hamilton on Kingsford Smith Drive with a great guy named John Gaffney—a real character. There were twelve units in the block: John and I in one and air hostesses in the other eleven. Heaven.

I saw a job advertised for a barman/diving instructor on Daydream Island Resort in the Whitsundays… and got it. My diving credentials were fine, but I was told to do a 'crash course' in learning the bar trade. I could not have done better. Gaffney knew 'Warren' from 'Warrens Bar' at the famous National Hotel. Warren was Australia's best known barman and openly gay—a rarity in those days. He was a top fella and brilliant at his trade, and generously gave me two weeks behind the bar at the National. I learnt heaps and was ready to fire. So, in March 1968, I headed north to begin the next phase of life. Daydream was to be the start of a fantastic 'ever after', It had taken me twenty-five years to get to the 'starting blocks', but was worth the wait.

CHAPTER 9

DAYDREAM ISLAND AND THE WHITSUNDAYS

He deserves paradise who makes his companions laugh.
...The Koran

This is where my 'fairy tale' took a huge turn for the better. Paradise found, and I met the lovely 19-year-old Helen.

What a breathtakingly beautiful part of the world Daydream Island is. Only 33 acres in area (it's original name was West Molle) and south of Hayman and Hook, Nara Inlet and Cid Harbour. All nestled behind the big one—Whitsunday Island. Named by Captain Cook back in 1770, the Whitsunday passage is full of tiny bits of paradise—including the beautiful Whitehaven Beach, the inlet and Lookout. Shute Harbour was the perfect launching site for those wishing to explore the Great Barrier Reef and Island.

The Whitsunday and Barrier Reef diving is second to none. A treasure trove of colourful varieties of coral and the hundreds of different sea creatures large and small are eye-openers for the hundreds of thousands who visit every year. I spent many, many days diving in the crystal clear waters of the spillway between Hook and Hardy reefs. Another world.

My introduction to the Daydream Island Resort was to meet the feared General Manager, Joy Collins. Miss Collins advised me there were three steps before instant dismissal:

"Firstly, I ask you to do something.

Secondly, if you don't, then I tell you to do it.

Thirdly—if you still don't do it—pack your bags."

Miss Collins also warned she would not tolerate any member of staff saying a negative word to a guest about the Island, our operation, or any other staff. Again, instant dismissal. She stated the guest was paying good money for a great holiday and we weren't to dampen their enthusiasm. She carried out the threat many times.

The constant humidity and heat took a bit of getting used to but I went from fifteen stone to eleven stone without giving up a thing, and soon got used to it.

The whole staff were rostered to do forty hours per week in their 'principle role', but you were expected to do many other tasks. After six months, I was promoted to Bar Manager—my principal role. However, I was also:

1. In the three weekly floor shows—Saturday's Luau Night, Tuesday's Roaring 20's show and Thursday's Roylen Cruise Fashion Parade

2. One of three diving instructors (Gary and Gavin were the main ones)

3. Part-time food waiter

4. Pool cleaner

5. Glass bottom boat skipper for daily coral viewing cruises

6. Speedboat driver—ferrying guests to and from Shute Harbour

7. All male staff were also expected to unload all deliveries. At that time we did not have a jetty, so everything was unloaded down the scoop ramp from the ship, no matter how big the seas were.

8. Fire chief—including the Briggs and Stratton suction motor

9. Nightly Island drummer—at 6 p.m. we lit the pool flares, belted the log drums and announced dinner and bar services were open in the main area. Very picturesque as the sun set.

10. A member of the welcome and farewell band.

So we were on the go day and night and loved it. If anyone thought we were being overworked, they were quickly reminded there were hundreds of

THE BRIGHTER SIDE OF A DEATH THREAT

backpackers at Airlie Beach keen to do their job.

The pay? Forty-three dollars per week plus board and lodgings. Most of us made much more on tips than we did on wages.

It would help if I described the cast:

- Joy Collins: Part owner and General Manager—late 30's (at the time I thought she was old). Tough, fair and very stylish.
- Her partner in the Island, and 'fiancé', was Gold Coast Identity, Bernie Elsey, a mean spirited crook. Didn't bother us much as he was rarely there. Bernie and Joy started the Gold Coast Meter Maids back in the early 60's, when they operated places such as Tiki Village, The Beachcomber (pyjama parties), Ski Lodge and Beachcomber Coolangatta, amongst others.
- The lovely Patsy and stunning Melva. Patsy Walsh, a Kiwi, and Melva Hickey, ran the office and were our two leading hula dancers on the Luau floor show, and models in the fashion parades—very talented and beautiful girls. They were 'executive staff'.
- Cranky Franky, honest Andy Donovan and John 'the flying Dutchman' Visser made up the original Daydream Island band trio. Cranky resigned almost nightly. Andy was the only deaf drummer I ever met, and John, 'the squeeze box', spoke strange English. They were soon joined by Gavin Power on lead guitar. Gav and his buddy Gary Flanagan were both from Perth. Crazy guys, an electrician and a boilermaker by trade. Much more later.
- Our fleet skipper: Captain Graham Mee, and his gorgeous wife, Kaye. Meesy was a total disaster, yet we loved him. He skippered the 250 passenger Fairmile, *The Daydream II*. (formerly the *Tambo Princess* from Victoria).
- 'Uncle Bill': Barman and host on the 'D II', and we had a full time deckie, Billy. By law, they needed an engineer on board when cruising to the outer Barrier Reef—either Gavin, Gary or myself fitted that role. I looked great in a uniform, but I only knew how to keep topping up the water in the port side engine, which leaked for years.
- Stan and Val Cushway: Owner/skipper of the *Dirojan*, and daughter, Sonja.
- Lee Thommo: our hairdresser

- Bob and Lola Playfair: Lola was head of the housemaids and Bob was our handyman.
- Adrian Ross: Bernie's pimp. A weak useless speedboat driver who rang Elsey daily to report what men had 'lingered' too long in Joy's unit or the many things the rest of us did wrong… a never ending story.
- Dennis Pollard: The pompous Assistant Manager—way above our status, 'Fig Jam' style—and his wife, Sue, who worked in the office.
- The beautiful Veronica Taylor: Veronica was the Gold Coast's very first meter maid. A classy lady—she ran the Island boutique and was our top model.
- Peter Cherry: married Veronica on the Island and the images of the wedding on the Island Bar bridge over the pool went world wide. Peter still has the first sixpence he ever earned and invented many schemes to enhance his bank balance.
- 'Pluto'. Denis Putello: The 16-year-old wizz kid who could operate any piece of equipment known. Spoilt by all.
- Finky—Wayne Fink in the kitchen.

There were others:
- Spider.
- Pommie Angie, our nurse.
- Big Tony.
- Simon the dobber.
- Vaughan Bullivant, our ski instructor (who later bought the Island and spent over $100 million on re-development),
- Graham and Margie Dare, boat thieves from Kiwiland.
- Ray Buschel, one of Meesey's skippers and fellow drinkers.
- Inge Visser in the coffee shop, plus the lovely Kerrie and Sue Salter.

And, of course, our Island 'mum', Margie Horan. What a lady. Margie was head Chef and ran the kitchens with a very tight rein. She looked after the likes of Pluto, Gary, Gavin and I in so many ways, and saved our necks often. She was ably assisted by Finky.

And finally, Joy's two dogs, Duke the Alsatian and Mr. Pimm, a yappy, snarly overgrown rat or terrier.

THE BRIGHTER SIDE OF A DEATH THREAT

We had mates on the mainland too. Don and Joy McLean, from Bowen owned Magees—they were our biggest supplier.

The Mullers, the Brooks and later the Weston families in Airlie Beach and, of course, Iris—the famous elderly barmaid with the hibiscus in her hair at the Airlie Beach pub, plus 'Captain Seaweed'—Billy Williams.

On the other Islands, we had some great colleagues:

- Sybil and Audrey on Palm Bay
- Andre Mestrace on Hayman,
- Basil and Shirley Keong from Mandalay Coral Gardens.
- Bill and Lean Wallace from Coral Art Dent Island
- and the Bauer clan from South Molle—all close.
- Plus the lecherous Bob Porter—Mr. TAA—major travel agent and ran Shute Harbour—his lovely wife Ann and great dad George.

Where do we begin. I guess at the 'top'

Bernie Elsey was a no good, shifty individual. One guy from the Gold Coast spent a month on the Island building and stocking a massive fish tank in the main dining room. He was getting increasingly nervous because the promised progress payments didn't come in, and Elsey wouldn't return his calls. Job completed—it really looked amazing. Elsey flew in and promptly advised the bloke, "I will pay in twelve months if it doesn't leak." He was shattered.

Middle of the night, the guy went into the dining room with an axe and smashed it all to smithereens—flooded all the staff quarters below and killed all the fish.

Another time, Elsey bought a huge coral crusher. The company had heard of his 'ways' and refused to bring it over until it was prepaid. Elsey said he had cash and would pay them before it was unloaded from the barge. They fell for it. When they arrived, he advised he had chartered the barge from here on and they had to unload it—and he would pay them in twelve months, if it doesn't break down.

Slimy bastard, he became so miserable in the end Elsey committed suicide. Karma.

He was a 'master' with fire insurance claims. His spy on the Island,

Adrian Ross, was a walking disaster. In just one week, he sank our two best speed boats—the *Riviera* and the twin rig. Don't know how he lived on an Island where no one spoke to him. He was a protected species.

Miss Collins, an amazing lady, loved and feared at the same time. She would press the fire alarm in the staff quarters regularly around 3 a.m. and see who came out of whose rooms. Cranky and Gavin were certain to be caught out every time. Some very embarrassed guests and staff.

One night, the Powerhouse caught fire and we all went into action for a few hours (more later). When it was out—and the sun was rising—Joy made us pretend to be playing cards on the Island bar and make a lot of noise, so the guests thought that's what they were hearing all night. We were wet, miserable, tired and smoke-filled and most unhappy, but she was paranoid about the guests finding out we had a problem so had us 'take a fall'.

One night, it was blowing a gale and the cargo barge arrived to unload the supplies from Magees at Bowen. Pluto and I were the only two waiters serving dinner to some 80 guests and were flat out when Joys 'measured' voice called, "All male staff to the beach" over the PA.

Pluto and I looked at each other, but there was no way we could 'down tools'. No one would have been fed.

Then—Joy again—this time a bit agitated, "All male staff to the beach… immediately". Again, Pluto and I were told by Chef Margie, "No way. Keep working."

About five minutes later, Joy stormed into the dining room and yelled at Pluto and I, "Haven't you two got balls?"

The supply barge was being washed ashore and cartons floating off everywhere and we were all swimming in the waves in the dark, trying to rescue the floating stock!

Joy really 'starred' one night. We had the 'King Island Ranch' boys in from the Northern Territory (about a dozen of them). All huge. Boy could they drink—usually pissed before breakfast. This night, Joy was fed up with their antics and lined up all twelve of our male staff. She told them, "I have twelve strong men lined up here who will throw you off this Island if you don't settle down." We were terrified. But before these hulking monsters tore us apart, Cranky, the smallest of us all, diffused the situation by taking one step forward and yelled 'Eleven'. It bought the house down and, fortunately for

THE BRIGHTER SIDE OF A DEATH THREAT

us, the ranch boys bought us all drinks. Phew!

Talking of Cranky—100% miserable by day and night—even on stage, but we all loved him—and still do. He is without doubt one of the most talented, creative geniuses on earth. His music, song writing, lyrics, those fantastic murals and the magnificent paintings had to be seen to be believed… and a real ladies man (he thought). Cranky wrote the beautiful Daydream Island song, which we sang in every floorshow and at every arrival and departure, along with 'Pearly Shells' and 'Island in the Sun'.

He would often tell a young lady guest that he had to meet the 'midnight helicopter' at the southern end of the Island. He had the knack of grabbing a lilo from the pool side stack as he walked past, and the lassie never saw him. But one night, Duke, the Alsation, did. Duke chased Frank and took a bite out of his bum. Hilarious.

Cranky was a builder by trade, and built the nightclub for Peter Cherry and I. He then painted the murals, then played the music every night when we opened at midnight.

Gary, Gavin and I would swim out from the unused 'back jetty' every day and spear some nice fish, which would be barbecued fish steaks at the nightclub every night. Bernie Elsey hated us for making such a success of it. I would love to have seen his face when he stepped off the chopper after Cyclone Ada to see the nightclub was the only building on the Island to be almost intact. They tell me he was furious.

The best thing about working on Daydream: Our staff 'uniform' was a lap-lap and lae. Nothing else. Day and night.

Fires—one of my roles. We had a few. One rainy night, Patsy and the girls were handed their diesel-dipped flares alight, so they could enter dancing 'Tamore' along the bar rail. Cranky was cranky, again, so he had over-dipped them, and the flares set alight to the ceiling.

Another night it was Luau night, and the practice was for two staff to carry a plastic pig—full-sized—set on a board surrounded by fruits and vines. It had a kero flare burning front and back. The lads had to descend four stairs. Somehow, Tony, 6 ft 2 inches, was at the back and Sparrow, 5 ft 1 inch, was at the front. It was never going to work. The flares fell forward onto Sparrow, and they set fire to him and the grass matting and trees next to the stage. The band escaped *real* quick... except Andy. Being deaf and having his eyes closed, he just kept drumming.

But the biggest fire was the Powerhouse, and it was well alight by the time we got the suction pump working. Gary, Gavin and I were on the hose and the water pressure was good. And then we saw it—irresistible. Both Dennis Pollard and Adrian 'the pimp' were between us and the fire. We let them have it. Nearly got them both in the fire, but they skirted the Powerhouse and headed for the bush. We kept the water on them till they disappeared. At the subsequent dressing down in the office, Joy had trouble being serious and not laughing.

Another Luau night, a guest walked straight through the glass doors at the bar—cut to pieces. Angie was brilliant and we hurriedly built fires around the helipad for the rescue chopper to land. It was times like this you realised your isolation.

You will like this—in the Roaring 20's floorshow, Kerrie and I sang an 'Al Capone' song. I was Al Capone and had to wear a pillow under my shirt to look fat. Not today.

One night, I was a waiter in the restaurant and the first course was Margie's Oyster soup. A lady politely refused and told me, "I am allergic to oysters". Fair enough. But her 'friend' told her she had paid for it so she decided to have it. Fortunately the soup looked like a Japanese POW camp recipe. I think Margie used one oyster to make the fifty or so soups. The lady was okay.

Sunday night was guest movies and our night off, except for the rostered movie projectionist, Adrian Ross—yes!

Usually, Graham brought the D2 over from Shute and the 20 or so staff all went cruising. We spent many a good night around the piano with Sybil and Audrey at Palm Bay, the Keongs at Mandalay Coral Gardens, the Bauers in the 'Pirates Den' at South Molle and went occasionally to 'Hernando's Hideaway' staff bar at Hayman. Uncle Bill was very busy in the bar on those nights. Andy's beer-can-top necklace usually went down to his navel.

One day, Captain Mee said he was taking the D2 dingy across the passage to the Airlie Beach Hotel. Andy immediately asked could he go, so there was Graham, Andy and I in this tiny dingy setting off on the 10 mile journey across the passage. About a mile out from Airlie, the propeller pin

THE BRIGHTER SIDE OF A DEATH THREAT

sheered and we came to an abrupt halt. A few minutes later, a fin appeared and the shark started circling the dingy. Andy was petrified. Then bloody Graham started to laugh and rock the dingy. We were rescued and towed to Airlie. Andy was first in the bar... by a mile.

Talking of sharks, we used to see heaps of magnificent, harmless reef sharks when Gary, Gavin and I were diving, but one day, Peter Cherry and I decided to swim from South Molle to Daydream—about five miles. The passage had a fair swell that day, but we had swum it many times so didn't worry. We were almost at Daydream and both saw it at the same time—a huge black shark in the next wave. Both of us suddenly realised we could walk on water—sort of. As buggered as we were, it wasn't till we got our breath back that we looked out to sea—only to see a big black mooring drum bouncing up and down in the waves.

Everyone had heard of a 'black coral' forest in a deep part of the passage near Abercrombie Reef. Black coral was worth good money and Bill Weston from the Airlie Beach Hotel engaged Gary and I to find him a good specimen to put on display.

We set out one day—very smooth waters and hooker gear. This was a twin-tank motor in the dingy which sent air through 200 feet of divers hose and into the mask. Gary went down first and was working in about 150 feet depth. My job was, every 20 minutes or so, to remove the wing nuts, one at a time, to clear any water from the bottom of the two air tanks. I decided to short circuit the job and do both at once. The boat was hit by the only wave of the day and I dropped both wing nuts into the bilge—***panic***. Where are they?

Meanwhile, Gary ran out of air 150 feet below and had to do the unforgivable—race to the surface. You normally took 15 to 20 minutes to keep adjusting the pressure. He took one minute and was buggered. How he lived, we will never know. He did take a long time to forgive me.

Helen and I surprised Gary and Allison recently, on their return to Sydney after a world tour—50 years after I almost killed him.

Over the years, we have stayed with the Flanagans and Gavin many times in their hometown, Perth. Drank gallons of coffee on the senate seats at the Hillary's Wharf, told lies and sang with the ukele band.

LANCE SMITH

One highlight of my time on Daydream was my Mum visiting in 1969, to spend a week. The whole crew spoilt her and we had a wonderful time all around the various Islands. It was the first time in my life I had ever spent one-on-one time with Mum and here she was in her late forties. I was totally oblivious to the fact she would die so soon after. Tragic. A beautiful girl was lost. Mum would have been 100 in May 2020.

Back in those days, the Daydream staff numbers varied between 25 and 30, depending on the season. More than half of them were 'core' long serving team and the survivors are still close today. We have had many a reunion on Daydream itself, and even more on the Gold Coast over those 50 years. Fifteen of us took Miss Collins back to Daydream for her 81st birthday. It was her last trip, as she was developing severe Dementia. Three of her old staff became Joy's Power Of Attorney and Executors as she had run out of family.

In late 1969, Palm Bay, on Long Island, went into liquidation. Miss Collins got involved, and I was appointed Manager. I took Gary, Gavin and Kerrie with me to run Palm Bay, along with existing staff, Sybil and Audrey and their team, including the German Chief Manfred.

Sybil was a legend in the Whitsunday. Dame Edna copied her glasses and she was famous for her collection of highly colourful parasols to keep the sun at bay.

Sybil later became known as 'Mary Poppins', she was tiny, and one windy day, on the end of South Molle jetty, the wind picked up Sybil and her brolly and gently floated her down into the ocean.

She was the best hostess we had ever seen. Never stopped laughing, **until**—January 1970. We received a warning via telex. Cyclone Ada was brewing. Friday night. Winds up to 100 kph. We swung into action and evacuated all guests back to the mainland, except the eight who elected to stay. Gavin, Gary, Manfred and I started tying down everything we could imagine and we waited.

Ada 'arrived' around 2 a.m.—wind gusts up to 270 kph! Terrifying. I had elected to do the midnight to 4 a.m. shift. Around 1.30 a.m, I went to Gary and Gavin's house to wake them as things were starting to fly everywhere. I will never forget that split second. Gavin got up and was dressing. Flanagan didn't want to get up, when suddenly there was an almighty crack—and the

THE BRIGHTER SIDE OF A DEATH THREAT

whole roof took off. I swear that Flanagan was up and dressed in his wet suit in 2.7 seconds, as the walls of the house started to blow out.

We could hear Audrey and Sybil screaming and the three of us made our way to their house. The roof had gone, but the rest was okay and they were both in the bathroom under a mattress. We could hear this huge grinding and smashing sound over the wind, and then saw the Hotel/bar and dining area breaking up and being blown out to sea.

Gary, Gav and I decided we best see if we could help the eight guests—all in the top motel style accommodation. Our hearts sank when we saw a huge tree had taken out the first two units and they had guests in both.

What we now know it is that one of the guests, Maitland Lowe, a well known McKay identity, had collected all eight guests and mattresses and put them in a middle unit away from the biggest trees. Phew. Onya Mr. Lowe.

Try as we could, only Gavin made it to the units. Flanagan and I were caught up in a flying tree and blown a long way out to sea. Once it hit the water, we were able to break free and start swimming back to the Island, heading into the wind. The water was flat on that side from the cyclone wind but full of building materials, trees and the like.

Cyclone Ada's eye was about 2.5 kilometres in diameter and, later, the Bureau of Meteorology in Brisbane issued a report that the cyclone's maximum wind would pass directly over Palm Bay totalling destroying the resort… but it had already happened.

The *Daydream II* (D2) went down. Uncle Bill was killed. Graham and Kaye Mee were washed through the glass windows in the galley—Kaye receiving cuts from head to toe. Miraculously, along with Billy the deckie, they were thrown ashore in the trees above the rocks in Shute Harbour. Incredibly, the DII first aid container (which Graham had unbolted in the cyclone) was washed ashore right next to them and Graham was able to stitch and bandage. It also had flares which Graham fired to lead rescuers to them. We still don't know how Kaye survived. She today lives happily in Proserpine with hubby, Nick—a beaut bloke. In January this year, we all went back to Airlie Beach where they were finally unveiling the first memorial for those killed—50 years later.

Guests were killed on South Molle Island, but most of the fourteen deaths were on the boats. Seven of these were on the *Whakatane*, close to where we were, at Palm Bay/Long Island.

Joy Collins was awarded a Queensland bravery medal. She made some great decisions and saved all staff and guests on Daydream Island.

Margie Horan was very proud of herself. Next morning, she was able to start a fire and she boiled water for tea/coffee. Then it was discovered the water was salt water. Uggghh!

Back on Palm Bay, we were able to get all fourteen of us into the only remaining house in 'the eye'. You cannot imagine the stillness and silence of the eye of a cyclone. But peace was short lived as the winds returned from the other direction. Yikes! Mrs. Brooke's house was protected by the cliff face in the first onslaught, but was totally exposed to the second. Waves came crashing into the house for hours, and we just held our breaths.

Toilet breaks were fun. As one wave drained, you raced into the front room—but had to get out before the next wave. I remember Sybil keeping us in stitches with poor jokes. She is now telling poor jokes in heaven.

Talking of stitches, about a week before the cyclone a guest—a young army bloke on his honeymoon—was stung by a sea wasp. It was low tide, and we could not get a rescue boat in for a couple of hours. I told Sybil to boil water and put instruments in it for sterilisation. I also asked her to get fishing lines in case we need to stitch him. She put the line in the boiling water and it melted like glue. It was our every nightmare.

We had the mainland on the phone, and we knew water police were on their way. The young bloke was in real agony, changed colour to a waxy grey and was fading. The only thing we could do was make him think he was going to survive, so I told him we had special medicine to fix sea wasp stings, and we gave him junket tablets from Manfred's kitchen. It worked. The police arrived, and he did survive.

Talking of Manfred and survival: When the cyclone 'left', we had no contact with the outside world and no food and water except for some vegetables and bottled water that were in the hotel cellar—the only things left. But they were all underwater.

Gary went under and retrieved the water and spuds. Manfred made a homemade bow of sticks and vines and 'honed' some arrows. He went off into the bush, and we were all amazed when he returned, a couple of hours

THE BRIGHTER SIDE OF A DEATH THREAT

later, with a wild goat. We ate goat and spuds for two days.

On the 20th January, we heard a loud boat horn as the Royal Australian Navy approached. Boy, were they a welcome sight! They came ashore in a tender and took us back to the destroyer. Our joy turned sour when they advised us that Uncle Bill was missing, plus others we knew.

We then cruised to South Molle and Daydream to rescue the forty or so people left, and we set out for Shute Harbour. The Captain got on the loudspeaker advising we had two choices: disembark at Shute Harbour or go on to Bowen with them and fly out.

Cara Coaches and 18 passengers who were on board opted to go to Shute with us until we rounded the corner and saw their coach upside down at Shute Harbour jetty. They went to Bowen.

Gavin and Gary's car was upright—but with every window smashed. We found accommodation with mates and set about organising searches and salvage for missing people and the various boats.

Gavin and Gary did an unbelievable job re-floating many boats. They went on to become two of the world's leading deep water divers on the oil rigs and worked all over the planet, diving at depths of over 1,000 feet for forty years.

The insurance companies decided to close Palm Bay permanently. Years later, APT Coaches bought it and built an upmarket camping/glamping resort. Daydream, Hayman and South Molle Islands were all closed and repairs began.

A few of us borrowed a car and went to the gem fields at Sapphire for a few weeks. Brilliant. Gavin and Gary stayed in Airlie, but most of us headed to the Gold Coast for work until the Island was re-opened. I flew back to Proserpine about two months before Daydream was to re-open. I was to live in Airlie but work at getting all the bars stocked and operational, plus employ and train four staff.

I heard about the smashing new barmaid at the Airlie Beach pub—Wow! The first time I set eyes on Helen, my heart missed five beats. I was on my best behaviour for weeks to convince her I was 'Mr. Right'. I had some work to do, but I persevered.

Captain Morgan Rum decided to make a world wide TV advert to coincide with the re-opening of Daydream. I auditioned and won the role of Captain

Morgan. The plan was for a band of pirates aboard the *Dirajan* to sail up to the old multi-masted tall ship being used by Fauna Productions on the TV series *Barrier Reef*. Then for Captain Morgan and his bunch of pirates to jump from the *Dirajan* onto the tall ship, fight and beat the crew, fire the cannons, and then throw small casks of rum overboard and swim them into Daydream where the 400 people celebrating the re-opening were to be given 'a tot of Captain Morgan's best'.

Did it go according to plan? A big *no*!

As the *Dirajan* set out to approach, we broke a shaft which took two hours to fix. All we had on board was a carton of Captain Morgan Rum and one large bottle of coke. Some fool suggested we sample it.

When the *Dirajan* restarted and cameras were rolling, my 'pirates' (mostly from Mackay) were smashed. Some jumped even before we touched the tall ship, and ended up in the sea. Two were hospitalised when jumping onto the ship and falling face first onto the raised hatch.

Some of the crew were hurt by 'pirates' who overdid the sabre cutlass fighting and then, to cap it off, the pirates who waded ashore with rum casks got carried away protecting their treasure and injured some of those who, under instructions, had run onto Daydreams beach to sample the Captain Morgan.

However, we survived and gave them some unexpectedly good footage for their TV advert and a few court cases for damages.

What with my 'newfound' fame and continued good behaviour, Helen and I went diving off Whitehaven. On that beautiful white sandy beach, I went down on one knee and begged. Thank goodness, she said 'yes'!... and the rest is history.

Cranky and Sue, Helen and I were offered a real job on the mainland, way down in Sale, Victoria. We accepted.

CHAPTER 10

SALE AND LAKES ENTRANCE TO BATEMANS BAY

*Optimists are often as wrong as the pessimist—
but have a lot more fun.*

…Author unknown.

Just before the cyclone, there was a bunch of Victorian businessmen on Daydream Island for a conference. One of them was a Russian, Vladimir 'Wally' Eremin. In July 1970, he offered Cranky and his wife, Sue, the general manager's job at the Wurruk Hotel Motel in Sale. Cranky accepted, provided Helen and I came as his assistants. They agreed.

At the time the 'new' Island wasn't the same. Lots of new faces, new rules and we weren't having as much fun. Miss Collins confided in us that they were going to sell. So the four of us set out south to face new challenges, plus a Mexican winter. Bear in mind, my entire wardrobe was two lap-laps, two pairs of shorts, two shirts and that was it. I hadn't worn shoes on the Island, but I did have an old pair from the Gold Coast trip.

We flew to Melbourne in June 1970. It was freezing. We boarded an old train at Flinders Street, Melbourne, bound for Sale, and they threw a huge metal hot water bottle into our 'compartment'. The heat didn't last long.

The Wurruk comprised 68 units, a bottle shop, five bars, a restaurant and two convention rooms. We were welcomed by the Board and Chairman Wally and set about running the place—about a mile west of Sale and set on a small lake.

The staff were a mixed bag. Mrs. Jackson ran reception—a great lady whose husband, Lionel, was Governor of the big Sale prison. Another Jackson, Gordon (no relation), was Bar Manager, and we had a lot of 'permanent casuals' who were Air Force personnel from the RAAF East Sale base. Firemen Dutchy Holland, Ray Brinsmead, and chef George Bell (whom we later worked with at Country Comfort) headed up the fifteen or so Air Force staff. Then there was the chef, Leo, and wife, Benildis, plus the counter lunch cook, Carol, whom I remember best.

Cranky was cranky. He resigned most days and only lasted two board meetings. In September, they accepted his resignation and he and Sue took off back to Queensland.

Meanwhile, Helen and I had shopped, bought a few clothes and settled in, and the board asked us to take over.

The first thing the board advised was that I had to have an Aussie rules team to follow so I could talk to locals in their language. I was reading the *Melbourne Herald* and looking at that week's AFL draw, and I saw an article written by 'The authoritative voice of Louis Richards'—boy, was he up himself. He was commenting on a game, St. Kilda versus Carlton. St. Kilda were going to win easily. "The only guts Carlton have is the guts to turn up!'—those 'weak-livered useless Carlton buffoons would be thrashed.'"

Now, I did not know where either St. Kilda or Carlton were, but immediately made Carlton—the underdogs—my team… and they won!

Chef Leo was a hoot—Swiss born and miserable. Every week, when he opened his pay packet, he winged that he was worth lots more—week after week. He was getting much more than we were!

One night, we woke to the sound of fire and screaming. One of the guests had fallen asleep smoking. He was burnt—not too badly—and was running naked around the courtyard. Benildis wrapped him in her fur coat. It was a funny sight seeing him loaded into the ambulance.

We let Leo and Benildis go and appointed an Austrian chef, Peter Michelsz, and his wife, Connie.

THE BRIGHTER SIDE OF A DEATH THREAT

We were having problems with theft. Alcohol, smokes and even housemaid supplies were disappearing. I needed help. The board suggested we double the times the local long-time security company came each night. I discussed this with them, and we set up a plan. It didn't work, and things kept disappearing.

In desperation, I decide to sleep inside the hotel on a mattress and—guess what—bingo! I caught the security guys stealing cartons of grog and cigarettes. I was chuffed with myself. They were charged and their business folded.

A couple of years before, the board had decided to build new units on the lake front. Instead of going to the bank, they decided to go public and offer locals shares. It worked for them but not for us. Every local who had $50 only in shares thought they owned the staff and gave them hell. One, a pig farmer named Charlie McLaren, became aggressive every night and wouldn't leave. "You bastards work for me. I'm a part owner", he would say. He owned about one brick. But the worst night by far was New Years Eve 1970.

We had a huge night planned—everything sold out. Dinner and show was $55, an enormous amount back then. Plus we had temprites and kegs ordered from about a dozen big home parties. The bottle shop was flat out all day.

Our Melbourne jazz band arrived and set up mid afternoon, and all were excited about our $300 winner-take-all dancing competition.

My Mum and some of Helen's mates were coming. The board had a V.I.P. table of eighteen, including their Melbourne legal team, the bank manager and the Mayor of Sale. It was going to be the biggest night of our lives. Around 5 o'clock, Mrs. Jackson paged, "Mr. Smith to the office immediately". I ran, as she had never done this before. She said, "Gordon Jackson has had a fight with his wife."

I said, "What's that got to do with us?"

She said, "A fist fight, in the bar downstairs. We have rung an ambulance and Gordon has taken off in our truck with all the kegs and temprites."

Ouch!

Meanwhile, around 6 o'clock, I had to start sending bottled beer to those parties whilst we looked for the truck. I rang the police and reported it stolen. It was not found until early next day. Disaster? Yes! But worse was to come.

Around sevenish, half an hour before the big dinner and show, Mrs. Jackson's voice came over loud and clear. "Mr. Smith to the office immediately."

What now?

It turned out our chef, Peter Michelsz, had heard the dumb waiter come up from the bar and went to investigate. He found a delicious cocktail and a love note from a barman to his wife, Connie. They had a huge blue, and he stormed off "to kill myself". Drama!

Connie was inconsolable and we all started looking for him. He wasn't at his house. Couldn't find him in town, and guests were arriving and we had no chef.

I will never forget the look on our counter lunch cook, Carol. As she came in dressed to kill, she looked great. I dragged her aside and into the kitchen, told her what had happened, and set her the task to fix it. She was not a happy girl.

Then a barman yelled they had found a body by the lake. Yep—it was Peter and he was still breathing and had lots of empty pill bottles around him on the ground. The ambulance took Peter and the police arrived.

Meanwhile, the 200 guests were all in and seated, the jazz band started, and there was no sign of dinner. Carol, bless her, had somehow pulled together a sort of alternate drop entrée which started to go out—very late.

Having been trained too long by Miss Collins, I was determined not to let our guests know we had a major disaster going on. The board were getting a bit agitated. I had told the staff to serve my table and the board last. Wally was ropeable, so I told him we had major challenges beyond our control and we were doing the best we could. He then instructed me to make sure the Mayor—a notable dancer—won the dance competition. I said 'no'—it was up to the judges, but I would make sure he was in the final three. Wal was not happy with me.

Carol was fantastic. She somehow managed to feed all 200, albeit late. But she did a brilliant job, and I will forever be in her debt.

The dance competition got underway, and there were a number of excellent contenders. Finally, the judges had only three couples left on the dance floor and the crowd was going wild as one was the Mayor and his popular wife. And then it happened.

THE BRIGHTER SIDE OF A DEATH THREAT

The Mayor was turning his wife under his arms. His sleeve button caught her wig and pulled it off and exposed her bobby pins holding down her gelled hair. She freaked, and immediately king hit the Mayor and knocked him out cold.

Mayhem.

That was the very first night I heard Helen swear.

In the aftermath, we were advised the hospital rang to say Peter had regained consciousness and Helen said, "Sack the bastard". We all laughed. But—I did. What a night!

Next day, the board held an impromptu breakfast meeting and I was summoned. I gave them the full story, from the bar manager beating up his wife in the bar and stealing the keys and temprites through Peter and Connie's fight and attempted suicide and Carole's heroism, and finally the Mayor's knock out. They were not impressed. Yet Helen and I were gifted a very rare and valuable Magnum of Beer in a champagne bottle for being in the top ten Bottle Shop sales in Victoria. Very impressive. We kept it.

However we were not happy there, and about a month later an opportunity came up that appealed to us. We were part of the Flag Motel chain, and Helen and I came under notice from their Executive Flag Chairman. Angus Taylor rang me and asked could he come down and see us.

He did, and told us he and his business partner owned other Flag properties—one of which was the prestigious George Bass Motor Inn at Lakes Entrance. He said the incumbent manager was ripping them off and he asked us to do six months there, help with the investigation and steady the ship.

Helen and I were already contemplating to buy a small motel in Batemans Bay and we saw this as a good stepping stone, so we agreed. We gave notice, and then drove a few hours north to Lakes Entrance.

As arranged, we went into reception and asked for the Manager, Bill Mackay. Bill came out and we told him we were relief managers for Flag with nowhere to go and they had advised us he and his wife Theresa were long overdue for holiday. They had never had any, so we were there for two weeks.

Bill told us in no uncertain way that he was not going anywhere, so I suggested he ring Angus Taylor. An hour later he drove out—angry. He told me that we were not welcome 'in our private unit' and would need to stay in a unit for the two weeks.

The first thing I did was ask the receptionist for the wage book so I could familiarise myself with who worked where and what kind of hours. She told me that the week's wages had been done and processed so there was no point. I again told her it was the best way to see who was what, where and when, and I need the book. Eventually she gave it to me and her shift ended. We never saw her again. It turns out she had come to the Motor Inn from Brisbane with the Mackays and was part of the 'team'.

First thing I saw was the name of the new chef 'Peter Michelsz'. I did a double take. He had gone from Sale to here some five weeks earlier. When he and Connie walked in, they froze when they saw Helen and I in reception.

There were a few awkward moments but, after a cuppa, we were all fine and shared a few laughs. We stayed close to them for many years and they were invaluable at Lakes Entrance.

The first thing we realised was there were more staff listed on the books than actually worked there. Some seven phantoms I think. The other staff members were very cooperative.

We found out that no local police who were friends of Bill ever paid for food or grog. This was not all the police—just a few duds. We found many invoices were for goods and services never received. It was a mess. I ended up as a prime witness and Bill ended up where he belonged.

After a few weeks, we had the place humming. The hanger-onners had disappeared. Local police who heard what had happened called in to eat, drink and pay. Good guys. One of them, Dick Ellis, went on to Inspector and is Warren's godfather. He later became Mayor of Lakes Entrance and is a great community leader.

Another policeman, Denis Drew, was a Slim Dusty tragic. He came up with two tickets for Slims show in Orbost that night and offered one to me. I couldn't go, but we talked Helen into going—a three hour drive. They were due home around 1-2 a.m. but walked in to the restaurant about 10 p.m. The Slim dusty concert in Orbost was the night before!

We are still in touch with Denis—another goodun. He is visiting us again this month.

THE BRIGHTER SIDE OF A DEATH THREAT

One afternoon late, Dick Ellis came in very stern faced. A gang of three hoodlums had committed a series of armed robberies from Sydney to Melbourne. In Melbourne, the leader bashed his girlfriend, who was with them. She went to the police.

She told them they had cased out a number of places on the way down to rob on the way home and we were one of them because of our isolation, and it was to be tomorrow night. They would be in a light van.

Peter and I switched out all lights as usual around 11 p.m. and, armed with a .22, sat guard.

A long night.

Nothing happened until about 5 a.m—still dark. A light van pulled up on the cliff top opposite. The rifle was aimed and we were petrified. That poor fisherman will never know how lucky he was not to die. He opened his van, pulled out his rod and tackle bag and disappeared over the fence to the path to the beach.

The crims were caught in Bairnsdale on their way north and never got to us.

Helen's mum came for a visit and witnessed a horrific car crash opposite our driveway, and a fellow died. Sad. The rest of her stay was fabulous. Shirley was a top lady—not necessarily 100% happy with Helen's choice. Sideburns, tattoos and a drinker! But she was always very polite, a super lady and staunch Methodist!

We started to get really interested in Batemans Bay. Dick Ellis came with me on a few trips looking at motels and flats, then finally Helen and I went up—did a deal and signed to buy the eight unit 'Motel Batehaven'. Champagne flowed.

We resigned from our fabulous six months in Lakes Entrance, but before we left, we had one wonderful event. Warren was born in Bairnsdale Hospital on Saturday 17th September 1971. What a gift. Probably the best day of both of our lives up to this point. So three of us arrived in Batemans Bay to start a fantastic fourteen years.

LANCE SMITH

The only other thing I must write about is that on one of our Batemans Bay excursions, Dick Ellis and I were returning home to Lakes Entrance overnight. Around 2 a.m., somewhere around Cann River, my motor seized. We hadn't seen a car for hours. I had just finished telling Dick how I had been lucky in life and everywhere I fell over there was a ladder to take me even higher. He straight away asked me if I had brought a ladder on this trip. Ha-bloody-Ha… at 2 a.m!

Just then, we heard a motor from the north in the distance and happily flagged them down in the dark. It was my mother's sister, Sheila. She and husband, Dick, were heading to Melbourne for the annual ski show. I hadn't seen them for two years. The ladder had arrived.

Oh… and one final tale. Dame Zara, widow of our late Prime Minister Harold Holt, had remarried Jefferson Bates, a shifty politician from Tilba Tilba. They stayed with us every time they travelled between Tilba & Melbourne. Often. Every time, Jeff would attempt to pay the bill with his cheque. Every time, I refused and Dame Zara would end up paying by cheque. (No Credit Cards in those days) Hers didn't bounce.

Despite him being miffed, they still stayed with us. Years later, the publican at the Tilba Hotel told me that when Jeff was in town he shifted the peanuts, chips & cashews etc. from where they were for sale on the bar to over the back, because Jeff kept taking and never paying. Nice bloke.

CHAPTER 11

BEAUTIFUL BATEMANS BAY

Life is a big canvas—throw all the paint on it you can.
...Danny Kaye

We sure tried to. Some of us live in a 'dream world', whilst others face 'reality'. I have continually tried to turn one into the other—and not always successfully.

In early 1971, we arrived in Batemans Bay, stayed a couple of nights with Jack and Bobbie Jury at the Hanging Rock Motel, then found a flat in Golf Links Drive. We had three weeks to 'kill' before the motel settlement was due. I read in the local newspaper. Big news: A home delivery postal service was to be introduced to Batemans Bay in four months.

I checked both Emmets and Thompsons Hardware. There were four letter boxes in total for sale between $15 and $30. I drove to Sydney and bought 300 letter boxes of varying sorts and came back and started door to door selling. I sold out in a week and went back for another 200 and, again, sold out. It was a very rewarding project—huge mark ups.

However, the following week a headline in the *Southern Star* proclaimed, "Con man, charlatan at large in the Bay," and a story written by an Eric Wiseman, advising residents that I had been claiming to be an official from the Australia Post. The two local shops were outraged.

What I, in fact, said, 'verbatim', was, "I am here in conjunction with the new mail service starting in a few months and if you do not have a letter box you will not get any mail." All above board and a very successful project. It is funny to see some of the flash letter boxes still there today, nearly fifty years later, although Ed Byrne is still arguing the price.

We settled and moved in to the Motel Batehaven in March and first up we had Jack Jury (apart from his motel, Jack was also a builder) draw plans, get approval and build a glass reception at the end of the motel. It looked great and worked well.

Just to put it into perspective, if the motel was chock-a-block full, the gross total takings for the day were $96. Yep, eight rooms @ $12 bed and breakfast. Our daily routine began at 5 a.m. I would start the wood-fire boilers to give everyone hot water, then set, cook and run the breakfast trays, collect them, wash up and clean up.

Helen opened reception at 7 a.m. and did all the checkouts. We then had to clean and make up the units prior to 2 p.m. check in, and we shared reception duties and answered phones—whoever was closest—all the while attending to our beautiful baby.

We did a deal with the main motels on the highway to not put up their 'no vacancy' signs until we were full out at Corrigans Beach. They were our main source of low-season business, as we were full most nights during the holiday season. Our repeat business was fabulous. Life was good. I convinced Helen to let me buy a boat to allow me to 'take guests fishing'. Later, I also bought a ski boat and we spent many a great day ski-ing and fishing.

A Lions Club was being formed—chartered by Canberra Valley Lions, led by Eris Pollard, John Trevillian and Ern Smith. We chartered with Jack Jury as our first President. Jack, Terry Smith and I filled the position of President twice over the first few years.

One of our first major projects was a billy cart derby down the huge, steep Vista Avenue hill. Half the town turned out and carts came from Canberra, Goulburn and Queanbeyan. We designed and built a fifteen-foot monster, 'The Lion Tamer', with massive wings on the back. Beautiful. Trouble was a fellow Lion, Des Phillips, was a sign writer but also a bad speller. The crowds at the top of the Vista Avenue hill erupted with laughter when we pulled off the cover to reveal our 'masterpiece'. Des had printed 'the

THE BRIGHTER SIDE OF A DEATH THREAT

Loin Tamer' down both sides.

At that time, the Bay had a champion swimmer in the making: one of the Innes lads, Grant. His mum and dad, Robyn and Merv, owned fishing trawlers. Grant was favourite in the feature race and was very nervous because he knew I was thundering down behind him—with no brakes. Grant made the mistake of looking back. He lost control and speared into the crowd. Three taken to hospital. Grant broke both arms and withdrew from next week's State swimming titles and the billy carts all went home. Robyn was livid with us.

One of our Lions Club members was Bruce Burgess, a local real estate guy and also a (bad) pilot. He donated a joy flight as a prize at one of our meetings and the then president, Jack Jury, was petrified of flying and wouldn't buy a ticket. What he didn't know was everyone else bought a ticket and put Jack's name on the butt. It was hilarious.

Two of our members were real larrikins, Derek Campbell, a builder, and Bill Lenehan, a plumber. I had bought an old double-decker bus, renovated with two bedrooms upstairs and shower/toilet, lounge, kitchen and dining downstairs. Magnificent. We used it every year as a mobile home at the ski fields. One night, I drove 'Goldie' to a Lions meeting at the R.S.L. Driving home. I realised I was illuminating every boat in the Marina on one side and shining into everyone's bedrooms on the other. Campbell and Lenehan twisted the bus headlights to face outwards.

Another night I drove our old 'Birdland' ute to a Lions meeting at the R.S.L., came out and took off home. I needed to brake for a car coming out from the Hospital Hill. I had not seen the truck behind me, but suddenly 'crash' from the back and the rear window exploded. Glass everywhere.

I was shattered. I extricated myself from the mess only to find there was no truck. Campbell and Lenehan had loaded one of the R.S.L.'s empty beer kegs into the back of my ute and when I put the brakes on it rolled forward and smashed into the back window.

One day, I had had enough. I came out of the R.S.L. and Campbell and Lenehan had filled the back of my ute with hundreds of empty cartons and packing cases from nearby Emmetts rubbish. I saw red & drove straight to the nearby Police Station. Gordon 'Honky' McSevney was on duty and I knew him quite well. I demanded that he take action and lock these two bastards up. Gordon calmed me down and then assured me that justice would be done. I felt better.

It was a week later when I found out Campbell and Lenehan had left early and, in fact, the bloke who did it was Honky McSevney himself—the policeman. Another bastard.

I played my last game of football—Lions v Apex at Mackay Park. We lost—the game and the fights.

Of course the two outstanding moments in the Bay were the arrival of Melinda, in May '73, and Ashley, in September '75. A brother and sister for Warren. We were blessed. Having kids is life's biggest thrill… and we were gifted with 3 gooduns.

Batemans Bay was a great place to bring up kids. It is strange, having lived all over the world, when people say to me today, "Where do you come from", I still say Batemans Bay.

Both Helen and I became involved in lots community activities: The Bay Theatre Players—we were both in many productions. Helen helped with Playgroup and Ballet. I joined the Chamber of Commerce and went on to become President. We ferried the kids from sport to school to dancing and everywhere else. They were good years.

It amazes me how many people think 'the grass is greener on the other side'. They would be surprised how green their own grass is. All you need to do is water it. We did—and love life.

A couple of things:

We started a group who went running on the beach then surfing at 5 a.m. to 7 a.m. Monday to Friday. On three days a week, it was followed by squash at 9 a.m. I would start the boilers at 4 a.m., set the trays and head out at 4.45 a.m., usually with Melinda joining us and occasionally the boys.

We were up to about 35-40 regulars until the movie, *Jaws*, came out and we quickly became 10-15. We ran for an hour, swam for 30 minutes, showered at the beach and home before 7 a.m. to cook, then to squash at 9 a.m.

One of our regulars, Tom Pitt, (Tom and wife Scottie owned the Batehaven General Store) was a classic. He was the most laid-back bloke I ever met. **Every** day he would forget his togs and towel at the beach and

THE BRIGHTER SIDE OF A DEATH THREAT

needed prompting to go back.

I think the best story I remember about Tom was the day a truck load of bricks arrived in town, and the driver went into Pitts store to ask Tom directions to 27 Joseph Street. Tom had no idea so yelled, "Scotty, fella here looking for 27 Joseph Street."

Scotty yelled back, "We live there, Tom", and it dawned upon him they were his bricks for the house extensions. Classic Tom.

One day, out of the blue, I received a phone call from Charlie Wedd—the primary school Principal, and he asked could I come straight away. I did. There were all the kids assembled and the presentations underway for the Athletics carnival that day. The main prize was the cross country champion 'Melinda Smith'. What? How? Then it dawned. She had been running with our mob five days a week. She went on to win at Zone and went to Sydney for the State titles. Came in mid-field, but a great experience.

My baby sister, Marcia, came to live in the Bay with hubby and son, Shane.

On a sad note, my beautiful mum only ever saw Shane and Warren. She came once to Batemans Bay, but died soon after.

Talking of Melinda, her birth was not without incident. We had friends staying and I had gone to an evening meeting at the Catalina Country Club and overstayed, drinking. Around 10.30 p.m., I received a phone call. "Get home quick. Helen has broken her water."

I had an idea to inject a bit of fun into the event and put on goggles and flippers before going inside. I was the only one who thought it was funny. We arrived at the hospital around 11.30 p.m. and stayed in the car. I was trying to reason with Helen that we could save over $50 if she wasn't admitted till after midnight.

Sister Williams saw the car and came over. She took Helen's side, but did promise to record it as after midnight.

I drove home. Just as I came in the phone was ringing. It was Dr. Blake advising Mel was born. I only just made it to the maternity ward! Hospital records still show Melinda born at 11.45 p.m. on the 9th May. Helen was admitted at 1 a.m. on the 10th May. Winners everywhere!

But it didn't stop there. I went back up to the hospital and came home around 3 a.m. Next morning, I was doing breakfast and the hospital Sister Nash rang to say Helen surprised everyone and had given birth to a twin. Wow! I jumped into the car and flew back. As I raced into the hospital Sister Williams was still there. She set me straight. Someone had set me up! It was Marie Patterson who had phoned, impersonating Sister Nash, and I fell for it hook, line and sinker. My excuse is that Helen, herself, was a twin, so I thought it plausible. The Lions Club thought it was hilarious.

Two days later, Helen was still in hospital and I was officer-in-charge of both the motel and Warren, doing breakfasts, when W crawled over the carpet joint and picked up a huge (2 inch) self-tapping screw. Before I could get there, he had eaten it. Panic! Up to hospital, an urgent X-ray and, **phew**, the blunt head of the screw was coming through first and he would pass it with no worries. I was so relieved I bought a lottery ticket for Matron Nash and I to share. I called it 'Our Screw' and matron was glad we didn't win!

Ashley's birth, too, had a few hairy moments. I was at the hospital with Helen and the doctors advised he had serious heart irregularities, and an ambulance was on the way. Canberra here we come. All turned out okay, and Ash's heart kicked into gear after a couple of worrying days.

During the early '70's, the Cootamundra gang were getting back together. Julie Lake, by now Julie Ceeney, and hubby Greg, bought a waterfront Caravan Park just along from us at Corrigans Beach, and then John Lord and Joy arrived to live. It was back to the good old days. Many of our Coota mates either came there to live or had holiday homes. Even our next door neighbours at the motel were the Thompsons from Coota.

One night, Helen was dancing in a show at Moruya to raise funds for a young man who lost both legs in an accident. Ballet teacher, Michael Anderson won the main raffle—a huge fifteen-pound Dusky Flathead. Massive. We had no fridge big enough—even the motel kitchen. Paul and Marie Patterson were with us and offered to hang it in their butcher shop cool room—opposite Ceeney's Caravan park.

Next morning, I hatched a plan. I rang Greg and Julie asking if I could fish off their beach. They said, "Of course." An hour later, we appeared at their office with our 'just caught' giant flathead. They were over the moon. Took photos under their park entry for their next brochure. Greg told us

THE BRIGHTER SIDE OF A DEATH THREAT

how lucky we were because dusky flathead always stay in the rivers and don't go out to sea. They called the newspapers—more photos.

He rang me that night to say he had sold over $500 worth of fishing tackle and bait that day—a record.

He was very pissed off when he found out we had won it in a raffle at Moruya.

Local police numbered only five. One howling-gale night, I got a call from the Sergeant, Max Love. They needed help with a cliff rescue at Malua Bay. Doug Drinnan and myself rounded up a dozen volunteers and we spent a few hours hanging off a cliff face in the wind and rain.

We eventually pulled the guy up top in a stretcher into an ambulance. The police superintendent from Bega came up next day to say thanks and we all received a commendation later in the year.

Talking of Sergeant Love and Malua Bay—a classic. Local character, Bob Hillman, was getting married to his gorgeous girlfriend, Annette, or Kelly as we called her. Bob had come to the Bay as a 'dropout' from his highly paid executive role at George Pattersons Agency in Sydney. It was in all the national papers.

Bob and Kelly were real favourites in the Bay Theatre Players and we wanted to give them something to remember. I rang Alan Head, Funeral Director from Moruya, and told him I wanted to borrow his hearse. He was not willing but I finally convinced him—along with a coffin. On the way driving home from Moruya in the hearse on the Friday night, I called in at the bowlo and, as I was leaving, Police Sergeant Max Love was about to ring his wife for a lift home and I offered to drop him off.

The look on his face when he saw the hearse and coffin was something else. But worse, as we drove along, I told him there was a body in the coffin and the morgue was full so I was taking it to Patterson's butchery to leave it in the cool room. Max fairly flew out of the hearse in Golf Links Drive.

Next morning, as arranged, I drove it to Brian Koorey's Bayview Hotel and we filled the coffin with grog and drove out to 'Wainbah' at Malua Bay. Geoff Lassau, Farmer John Casben, Brian Koorey and I dressed in our dinner suits, crammed in, and I drove.

LANCE SMITH

On arrival at 'Wainbah', Dr. Humphreys had a 'choir' lined up. The boys walked beside the hearse in their dinner suits as I drove up the drive to the front door. Hillman appeared at the front door—dressed in shirt and undies—mouth gaping. We heard Kelly scream to him to put pants on.

The coffin took pride of place on the veranda table during the wedding.

Just to give you an idea of Hillman's sense of humour, years later I was about to open as 'Tevye' in *Fiddler on the Roof* in Sydney. There had been a deal of publicity about it, and a lot of Bay people booked opening night.

I still have the letter from Hillman, and I quote, "Mr Smith, we are advised you are playing the lead role in the musical *Fiddler on the Roof* in Sydney. We have been invited to attend. Unfortunately we have heard you sing. Kind Regards, Bob Hillman."

A great mate.

Another one—again years later, in my Lend Lease days. It was a feature in the Sydney 'Sun' newspaper telling of my losing 23 kilos and raising heaps of dollars for the Children's Hospital at Camperdown.

Another Hillman letter quote: "Mr. Smith, It has come to our attention that an article in the Sydney Sun reports you losing weight and gaining money. Obviously it was the other way around. Kind Regards. Bob Hillman."

My weight loss challenges were well known. Local Bay Real Estate Agent, Brian Connolly, and I had a very public weight loss challenge. Brian was a massive 32 stone and I was around 19 stone. To weigh Brian, we had to use a tractor pulling him up on a block and tackle at the game-fishing club scales.

It was to be held over ten weeks. The pot was $1,000 and the winner was the person who lost the greatest percentage of body weight.

We both worked very hard. Brian lost an amazing 11 stone. The good news is—I won! Just.

Another wager, in 1978, Dr. Humphreys offered to put $1,000 in a savings account provided that Brian Koorey and I did likewise. Brian and I were both heavy smokers. The deal was that if either of us smoked during the next six months, the $3,000 would be split between the others—or, if we

THE BRIGHTER SIDE OF A DEATH THREAT

both went back on it, Dr. Humphreys got the lot. He lost his $1,000 if we both made it.

It was by no means easy for anyone. After three months, Dr. Nigel started sending us cigarettes and matches in the post. Brian and I have not had a smoke in the past 40 years and we split $1,500 each.

At various times, our kids caused a variety of concerns.

As a baby, Warren 'escaped' from reception whilst still only crawling—but fast. I heard the screech of brakes, saw Waz missing and froze. He had crawled out the door left open by a guest, down to and was crawling across beach road. The poor driver threw up everywhere. He thought he had hit him, but thankfully, not.

Melinda was hospitalised with a 'serious' virus and extremely high temperature. The hospital team were bathing her in ice on the veranda in mid-winter to get the temperature down. Dr Humphries arrived and immediately called an ambulance and off to Canberra, again. Thankfully into the care of a brilliant paediatrician, Dr Tony Crawford. Pneumonia. A week later, back home. All well.

Ash had a couple of 'moments'. The first was when I bought two Pee Wee 50 motor bikes from Ed Byrne. Ash was riding the bike in park at Corrigans Beach and froze, pulling the throttle onto full bore. He was heading straight to the main road when a quick thinking Jack Danzey, 1st grade Sydney referee, raced across and pulled Ash from the bike. **Phew.**

Another time, years later, it was Boxing Day and we were picnicking with the Lords, again, at Corrigans Beach play area, when Ashley came down the slippery dip head-first into the concrete pad. Ouch! Lots of blood and all top teeth all gone. Straight to hospital while we looked for his teeth in the grass and dust.

Local dentist, Ron Gifford, was about to drive out on annual holidays when he got the call. He didn't leave Ashleys side for 48 hours. Found all his teeth, up in his gums. He did perform remarkable surgery and we were very, very, very grateful. I must say I was dreading the bill, and it came a few weeks later. $1540. **Ouch**! A fortune back then. I could buy a block of land for $800.

But then, under the 'amount due' were the words, "However for what you have done for Batemans Bay...Credit $1540....balance: **Nil**."

LANCE SMITH

I cried.

Another Warren moment: Warren at the Ski fields. More later.

Melinda had another mishap, aged around 18 months, crawling along the motel veranda and into a unit as the wind slammed the door crushing her fingers against the metal door strip. Ouch. For two hours, I held her while Dr Blake sewed the fingers into some sort of shape.

During my 'get fit' endeavours, I started playing basketball two nights a week in 'B' grade. 'Honkeys Haulers' were a draw card. Honky (Police Sergeant Gordon McSevney, named after our Birdland wombat because of a similar gait), our star—Real Estate Agent David Hayes-Williams, Solicitor Graham Kennedy, (totally unco-ordinated), Dr. Nigel (I think he was Captain), Hot Harry from the Department of Transport, Phil Penman and myself were the founding team and regulars and we had **the** most beautiful and talented coach in Australia, Jenny Hayes-Williams. Jenny took us to the grand final, and we **won**.

The basketball association held their annual awards at the Catalina Club. I was MC and David Hayes-William's brother in law, vet John Laws, was to receive an award. I knew he was terrified of snakes, so I borrowed a large python from Birdland and had it hidden in my guitar case on stage. Lawsy's acceptance speech came to an abrupt halt and the scream is still reverberating around the Bay.

Talking of Birdland, not my best idea!

Around 1974, things were going really well. We had saved a few dollars. I was President of both Lions and the Chamber of Commerce. Warren and Melinda were growing up too fast. Helen was pregnant. Life was good!

Everyday I used to drive to town and over the bridge and look at Russ Farrell's Van Park looking over the creek at the She Oaks and bush. It looked like an Island and reminded me of Currumbin Bird Sanctuary on the Gold Coast.

I sat Helen down and told her I had the 'best idea ever'. Helen's eyes rolled.

I had searched titles and found the land had beach front to the Clyde River, a creek around two thirds of the parcel and a road frontage to the

THE BRIGHTER SIDE OF A DEATH THREAT

Beach Road and side road access from Hanging Rock. It was owned by the Department of Lands. We could develop an attraction along the lines of Currumbin Bird Sanctuary. Easy. So I drove to Nowra and presented my idea to the Department of Lands. They liked it.

I convinced my great friend, Doug Drinnan, and long time mate, Ken Paull (from my Sydney/Ed Byrne/diving days), to join me.

I digress, but around this time, Doug and I came up with another idea to have people do a bit more for nothing and the savings passed on. It was called the T.O.O. Campaign. (Think Of Others). The national and then international media grabbed it. Doug and I were flown all over Australia and New Zealand to address groups and we had dialogue with countries like Russia, Germany, the U.S.A. and the U.K. Batemans Bay was on the world stage.

During all these flights and drives, we developed all the strategies and plans for our wildlife park and chose the name Birdland Wildlife Park.

We submitted all the applications to the Department of Lands and Council and, after protracted negotiations, we received a forty-year lease and Council approval.

At the end of 1974, we got stuck into it with the backing of our Bank Manager, Bob Spruce. Our first job was an eight-foot-high plastic-coated wire fence around the ten acres, capable of keeping animals in and people out. We then began building the brick front office, bridge entry, interpretative centre, the brick café and souvenir shop in the area outback, and the kids play area. We bought in an old farm building from Mogo which ended up our machinery and storage area plus a 50-foot tunnel for the 'Birdland Express Train'.

Yes, that's right. We bought a fabulous mini-train engine and three carriages, plus nearly 500 metres of tracks from the N.S.W. cane fields which wound through the park—through the tunnel and over bridges, creeks and past waterfalls (man made).

Add to this, many cages of various sizes, thousands of hours work and major tree-planting and landscaping projects and some fantastic community support, and we were ready to open.

Yep—we had overspent the budget and Sprucy was not happy with me.

There is an old Chinese proverb, "Fall down seven times. Get up eight."

First up—our beautiful train had only one consistent habit: Derailing!

Some eight-minute journeys took thirty and we lost a lot of sweat putting the motor back on the tracks. The carriages were fine.

We were 'donated' birds and animals from all over the country in response to the media call out. We inherited 'Wally', the world's largest wombat, Ernie the emu, snakes, kangaroos. goannas, wedge-tail eagle, chooks of all sorts, Cleo the yellow-tail black cockatoo, a huge variety of finches, parrots and cockatooos, including Ken's mother-in-law's 'Cocky McCormack', a galah with attitude and lots of colourful pheasants. We had foxes, glider possums and more.

Ken's mother-in-law had smoked all her life and developed a really bad cough. Cocky McCormack had perfected mimicking the cough. We thought that was funny until the wildlife authorities started raiding us because of complaints from visitors about the galah who was close to death.

Ernie the emu loved red. One day he started to follow a very apprehensive gent in a red jumper. The fellow sped up, terrified! Ernie sped up, the fellow ran, Ernie ran. He eventually ran out of breath and collapsed. Fun over, Ernie just shook his head and walked away.

We had a revolving gate at the front entry and Ernie had worked out how to stand upright and push it around. He escaped often, and the only person he would follow was Helen. She used to go to wherever he was sighted, put her arms around him and walk back to Birdland. One day, somehow Ernie ended up in the new Batehaven supermarket and became spooked. It was a scene from Hollywood—a chaotic mess. Helen calmed him down and brought him home, again.

Wally the wombat, too, had worked out how to tunnel under our fence, and regularly escaped. Being so big, he frightened people. One night, he destroyed John Bamman's garage. Another time, Barry (our park caretaker), and I took two nights to coax Wally out from under a house at Sunshine Bay. He had already devoured their lounge chair and a divan on the verandah. Lots of blood—all Barry's and mine.

Wally's funniest escape: One day the phone rang and a distressed member of the Ison family in Catalina Heights yelled that, "Mum is trapped in the toilet and a big bear is eating the toilet door."

I knew straight away it would be Wally and was able to resolve the situation, but we did have to pay for a new door.

We had many fun times in Birdland: concerts, parties—even a regular

THE BRIGHTER SIDE OF A DEATH THREAT

lunch get together—the Frontiers Club.

However, the dollars did not stack up and we were in trouble. We had sold the motel and got the capital gains into Birdland and shifted into a shack we bought in Matthew Parade. The bank decided that because we couldn't sell Birdland, then we had to sell our home. It was Easter, 1978, pouring with rain and Birdland was closed due to flooding. We had a menagerie of birds and animals in our house because Helen thought they might drown in Birdland.

Rod Deadman, a real estate agent, had a very keen buyer from Goulburn prepared to pay $43,000 for the house. **A great price**. All she wanted was a quick look at the interior.

I told Rod impossible—we had too many issues with housing Birdland nursery babies from the cold and rain. He rang back. Just a thirty-second look. I said, "Give me an hour". Helen was not impressed with me. We took cages and animals, one by one, into our garage. It resembled Noah's Ark.

The lady arrived. It was still bucketing down. She walked through the front door just as 'Holly', a five-foot grey kangaroo, bounded out of the lounge room. I explained that Helen was worried because Holly was frightened of lightning and thunder and better off with us.

As she walked into the kitchen, Ashley, then three years old, had 'Harry', a young rock wallaby, in a choke-hold. Ash saw us and dropped Harry onto a lino floor. A wallaby's long legs pumping had no traction on lino, and when he finally jumped it was straight at the lady, who yelped. I promised her that was all we had in the house and proceeded down the hallway to show her the bathroom.

I opened the door and even I baulked. There was a black baby pig in a red and white jumper. I looked at Helen in despair and she said, "He was cold and shivering so I dressed him and bought him home."

The lady turned on her heels and walked out, never to be heard of again.

In the midst of all this, I had decided to stand for Council. Eurobodalla Shire stretched from Durras Lakes in the north, down to south of Narooma and back to the Clyde Mountain ranges. Spectacular coastline, inlets, rivers and mountains. As President of the Chamber, I was batting my head against a brick wall trying to get events started and promotion underway. I was really chuffed to top the voting count. Our team had worked hard.

My first three years were a learning curve, but I was mentored by two terrific men: Ron Prior, our local bus proprietor, 15 years on Council and was re-elected, and Jack Parker. Jack had retired but still keen to advise. My third councillor, also new, was the remarkable Robyn Innes. A great lady, tough and intelligent. Robyn's daughter, Liz, is the current Mayor and doing a great job.

In the third year, I became Deputy Shire President. At the end of three years, Ron P and Robyn stood down and the 'three Smiths' were elected: myself; Terry, a former policeman and now very successful businessman; and Joe, a solicitor who had arrived in town, fell for, then married a local delightful girl, Dianne Veitch. I was privileged to win the vote as Shire President so spent a deal of my time in Narooma, Dalmeny, Bodalla, Moruya, Mossy Point, Broulee, Tomakin, Malua Bay, Durras, Long Beach, Tilba Tilba and Nelligen areas as well as the Batemans Bay District.

It was all go. In those early days, we talked 'team' and the need to thrash out all disagreements and present a united front consensus and support whatever way it went.

Sounded good. Joe didn't get it. He thought 'team' described pouring rain. Even if he voted for something—including his own suggestions—he would immediately switch and agree with every dissenter. He would sell his Grandma for six votes and that never changed.

Terry was a no-nonsense bloke, but true to his word, and the three of us did very well, not just for the riding but the whole shire.

The job had it's setbacks and challenges. Being such a large area and split into three 'ridings'—loosely, the Bay, Moruya and Narooma districts—there were parochial issues. No one wanted to pay rates but everyone wanted road works, sporting fields, new hospitals, marinas, bridges, libraries, swimming pools etc. It was a balancing act.

As stated earlier, my first term had been with two great Councillors, Robyn Innes and Ron Prior, both of whom I respected and liked. Still do. Though poles apart in politics, Ron was President of the Labor Party, Robyn was campaign head for so-called independent John Hatton and I was Chairman of the south coast Liberal Party. We never once made a decision or statement along political lines. The same thing with the three Smiths. It was always what was best for the Shire, and it worked.

The Bay owed a gratitude of debt to Ron Prior. The Bay Hospital, in the

THE BRIGHTER SIDE OF A DEATH THREAT

'60's, was a ramshackle collection of 'huts' in North Street. Two adjoining doors were the operating theatre and the pit toilets. Fly swatters were standard in the operating theatre—especially on hot days—and the stench!

Years of requests from Council and the Hospital Board had fallen on deaf ears in the corridors of power. Not enough votes. Ron put together a brilliant presentation to put before the United Nations General Assembly asking them to consider a new hospital for Batemans Bay when deciding on grants for third-world and impoverished areas. It got world wide publicity.

Jack Beale was our State Liberal Member—a despicable power hungry creature who had followed his dad into politics. He was livid with Ron and Doug Drinnan and the rest of the hospital board. Within two years we had a beautiful, new twenty-bed hospital under construction overlooking the Bay and Tollgate Islands.

Thanks, Ron and Doug. I hope heaven is being kind to you both.

When the Liberals became the State Government, Premier Tom Lewis—who I knew well, and liked, rang me to send him the names of six locals he could appoint to the 'new' hospital board. I sent him the six best. Tom was furious when he found out three of them were card carrying members of the Labor Party. He got over it!

They were a terrific board and did a great job for the Bay.

My strangest call on Council matters came at 2 a.m. one Sunday morning. A distressed resident at Malua Bay reported a large lady had just gone into the pit toilets. There was a loud crashing noise—the toilet, the shed *and* the lady had all fallen into the sewerage pit. Yuk.

My funniest recollection was when we were seriously running out of water—very little left in the dam at Buckenboura. A team of top bureaucrats flew in Sydney and we took them bush to the dam site. We literally had seven days supply left. We first took them to local property owners, John and Jane Bassingthwaite (ex Cootamundra). Jane had freshly baked scones, just whipped cream and butter and freshly-squeezed iced oranges

By the time we got the delegation to the dam, they were our best friends. Thanks, Jane. We had media with us and they suggested I take off shoes and socks and stand in the water for a photo. I agreed—as long as cattle carcasses nearby were not in the photo. It was front page and no carcasses. But the following week's paper had a letter to the editor from a very distressed lady claiming her disgust at my feet in the towns drinking water, and advising she now boiled her water before watering her flowers! Thank goodness she didn't see the carcasses.

Shire Engineer, Peter Abbotsmith, was brilliant. On the day we took the delegation to an area we called 'The Botanical Gardens', just south of the Bay, and showed them plans, designs and a spot where two hills came together and a small dam wall would 'waterproof' Batemans Bay immediately.

Given the dire circumstances and great presentation, the bulldozers were on site in just seven weeks, and today the Bay has beautiful Botanical Gardens and a permanent water supply. I hope heaven is also looking after Peter Abbotsmith. Another goodun.

On the downside, Jack Horne was our town planner and a very poor bureaucrat. He caused us a lot of grief. One day, in the old council chambers I heard a ruckus and raced in to see Peter Abbotsmith about to deliver a killer hit to Jack—already lying on the floor. Even though I would have loved to see the end of Horne, it was not to be this way, and we pulled Peter away.

It wasn't long before we had a number of complaints—some from female staff, and sufficient to suspend and dismiss Horne. We contacted the whizz-bang lawyers in Sydney for the correct wording on the suspension.

Jack appealed. We all came to Sydney for the case, armed with lawyers, Barristers and Q.C. and a three-foot high pile of Jack's previous poor record and written warnings.

The case opened and closed within ten minutes. Our legal team had forgotten to put the words 'and his previous record' on the suspension letter and the Judge would not allow us to present it. Horne won.

We had two choices:

(i) Reinstate him or

(ii) Pay him out.

We chose number two. When we refused to pay the Sydney's legal team they insisted, "It was not wrong advice. It was poor advice." We should still pay. We didn't, and heard no more.

THE BRIGHTER SIDE OF A DEATH THREAT

Our Council needed a new home. We were working in two houses joined together in Moruya and way overcrowded. In came the 'big boys' from the city who all wanted to build the new Shire Chambers.

As we had just received our first ever canal estate proposal plus our first high rise proposal. We decided to fly to the Gold Coast to check out the good and bad points of their developments and drive home discussing our new chamber issues with the likes of Coffs Harbour and Port Macquarie, as they were coastal towns with similar development issues. There were also new council chambers in four places worth looking at.

Old Councillor, Reginald Murphy, was a fifty-one-year veteran of council. He lived in the bush at Neragundah, did not own a car, and he and his brother Dudley had once gone to Canberra on a trip.

Our party of eight drove to Sydney to catch a Gold Coast flight. Reg brought two huge brown paper bags of sandwiches. Asked why, he said he and Dudley had looked on a map how far it was and thought he would need food for four days. We boarded the flight from the aero bridge and sat on the plane. Reg then asked Peter Abbotsmith, "When do we go out to the plane?" He had never seen an aero bridge and thought we had to walk out to the aircraft and up stairs. Too many old movies.

When we arrived, we checked into the 'Chateau' at Surfers and took the lift to the 19th floor. Reg had never been in a lift. When he got out and looked out the window, he froze. All this is spot on… and Reg was one of nine votes. By the way, the Chef at the Chateau was Peter Michelsz from the Wurruk and Lakes Entrance days, and half of the duo band in the restaurant was Gavin P. from Daydream Island. He and Gary were diving instructors at Surfers. Small world eh!

I remember we took all Councillors on a bus trip to look at the newly completed coast road from Moruya along the river to the aerodrome, then north along the beaches, Broulee, Mossy Point, Tomakin (Dog patch), Guerilla Bay, Rosedale, MacKenzies Beach, Malua Bay, Lilli Pilli, Denhams Beach, Surf Beach Sunshine Bay, Caseys Beach, Corrigans Beach, Batehaven past the Clyde River Marina to Batemans Bay. The final Broulee leg had been completed that year. An eight year project.

Reg got up on the bus and gave a passionate 'congratulations', 'wonderful', 'amazing', 'superb' type speech to the 'A' Riding Councillors for this 'world class' coastal road. Ron Prior then reminded Reg he had his vote recorded against the expenditure five times in the previous five budgets. Parochialism at it's best.

One night, a group of us had a big night out at the Steampacket Hotel at Nelligen. Our great mate, Farmer John, and his wife Carrie, from nearby 'Farmer Johns', were, like the rest of us, glad they had a car. They were in no state to walk. Yes—pre RBT days.

We all put pressure on John to let Carrie drive. He did, reluctantly, and Carrie reversed in the pub car park flat out, into a telegraph pole. John took over and drove east into the fog and missed their driveway to the farm.

The Casbens had come into our lives in the mid '70's. Farmer John was the heir to the famous Casben Swimwear Company. His gorgeous wife, Caroline, was a former model. They purchased forty acres of prime waterfront real estate on the Clyde River at Nelligen and commenced living John's 'dream'. 'Farmer John. Orange Grove'. He wanted to develop an eco-style tourist attraction on the land. He saw an old barn done up for parties, weddings, barbecues etc. He wanted to sell local produce—mainly fresh fruit and veggies and also develop some accommodation.

To say we had many a great night in Farmer Johns barn is a huge understatement. We, along with their two bundles of joy, Trygve and Liv, all went on their journey for years. None of us will ever forget John's rich baritone voice singing his anthems, *Mine Eyes Have Seen The Glory*, on many occasions—with Bob Hillman conducting a make-believe orchestra.

John's in-laws lived there, Philsy and Joyce Southwell-Keighly. Joycey played piano at every Bay Theatre Players party night and often at Farmer John's dos. One day there was a snake in the house, and Joycey told Phil to 'get rid of it'. Everyone heard the shotgun blast. There was a hole in the floor for years and there were bits of snake all over the walls and windows.

Tragically, John died in his 30's. It was a devastating blow to all of us. I remember sitting in the Church in Sydney, still numb with disbelief and tears flowing.

Liv Casben grew up—travelled the world and joined the BBC in Scotland as a journalist before coming home, and has now been on the ABC TV for many years. Liv married at Farmer Johns and has two lovely children and grandchildren for Carrie. Little Trygve grew up and got real lucky. He

THE BRIGHTER SIDE OF A DEATH THREAT

married my brother's baby, 'Nicole', and they are living on Farmer John's waterfront block today with their two fabulous children, Zoe and Kai.

Our youngest, Ashley, and his gorgeous wife Marney, had their wedding reception in Farmer John's barn in 2003 and are still 'regulars'. Their wedding started with a river cruise from Batemans Bay on Merinda, a rose petal walk to the ceremony under a huge oak tree at Nelligen and butterflies released as they said 'I do'. A fantastic reception in Farmer Johns old bar.

John's ghost was there and Tryg sang all his old songs.

No Batemans Bay story would ever be complete without the tale of Paddy MacKenzie.

Brigadier Don MacKenzie (Rtd.) was a 'stiff upper lip' product of Duntroon Military Academy. His little Irish-rose wife of fifty or so years, Paddy, basically milked the cows, baked the bread and so on. Don did everything else. They lived on their idyllic property at MacKenzies Beach.

Don asked to see me one day and advised 'confidentially' that he had terminal cancer and wanted to 'do a deal' to ensure Paddy's financial future. He offered, at no cost to the public, MacKenzies Beach, the headlands and bays going south to Rosedale in return for permission to develop smaller acreage blocks along George Bass Drive.

What a gift. We all moved at great speed with the bureaucrats and the deed was done before Don passed away.

But Paddy was now on her own at 74 and had never driven. She purchased a white Honda and started to have driving lessons—a lot of them! She eventually got her licence and the whole district knew to watch out for her—and tell all visitors.

You see, Paddy drove with one wheel either side of the centre line and slowly. She would not drive at night thankfully. She came to our place one day to brag that she had driven home from Canberra in under seven hours—it took the rest of us under two hours.

At one council meeting, I sensed something unusual was happening. Eric Wiseman, a local journo and thoroughly miserable creature, had come in and nodded to one of the Moruya councillors who suddenly said:

"Mr. President. I would like to move a motion that we write to the Batemans Bay police for an explanation as to why they gave Mrs. MacKenzie a licence."

I hadn't seen this coming and called for a seconder, the other Moruya Councillor. I immediately said, "Okay, all those in favour say 'Aye.'" Enough did, so I said "Motion carried", and gagged the councillors who wanted to expand. Wiseman was furious. They had a plan to launch a 'headline' story and I stymied it.

On the way home, I called into the Bay police. Sgt. Max Love was there, and I advised him the letter was coming. He immediately called Ron Nunn and Ross O'Dwyer into his office and said, "You two are the traffic officers who issued the licence. Can you answer the question?"

After looking at each other, Ron Nunn said, "We took Mrs. MacKenzie on nine separate tests and failed her each time. We discussed it and decided not to risk our lives again." Enough said.

One day, John Gill called in to advise me a close friend of mine had taken over as General Manager of the prestigious Country Comfort Motel—set in acreage on the north side of the Bay bridge. His name was Bill Mackay, and he was keen to catch up! Yep, the same Bill Mackay from the George Bass Motel at Lakes Entrance.

Now, I am not a dobber, but this was too much. At the time, I was Chairman of the Region 8 Tourism Board which took in Thredbo, Queanbeyan and over to the coast—a huge area. Lend Lease owned Thredbo and all the Country Comfort motels and resorts around Australia and their Director, John Hagley, was on my board and we got on well.

I rang John to advise him he would have trouble getting a licence for Mackay given his track record.

"Tell me about it," said John. They knew his background but were going to give him a go.

Do you know the 'leopard' story?

Two years later, the police were waiting for Mackay at the Westpac Bank in Batemans Bay. They charged him with a number of offences.

Let's talk about John Gill—the Bay was lucky to have big Gillie and Carole. John was revered by the 'Mexicans'. He had won a Brownlow Medal playing

THE BRIGHTER SIDE OF A DEATH THREAT

for Essendon. At 6ft 6 inches, he was an imposing figure.

The Gills owned the Bay Newsagency and John was President of the Chamber of Commerce when a front-page story in the *Canberra Times* told the world the Bay was 'a rip off' in peak periods. It pointed out many price comparisons from winter to peak summer.

The Gills also owned flats at Batehaven-Taliva Lodge. Some members of our local Greek community were savaged in the article, particularly Michael Diacomohalis, whose bread prices in his convenience store went up at 5 p.m daily—as soon as the only supermarket shut.

Leader of the Greek community was a fabulous bloke—Sid Pashalidis, an oyster farmer. Syd had a delegation of his fellow countrymen at the hastily called special meeting of the chamber. Some seventy odd people turned up instead of the normal dozen.

Gillie spoke and said some of the stories were true and that those responsible should take a good look at themselves.

Sid rose and said, "Mr. Gill, friends of mine stayed in your flats last July for $150 per week. They then paid $475 for the same flat at Christmas."

Gillie, the master, replied: "Sid, $475 is my normal price. I discount in winter". Classic Big John. He was responsible for starting our first ever Batemans Bay Aussie rules team. Good fellow.

Talking of good fellows, Bill Lenehan, despite his damaging my bus headlights and smashing my ute windows—is also a good guy. He has done heaps for our Surf Life Savers over the years and early '80's was part of our National Titles delegation on the Gold Coast.

One night, no one knows who started it, a fight broke out in a surfer's pub. The police were quickly there and arrested the main thugs. Later that night Bill's wife, the beautiful Robyn, was very worried at his non-appearance at the unit and began ringing hospitals, police etc. Around 3 a.m. the whole Bay team went out searching.

Things were very grim until Bill walked in around 9.30 a.m.—about an hour after the police bailed out a John Smedley, who had been arrested for disorderly conduct over a fight in a Surfers Paradise pub the night before. 'Smedley' failed to appear at the court and forfeited his bail. Lenehan goes red when we call him 'Smedley' and he doesn't come to Queensland anymore.

LANCE SMITH

Another 'Bill'—this time Billy Mistakis—a young Greek boy kidnapped in Sydney. Police were broadcasting the description of the kidnappers car. Big Brian Connolly was out looking at Real Estate and spotted the car in the bush near Shallow Crossing. Brian hot-footed into town and alerted the local constabulary, mainly Mike Broadfoot. He was the only one on duty. Mike mustered up Gordon McSevney and a posse and they made a timely guns-drawn raid on the bush camp, scaring young Billy and arresting the bad guys. Much excitement and plenty of media and police dollars spent in the Bay.

Another Bay story worth telling: Terry Smith owned the Mariners Lodge Hotel Motel—the poshest in town and right on the waterfront. They had 'done up' an old large storeroom and called it 'The Captains Cabin'. It looked sensational and good for a 120-seat cabaret style night. Smithy was looking at an official grand opening night.

Helen and I were in Sydney and were recommended to go to a dinner and show at the 'Speakeasy' Theatre Restaurant at Kensington. Wow, an international act *Solomon and Goldberg* were on. Brilliant. After the show, Solomon and Goldberg 'did the room' to say hi to the patrons. Solomon landed at our table and I expressed my regret that those in the smaller towns like Batemans Bay never got the opportunity to see such world-class entertainment. One thing led to another and Terry had his 'opening night' act booked. They were keen to see some of Australia's coastline and happy to do it at mates rates. Great excitement. It was very soon a sell-out with a waiting list.

Helen and I weren't in town. We were on the Gold Coast staying at 'Paradise Towers'. At just twelve stories, it was then the tallest building on the coast. What happened next was a classic. Helen and I checked in and walked off holding hands. An hour later, I was walking past reception, again holding hands, but this time with Patsy—our Daydream Island receptionist. The lass at the front desk was flushed.

"Mr. Smith, Mr. Smith, an urgent phone call. Can you please ring Mrs. Smith in Batemans Bay immediately?" and she gave me the Mariners Lodge phone number. She had seen me holding hands with two gorgeous girls within the hour and then had to tell me my 'wife' wanted me to call urgently.

THE BRIGHTER SIDE OF A DEATH THREAT

Of course it was Mrs. Terry Smith telling me that Solomon and Goldberg had cancelled for Sunday and the big opening 'because of ill health'. She yelled at me, told me she knew it would never work and assumed they didn't want to travel that far and made up a story.

Panic—we had 48 hours. Terry was able to get Jan Adele and 'Mr'. Chris Shaw, a female impersonator, and by all accounts they brained them. Jan was without doubt one of the best Cabaret performers in Oz.

Solomon died in Sydney on the Saturday morning.

One of my bright ideas was to wear a toupee. I trooped off to Sydney, was measured up and purchased a very expensive toupee. So expensive I decided only to wear it at meetings and special functions. That was confusing.

I decided to have a bit of fun and wear it to the Catalina Golf Club. As I strolled through the front entrance the doorman, Stan Hillier, called me back and told me all visitors had to sign in. It had passed the test. Stan was a good mate and didn't know it was me.

One day at the Motel, I cooked, delivered and collected trays as normal and then showered, dressed and put on the toupee. As I was heading to a meeting, a guest, on checking out, told me, "I was talking to your older brother when he bought my tray this morning." Another endorsement.

But there were two close mates who wore toupees 100% of the time. One was our much loved Bank Manager, Bob Spruce, and the other a fellow Lion, Ben Ogden.

Ben and Val owned a fruit and veggie shop in town and tragically lost their son Rick to cancer at just 21. Ben was very sensitive about anyone knowing he wore a toupee, and one night was cleaning his using metho and he flicked it. The metho hit the gas stove, the toupee went up in flames and poor Ben was bald and hairless.

The phone rang at the motel—it was a distraught Ben. "You know how you only wear your toupee when you are going to special meetings. Do you mind if I borrow it for a month or so?"

What a classic. Ben's hair was a very different colour so he had a two-tone hairdo for about five weeks. Funny.

Talking of Bob Spruce, some people have a heart of gold. As our Bank Manager, Bob knew how tough things were. We had sold the motel and were about to lose the house. Things were not looking good. One Friday, Bob and Judy rang to say they were coming to see me at Birdland and could Helen be there. They came down the path, over the bridge and into the office. They gave us two return flights to the Gold Coast, leaving tomorrow, a voucher for a week's accommodation at Aquarius Apartments, plus an envelope with $500 in it. They were going to look after Warren, Melinda and Ashley for the week. All out of their own pockets.

I still get choked up. It is awful having to face reality when you have made a bad call, but people like the Spruce's certainly soften the blow. Bob always looked dapper in a white sports coat with a pink carnation.

Judy Spruce, like a Gold Coast friend of ours, Jai, has a dreadful 'disease'. She just cannot be on time. Used to drive Bob batty. Always late—not sometimes, not often but always. One night they were late at David Craig's Christmas pool party. Some of the guests were being thrown in the pool and Judy got quite stroppy. She did not want Bob thrown in because of his secret toupee. She proceeded to get a few drinks on board and we ended up back at their place for a nightcap. Judy went to the toilet. We all heard a loud crash and splash. She came walking back in like a stunned mullet. From the front, it was obviously Judy, but she had tripped on her undies and, because she was late, had not let the bath out and fell backwards into it. She was soaked, and I mean soaked.

Another Spruce story. As a Bank Manager, Bob was in his office signing house documents with a local solicitor, Junior McHugh (who went to gaol for ten years for fraud, but that's another story). Bob looked up and saw a house being driven past on a low loader. He immediately realised it was Bob Heron's home, and Sprucy blurted out, "Stop—I've got a first mortgage on that house."

Junior quickly replied, "Not now you don't. It's going out to his farm at Cullendulla."

Bob was shattered.

Bob always had a frown on his face. One day I asked him why he always looked worried? Silly question. He then spent days worrying that he always looked worried.

Special people, the Spruces. We love them.

THE BRIGHTER SIDE OF A DEATH THREAT

There were many days that produced frightening moments. One of these was when I headed out to sea in our wooden ski boat to do a spot of fishing. I think it was Paul Delves, a mate from Sydney. Robyn Delves and Helen were old school buddies and Paul was another C.B.C. Bank Manager like Sprucy.

We were some ten to twelve kilometres out to sea when Delvesy hooked a shark. We got it into the boat and I noticed big black clouds coming from the south and the seas were rising. We decided to head for home pronto and I was travelling too fast. We soon smashed into a wave and split the wooden slats the full length of the boat. Panic stations! We were still way out at sea. No mobile phones in those days. We both sat on one side and kept the crack 'sort of' above water and kept bailing.

Somehow, an hour later, we cruised past Tollgate Islands at the mouth of the Clyde into relatively calm water. By the time the boat sank we had been seen from the headlands, and a boat came to our rescue and fished us out of the drink.

Another story on the Bay is a goodun. Local vet, John Laws, and horse trainer (and builder) Jack Jury were going to the yearling sales in Sydney and asked me to tag along. Near the end of the sale, they brought out an old 'warrior' who had seen better days, Tangalooma Lad. He looked buggered but had a really friendly face. No one bid, so I bought him for $500 and registered him under Helen's and Bobbie Jury's names. I did it mainly because Melinda had begged for a horse to be kept with 'Duke' at Farmer Johns.

Turned out Tangalooma was sired by 'Even Stevens', winner of both the Melbourne Cup and Caulfield Cup and his mother was a classy Kiwi mare—Blue Camellia.

A local acupuncture healer, Arthur Newman, asked me could he do some work on the horses back with his new laser. A month later, Tangalooma's back, which had looked like a corrugated iron roof, was flat and straight and Arthur had also found bad stone bruising and was able to fix that. Vet John Laws said his teeth caps had never been maintained and it was a wonder he could eat. So John went to work on these.

Well, with all that done we had a new (but old) racehorse. He won nine races including the Cooma Cup, the Pambula Cup, and the Merimbula Cup. One day he ran second to Tommy Smith's horse in Canberra Black Opal

Stakes Day at sixty six-to-one. We had a ball and, for whatever reason, I have never had a bet since—even on Melbourne Cup days. Just sweeps.

Tangalooma was retired to stud with Jack and Bobbie and lived many great years.

Life is a roller coaster... and the Bay was no different. Neill Lassau was a great mate, a great guy and a terrific pilot. Brian Connolly and I won't ever forget how he coaxed that little plane to clear the trees on the top of the Clyde Mountain, with the two of us over fifty stone! We just made it. Canberra never looked so good.

But I also won't forget the police knocking on my door advising Neill had been killed in a plane crash and they were unable to track down Sandy. A few phone calls and we found she was at a meeting at the primary school. I was elected to break the news.

Two things:

- Neill was delivering a brand new plane and the tail malfunctioned causing the crash. There was nothing he could do and criminal charges were later laid against the manufacturers, and
- Sandy did a super job raising the three boys but, equally sadly, died of cancer in her late thirties. Life can sink the boot in!

The funeral celebrant at North Sydney was a shocker. The only thing that 'saved the day' was Melinda fainting at the service. She had lost four wisdom teeth and lots of blood in the week leading up to the funeral.

Another mate, Harry Patrech, had a disaster of a totally different kind. Harry was a super-intelligent drop-out and did precious little but grow and smoke the green stuff... but we all liked him. Harry had easily been dux of Moruya High, so it was not a surprise to see him on *Who Wants To Be A Millionaire*.

Harry had used two of his three lifelines and had achieved $16,000. If he got to $32,000, he then got to keep it as a minimum. He balked at the question and asked to 'phone a friend'—his last lifeline. The 'friend' was Moruya Headmaster Brian Passmore—another whiz.

Brian said, "B".

Harry asked, "How certain are you."

Brian replied, "One hundred per cent."

THE BRIGHTER SIDE OF A DEATH THREAT

Harry said, "No, I don't think so. I will go with 'D'. Lock it in."

It was 'B'. That was Harry.

Another classic. Back to the Mariners Lodge. Terry had employed a pommie girl, Annie, in the public bar. A great lady with a great sense of humour. One busy Friday night, a bloke kept saying something to her 'on the quiet'.

Annie stepped back, reached under her skirt, took off her knickers and handed them to the bloke. She said, "Go on—get into them then." Brought the house down.

At one point—another of my bright ideas—we purchased *Merinda*, the small ferry which had plied the waters between Palm Beach and the central coast. It was to cruise the beautiful Clyde River. We were backed by a great guy, Jack Riley, who really got behind us. I did a terrible job with the marketing and promotion and the whole venture did not go well.

Fortunately, the Innes's took it on and made it into a great success. They are still cruising nearly forty years later, but in a magnificent new boat.

One beaut story on *Merinda*. Local mates and surveyors Bullock and Walters organised their work Christmas party on board. It was booked—an evening cruise for forty people—on December 17th 1982. This happened to be the first ever night of random breath testing in N.S.W.

During the day, I had received a call from a good cop. He knew of the cruise and realised our usual practice of driving home after the event. He told me half the Wollongong police team would be in town to have a 'dress rehearsal' before rolling the RBT out in the 'gong' next night.

I rang Ralph, and we organised for everyone to be picked up by Priors Bus Service and then driven home after the cruise. Job done. As we cruised back to the Bay and along the waterfront, we could see the 'operation' in progress. A number of our cruise guests offered some 'encouragement' to the visiting police.

Our bus was then pulled over for a driver breath test on the way home and, again, our guests had all sorts of advice for the police.

Everyone was delivered to their doorstep by midnight, and then realised they had to get the baby sitters home! Shock, horror! There were no taxis in Batemans Bay. Our phone rang hot. Helen was the only non-drinker in the team and was breathalysed five times before delivering the last baby sitter home around 2.30 a.m.

Talking of Innes's: years later we were in the Bay with Glenn T. in his SAAB convertible. We went to visit Robyn at their fabulous guest house overlooking the Bay and islands. Sunny day—roof down—pelicans flying overhead! Not a good finish. It took months for GT to get rid of the pelican poo. We didn't believe how much there was. Must have eaten a small whale!

Another good story. Local playwright Ron Seymour wrote a musical: *Wouldn't Be Dead For Quids*. The world premier was to be staged at the Bay RSL, upstairs. A huge crowd turned up. The crowd filled the street outside to watch the red carpet arrivals. Hillman was doing live radio interviews on the carpet as were WIN TV. A big show. Every 'second' arrival came in a gold Rolls Royce we had procured from a Sydney developer, so therefore every second arrival was in another vehicle of some sort.

Helen and I arrived in formal attire in the Batemans Bay sewerage removal truck. The best arrival was our Bay Theatre Players President, Neill Lassau. The crowd heard sirens, saw flashing lights, and became silent when the ambulance drove up to the RSL and stopped.

There was a brand new doctor just started in town that day, John Berrick. Dr. Berrick pushed through the crowd and said, "I'm a doctor, I'm a doctor," as they opened the rear doors of the ambulance to reveal Neill on the stretcher with a slab of beer on his chest and one beer in his hand. The crowd roared. Dr. Berrick said, "Oh Shit," and walked off.

What a night it was. Leslie Wiles played the part of 'Racecourse Red'—a voluptuous lady of questionable morals. RSL Executive, Geoff Lassau (Neill's brother, Geoff is still one of Batemans Bay's finest) next day denied balancing champagne glasses on Leslie's boobs—until the photo appeared as a full page in the *Australasian Post*.

That night also saw the introduction of our new town solicitor and his wife, Rick O'Neill and Janice Fox. What a pair. The foxy lady soon became a real favourite with everyone and just about took over the Bay Theatre Players. Years later, in Queensland, they split and it was not pleasant. The Fox's best mate, Annie Hillman, and I were 'summoned' to an up-market nursing

THE BRIGHTER SIDE OF A DEATH THREAT

home on the Gold Coast to sign her last will.

When she passed, we were sworn to secrecy and she had no funeral because she was afraid her ex would find out and contest the will till all monies were exhausted—into his practice. A very, very sad end to a much loved lady.

During all this, the motels, Birdland, Shire President, Bay Theatre Players and helping to raise three kids, I also successfully auditioned in Sydney for some national TV commercials. One was for the 'Clean Up Australia' campaign, one was for the introduction of fringe benefits tax. Another—a world wide campaign for Levi Jeans—saw me in Broken Hill for a week of filming and also introduced the American male model of the moment, Eudon Whitfield, to our family. Eudon has been a favourite son ever since and has visited often.

I also won a principal role in Mike Willisee's series on famous Australians, filmed in the early eighties.

I mentioned earlier that Mum had been in *Ten Little Niggers* in Cootamundra, so I was pleased to win the lead role of the judge in the Bay production. Trouble was, the judge was unmasked as the killer!

One day, young Patrick Kennedy, ten-year-old son of Graham and Liz, (cast members) saw me coming towards him and ran out in front of the traffic in the main street the day after he had seen the show. I had certainly convinced him.

And finally, probably the most satisfying success in the Bay was in 1974. As Chairman of the Eurobodalla Shire Tourism Committee, we joined forces with Bega and Imlay Shires to stage a seven-day international surf boat race along the original George Bass route from Batemans Bay to the Victorian border. This will have a chapter on it's own and appear later.

Queensland was calling, and we were ready.

Batemans Bay will be forever 'home' to me, the place where we enjoyed our three absolute treasures—Warren, Melinda & Ashley. Wonderful years. But before I move on to the Surfboat Marathon, I do have to tell you about my great mate—Wilfy Reid.

CHAPTER 12

'A FABULOUS REID'!

Great lives never go out—they go on.
...Benjamin Harrison

This chapter is definitely *not* for the politically correct.

The Shire had some wonderful characters, but none came close to Wilf Reid. I could write a full book on just Wilf. Loved by many, hated by others, Wilf's colourful escapades are legendary.

Sometimes the thoughts in his head got so bored they went out for a stroll, through his mouth. This was often not a good thing, as Wilf had a direct way of expressing himself. He was often misinterpreted.

I remember the Liberal Party brought down two of their 'finest'—Nick Greiner and a fellow named Azzopardi, for some flag waving and whistle-stop meetings. Joe Smith was MC, and when question time came up, Joe pointed to everyone else—but carefully avoided Wilfy's hand up. As the pollies got ready to leave, Wilfy loudly asked, "So you take our money for lunch but I can't ask a question?"

Greiner made a rare mistake. "Of, course you can", he beamed.

Joe choked.

"When are you going to stop giving our hard-earned white fellas money to these black fellas."

The room went into an uproar. Dolly Swift, a Swiss art gallery owner from Rosedale, demanded he be evicted for such blasphemy. Wilfy's reply, "It's time you thought about going back too—lady."

More uproar.

To set the record straight, Wilfy had lots of indigenous close mates and often helped them out, **but** he was fed up because so many bad eggs had their noses in the aboriginal industry trough and were ripping it off. He was sick of it, and so was I. It's just that he never phrased his questions 'correctly'. The point was good.

Let me set the scene. A Young Wilfred Reid was from a poor family of nine children living in the hills outside Moruya. He fell in love with the beautiful Thelma Reid (that's right. Same spelling, and it's not Tasmania) from a family of six in the same area. They married, built a block 'home' on an earthen floor on the Broulee turnoff and started a very messy car wrecking yard.

Wilf and Thelma had three wonderful boys, Wilf Jnr., Marshal and Locke. There is no way I can tell all the stories and there is one Helen has forbade me to write, but I will certainly give you a good insight.

For a bloke with no money, a non-drinker and a hard worker, Wilf was a Liberal party member—but they were always trying to get rid of him because of his blunt questions. He hated corruption and sly people with a passion, and it showed. But he was also a bigot. For example, if you went into his wrecking yard for something worth, say $20, if you had A.C.T. number plate (Labor voter, according to Wilf) it was $30 but if you had A.C.T. plates **and** a beard ('those bastards are always hiding something' says Wilf), it was $40, and he stuck to it.

One day he had a call from Canberra from a fellow who has searched the nation (no Dr. Google in those days, no Ebay etc.) for two years for a 1940 Peugot windscreen, and a friend thought he had seen one at Wilfies.

"Yes, I've got one," said Wilf.

The excited bloke said, "I'm on the way. See you in two hours."

Sadly for him, his A.C.T. plates meant Wilf wanted $50 for the windscreen. The fellow baulked. "No one else would ever want it. It's worth $30 at the most."

THE BRIGHTER SIDE OF A DEATH THREAT

Wilf said "You might be right", and picked up a rock and smashed the windscreen. That's Wilf.

One day he set up his fruit stall in our Birdland Car Park. He was selling rockmelons from his Deua River farm for 50 cents each. A lady pulled up and said she would take the lot—some one hundred melons. Wilfy asked her if she was the lady from the Batehaven fruit shop. She said 'yes', so Wilfy said, "You will buy them for 50 cents and sell them for $3. No deal."

That's Wilfy. He took five hours to sell 100 melons at 50 cents but went home happy that one hundred people had saved $2.50 each.

I served a term on Council with Wilfy's lovely wife, Thelma. She was the High School librarian and the sweetest, nicest, knowledgeable calm person I knew; the exact opposite to Wilfy.

We often had floods in Moruya, and the Princes Highway at Mullenderry Flats would close to all traffic. Wilfy had a tractor and high trailer and he would tow people through the floods for $10 each way. He would pull up in the deepest section, with water flowing over the trailer, and he had Thellie's handbag around his neck. He would climb up to the driver for his $10. If they only had a cheque, he told them he was Johnny Cash's nephew and to make it out to 'cash'.

One day, John Nader, President of the local Chamber of Commerce and prominent Moruya businessman, was there with the grubby reporter, Eric Wiseman, who had his camera ready to set Wilfy up. As he dropped a car in Vulcan Street, John strode up and, in front of fifty or so locals and tourists, loudly asked, "Wilf, wouldn't it be kinder to offer the stranded tourists a free tow through the floods?"

Wiseman clicked away. Wilfy thought about it, and then walked over the road to John Nader's Menswear shop and yelled out, "Free shirts and shoes for any stranded tourist."

John closed the shop instantly.

That was Wilf.

To his great credit, John and his brother, Michel—who between them owned half of Moruya it seemed; both good blokes and solid community leaders—chartered a plane in the middle of winter to Wilfy's funeral, on a rainy day in Temora, western N.S.W. Over five-hundred people had come from near and far to farewell a legend, and it was great for Wilf's grandkids to see 'Poppy' could draw such a massive crowd—particularly as he was just out of gaol. We flew down from Queensland for the send off.

One day, when Wilf himself was on Council, they were resurfacing the main Street, Vulcan Street. Wilf was walking down one side of the street and noticed Mike Steer, the Engineer in charge of the job, on the other side. Every worker was either sitting, leaning on something, or chatting to each other. Not one of them was working.

There were some fifteen or twenty workmen on the job and not one of them was active.

"Hey Mike," Wilf yelled.

Mike Steer and everyone else, looked at him.

"Congratulations, Mike—you've got 'em so shit scared not one of them is game to move."

Mike was not the only council employee to lodge a complaint about harassment by Wilf.

Sadly, Wilf ended up in gaol and in a prison farm near Tumut for the last bit of his life. One day in Moruya, Wilf was backing into a parking space and knocked over a motor bike. The bike's owner took exception and a fight ensued. Both Wilf and the other guy had witnesses to say the other had thrown the first punch. The case was dismissed.

Some time later, Wilf's 'witness' put in an application to Council for something outside the regulations. Wilf pointed this out and the bloke reminded Wilf that he had done him a huge favour in the court case and it was time for payback. They can say what they like about Wilf Reid, but he was a man of real principle and said he would not support it.

The bloke went to the police. Wilf was charged with coercing a witness and perjury and gaoled. There were a few who had waited for years to get square, including the magistrate. I was filthy, and Eric Wiseman kept it in the news as long as he could.

I am going to quote from a letter Wilfy wrote to me from the prison.

"My dear mate—Sir Lancelot. Well, at last I have some glasses so I can attempt to write to you. The glasses ain't too good but they have one good thing about them. They make my dick look bigger. I am in the common room. Beside me on one side is a murderer and the other side a bank robber. Across the table is a rock spider and down the other end of the table is

THE BRIGHTER SIDE OF A DEATH THREAT

a chronic masturbator (sic) who was caught recently trying to get a milk carton pregnant.

"Mate, you are so right about people. Half the bastards are not worth representing. Both Thelly and I have helped dozens over the years but only a small portion step forward to help. Young Wilf always said we should have left when you left."

That's Wilf. He once told me, "The fact that there is a 'highway to hell' but only a 'stairway to heaven' speaks volumes about expected traffic numbers." He went on to 'save the world' and Council, saying they should have heeded his warnings.

He was wrong when he said he and Thelly had helped 'dozens'. We know of 'hundreds', but he never bragged about it. He just helped battlers. A great, great man.

Couple of quickies on Wilf that must be recorded. He was leant on by the Bank of N.S.W. who tried to break him. The Bay Manager was Arthur Eastman. One day, Wilf went into Brian Koorey's pub and drank a schooner of beer—news for any of us, including Brian. Wilfy didn't drink.

He then walked across the road to the bank and his appointment with Arthur. He got into the office, unzipped his fly and peed all over him.

"That's what you have been doing to me," and walked out.

The final word. Wilfy had bad diabetes but did little to help his cause. One day in the shower, he was in strife. His old fella was badly chaffed because of the diabetes, so he reached up and filled his hands with Johnson's body soothing cream to relieve the pain. Trouble was, his eyesight was bad and it was, in fact, Mentholatum Deep Heat Rub he used. You could hear him screaming in Moruya, twelve kilometres away, and to hear him describe how he tried to dip it in ice blocks is pure comedy at it's best.

I really miss him, and see Thelly and the boys as often as possible. I should mention that Marshal recently stayed with us on the Gold Coast and was badly bitten by one of Helen's pet water-dragon lizards. He is in good company. So was Tania Kernaghan.

Vale Wilf.

CHAPTER 13

THE GEORGE BASS SURFBOAT MARATHON

Don't say 'No', say 'How'?
...Rob Chandler. Mayor of Barcaldine.

There is no doubt our beaches, rivers and ocean are the major draw cards of Eurobodalla Shire. Batemans Bay, alone, has ten beaches both in the mouth of the mighty Clyde River and the open ocean. I think they were all full in the recent tragic bush fires. So, when Curly Annabel, the 82-year-old editor of the *Bega Times* (and still skiing competitively) and Merimbula Tourism chief, Peter Caruth, approached me as Shire President with the idea of a surfboat marathon right down the south coast, I jumped at it, and said, 'how'?

After a few meetings we had a plan. The event would showcase Captain George Bass and his epic rowing journey back in 1797 in an open whale boat, with a crew of six, along the south coast.

(Captain Bass later set sail in February 1803 in the *Venus*, bound for Tahiti, but neither he nor his crew of twenty-six were ever heard of again, and never found. The perils of the wild ocean.)

Our council then agreed to call the new coast road from Moruya to Batemans Bay 'George Bass Drive'.

Our plan was to invite surfboat crews from all over to enter a seven-day surf-boat marathon, starting in the Clyde River at Batemans Bay and finishing near the Victorian border, with overnight stops along the way at Moruya, Tuross, Narooma, Bermagui, Tathra, Merimbula and Eden.

Each crew was to nominate eight rowers—a sweep with six rowers in the boat at all times, and two relief crew as required.

Scoring was easy. First across the finish line each day lost zero points, second lost one, third lost two and so on. The winner would be the crew with the least amount of points lost at the end of the seven days. There would be a daily 'leg' prize presented in each stopover town.

January was selected because summer holidays were the only time surf clubs in Australia could get crews for that length of time away.

A committee was soon established with the South Coast Surf Life Saving branch now involved and 100% behind us. It was to be the longest, toughest surfboat race in the world—and still is. It was to be a biannual event.

The new year weekend of 1975 was chosen as a starting date. My mate, New South Wales Premier Tom Lewis, was to fire the shot gun right opposite our Batehaven Motel at Corrigans Beach. Camping areas and presentation venues were booked and we sent out invitations to the surf lifesaving fraternity.

Our first major support came from Cronulla sweep, Nick Dixon, who later shifted to Moruya and became Principal at the school. Nick swept his Cronulla crew to victory in that first race, followed by Bulli, Point Lonsdale, Burning Palms, Long Reef, Moruya, Seaspray, Portsea, Tathra, Maroubra, Mona Vale, and we also had a crew from the Atlantic College in Wales, United Kingdom. What an incredible event. There was much excitement at the Catalina Golf Club briefing the night before the start.

The news that the U.K. had sent a club to challenge meant we had TV and print media from all over the world, choppers in the sky, journos in boats and on land and at many vantage points.

Most crews had huge support teams, doctors, physios, cooks, managers, drivers, rubber ducks and crew being the minimum. Most teams had trained for twelve months in the lead up and were fresh, fit and ready to row. I was the beach announcer and presentation MC for the week.

My memories of that first day are still really clear. The first thing that went worldwide were the crew changes out at sea. These were made when

THE BRIGHTER SIDE OF A DEATH THREAT

the team's rubber duck dropped two fresh rowers in the open ocean in front of their approaching surf boat, then scooting behind the boat to pick up the two rowers who 'fell' out of the boat as they approached the two in the water—all very slick. The TV footage from the chopper overhead showed it all, along with a massive shark circling the boat and unseen by all at sea level. If anything, that footage made future crew changes even faster as we went south.

Then there were the blisters on hands and bums. Ouch! Cronulla were the only crew to have sliding seats that first year. The rest used the conventional and Vaseline shorts. Never again. All crews thereafter would have sliding seats.

What amazed all of us was that the crews kept up an attacking pace the whole way—incredible.

We allowed about six hours for the first leg. They finished in just over four. A huge effort out at sea.

One downer. That first night we had a celebration in our private bar in the back of our motel. I heard a champagne cork pop and then a voice said, "It tastes like beer".

Some idiot had helped himself to my special 'prize' magnum of beer from the Wurruk Hotel in Sale. $800 gone!

Later years saw some southerly head winds and rough seas. This made every leg way tougher and longer.

Another story from that first year. The fifth leg—Bermagui to Tathra—thirty-five long kilometres at sea in a southerly. By this time there were many tired lads and the Victorian club Portsea, under the watchful eye of 'Tricky Dicky' Fisher, were to be presented their first-ever leg prize at the Tathra Country Club. The entire team turned up, resplendent in their special George Bass Surfboat Marathon team uniform—a beautiful polo neck with the race map on the back. The overzealous doorman stopped them. "Read the sign. No collar, no entry."

Their classy polo necks didn't cut the mustard with this old-timer and he was determined to show all of us his powers.

Despite pleas from race officials and surf lifesaving executives, he would not budge, and the team was refused entry.

About half an hour later, I heard this great commotion, turned and saw the whole team had come back—in women's clothing! He had to let them in, and boy were they ugly. Many great photos when they received their leg award.

That night, the Portsea sweep—Nigel (bigger than me), fell out of the team truck as it went up the steep hill at Tathra and no pain was felt, but I think Portsea was dead last on the final two legs. Nigel passed away a couple of years ago. We still have annual visits from Tricky Dicky, these days a teetotaller.

There are way too many tales to tell. That first marathon finished with a huge night at Boydtown at Twofold Bay. One crew member somehow climbed the 60-foot hoop pine tree and did a 'mooney' for all to see. The officials were not impressed.

None of us will forget the final leg in that first race. Bulli were determined to beat Cronulla on one leg and decided to tempt fate by rowing through the massive rocks on the final headland instead of going the long way with everyone else. Luckily, it was a high Christmas tide and we all held our breath. History shows they made it and won the last leg but the sweep, Robbie Meijer, was officially reprimanded and no crew has attempted it since.

The long recognised face of the George Bass was Moruya legend Bert Hunt—an incredible human being. Bert has rowed, swept and been race controller for the first forty years. What an achievement. He went on to become long time President of the Australian Surf Rowers League, captained the 2015 surfboat landing at Gallipoli and was responsible for bringing the Navy in as the major sponsor for many years. Bert 'owned' the race and history will be very kind to both him and his legacy.

Again, I could write for hours just about Bert and his band of officials—Hal and the *Sarah Jane*, Dave and Leslie Pheeney—Doctor Chris Fen, Race Referee Barry Smith from Victoria, Laurie 'Marmite', the Tathra Parberry's, and so many long serving key players like Eurobodalla Mayor Fergus Thompson, our last Shire President and first Mayor, the unstoppable Chris Vardon, the Navy's Commander, Rod Harrod, and photographer, Les Herstik, just to name a few. I had the privilege of working with them for that first forty years and delighted with their success. Crews from New Zealand, Europe, U.K. and all over Australia proudly wear their George Bass 'badges' today. I was very humbled to be placed into the George Bass Surfboat

THE BRIGHTER SIDE OF A DEATH THREAT

Marathon Hall of Fame in 2015.

By 1990 we had thirty-eight open crews facing the starters gun.

The one famous deed I want to recount happened at Coila Beach in the early 2000's. Over the years the race had expanded and now included Women's and Veteran's teams and also ski paddlers. This day, there was an enormous sea running and huge waves, and the whole team of officials were very concerned about the safety of boats, crews and paddlers trying to navigate the massive seas over the rocks and onto Coila Beach. One of the ladies teams, North Steyne, were absolutely buggered and made the heartbreaking decision to abandon their surfboat at sea and be picked up by the rescue craft. This meant their boat would be smashed onto the rocks and wrecked. Bert Hunt watched all the drama unfold from the race referees boat nearby.

None of us will ever forget the sight of him diving overboard into the boiling seas, swimming to the abandoned surfboat, clambering in and grabbing the sweep oar. No one breathed as we watched him single handedly steer that boat through the massive seas, over the rocks and into the beach. There were tears and cheers all round. That is Bert Hunt.

One of my favourite memories was the reaction of the Dutch crew of the final presentation in Eden. Again, early 2000. They were fantastic people—a mix of guys and girls but were way outclassed. At the final awards ceremony I announced to the 500 present that the Dutch had amassed so many points they could all fly back to Holland 'first class'. It brought the house down and they took it in great spirit. They were justly proud to finish the whole course.

You can always Google GeorgeBassMarathon.com.au to get more details on this amazing event moving forward. I really hope the current committee can lift this event to the high profile it richly deserves. Helen and I certainly had a ball for the whole forty years. Thanks Bert and Co.

This year 'the Bass' was called off mid race. Those massive bush fires. Crews from all over Oz and N.Z. spent the week assisting locals. They did an incredible job. They'll be back at the end of 2021—unfinished business!

CHAPTER 14

COUNTRY COMFORT AND THREDBO

Imagination is more important than knowledge. Knowledge is limited. Imagination encircles the whole world.

...Einstein

My terrific nephew, Shane R, disagrees. He has faith in the over educated green riff-raff.

As Chairman of the Region 8 Tourism Board, I had many meetings with fellow board member, Lend Lease Director John Hagley, who was the Chief of both Thredbo and the Country Comfort Resorts and Motels around Australia.

At a meeting in Queanbeyan, John ventured that I could have a great career opportunity with Lend Lease—in Lend Lease Leisure. He made me a good offer.

It seemed a new start was just what we needed. We were burnt out in the Bay, and our 'empire' was no more. John reckoned the experience I had with all my misadventures would make me a very valuable team member.

After lots of negotiations, I accepted the role of 'Groups Sales Manager', with the task of getting Australia's coach industry and group tour operators staying at all Country Comfort properties and skiing/staying at Thredbo.

They allowed me to live in Queensland and work out of Australia Square in Sydney.

It was a wonderful move—a decade of happiness and regrouping.

Leaving the Bay was not easy. We loved the people, the environment and the lifestyle, but my 'dreams' and enthusiasm had cost us everything. It was time to go.

One final story. We were packing our entire possessions into two old cars to head north—including three kids, furniture, clothes, crockery and cutlery. It all fitted. We were heading out with heavy hearts, great people, great place, great memories—and looking forward to getting back on our feet in Queensland.

There was a knock on the door. Bob Wales, a born and bred Bay identity, just handed me an envelope and said, "This is a small thanks from all at the Bay Tigers League team", shook my hand and walked off.

I opened the envelope—one thousand dollars—back then, a fortune.

I was devastated on the one hand but so, so thankful on the other. It's times like this the Spruces, the Lassaus, and Ron Gifford (the dentist), that you take a deep breath and say thanks for caring people.

This spurred us on to bigger and better times ahead—starting with Lend Lease and Country Comfort, and some more dreaming (cue—Helen's eyes roll).

I had negotiated a starting wage plus a bonus scheme. Lend Lease had accurate figures of 1981-1982 coaches, groups revenue in all their motels, plus lift and lessons and accommodation sales at Thredbo. Easy—my aim was to increase these figures by 15% in the 1983-84 financial year and my bonus was 5% of all revenue over and above those figures. Thereafter, a 10% increase target each year plus 5% bonus over that.

I took to the task with great enthusiasm—and it turned out to be very rewarding for all, in a positive way.

First up, I set out a plan:

- I would knock on the door of every major coach company/tour operator in every city and regional centre in eastern Australia
- I would attend the annual national Bus and Coach Association three-day conference, wherever it was held in Australia, plus the annual two-day conferences for the State Associations in Victoria,

THE BRIGHTER SIDE OF A DEATH THREAT

N.S.W. and Queensland, plus the annual Coach Show at Warwick Farm Race Course.
- I would get close to the motoring organisations tourism chiefs e.g. NRMA, RACQ etc. and
- I would attend the annual seven day ATE—Australian Tourism Exchange. This is where the Australian Tourism Commission and major airlines and hotels flew and hosted the top 1200 tourism suppliers from all around the world to Australia.

They were my only priorities—and I stayed focused. My first day was a real challenge. In fact, I decided after a few months to record my memories of that first day and it meant a lot to those who were there at the time and nearly got me the sack.

The accountant was an obnoxious ignoramus named Brian McGarry, and my first impression of him that day was not good. It was all downhill from there. After leaving Director Ros Matthew's office, he was my second call to sort out pays, bonuses and car usage. I told him I was happy to use my car if they wanted. He immediately scotched that.

"You will be driving all over the country, and the going rate of fifty-two cents a kilometre (in 1983 that was big) is way too much."

So I said a company car would be fine.

"No way—you need to be with the company for twelve months and be top management. You are neither. And that is strict company policy."

"Okay, I can't use my car. I can't have a company car. Do you want me to lease a car?"

"No way. That would be the same as having a company car."

In the end, he decided I would hire a car for 48 weeks per year, not on my holidays.

Later that week—Luke B., my mate at Budget, thought I was nuts. He pointed out a Commodore for 48 weeks hire, even with corporate discounts, was still five times the cost of a 52-week lease.

I rang McGarry and he said, "Don't you understand plain English. Hire it," and slammed the phone down.

Luke then upgraded me to their top of the range vehicle—a brand new imported Volvo with all mod cons, and said I could have it for 52 weeks and pay Commodore rate for 48 weeks.

LANCE SMITH

Within an hour of getting back to Australia Square, word was out about this flash car. I was summoned by Sue, 'The cupboard', to Mr. Hagley's office and asked to explain. I did. Within thirty minutes I had handed over the keys to the new Volvo and was given the keys to a two-year-old Ford Fairlane. Problem solved. I had a company car. The Fairlane was stolen from outside our Queensland unit a few months later.

John Hagley was the big boss Managing Director of Lend Lease Leisure. A really top guy and very successful. Gave me many bits of great advice. Turns out John and his wife Pat lived just around the corner from Helen's family home in North Epping, and still there today, over forty years later. I became good friends with his brother, Bob, years later in Queensland.

John's PA was Sue, who sat in a very small cubicle (the cupboard) outside John's office. Again, a great lady and an even better PA. Sue and John taught me some of the most valuable lessons in corporate life. I learnt very quickly how to get an answer from John—ask Sue first. She had an amazing ability to find him quickly and get the answer.

Over the years, just once John called me in and said, "The answer I gave yesterday was wrong. On reflection, I want you to do it this way," and on it went.

Later he confided in me two things I have never forgotten:

- Sue made all the decisions herself and let John know daily. On the rare occasion, he disagreed he took 'the blame' and said he had changed his mind.
- John could never say yes to any meeting request or social invitation until Sue said okay—even personal invitations.

That, folks, is how you become one of the most successful Directors in any corporate organisation. Simple.

I certainly learnt from it, and my 'right arms', Jenny and Gayle, over the years had that exact same arrangement from me—and it worked.

The other Director was Ros Matthews. She and her man, Richard Harper, were Lend Lease favourites and on many boards and we all got on well.

The General Manager was Darryl Courtney-O'Connor, a Kiwi with great credentials and climbing the Lend Lease ladder quickly. It wasn't long before Darryl was promoted to another part of Lend Lease and the new G.M. was an industry hot shot, Rob Annis-Brown. Rob and I became sparring

THE BRIGHTER SIDE OF A DEATH THREAT

partners over many years and many meetings and conferences. Somehow, we have remained good friends and we see and stay with Rob and Trish regularly. But we sure had our moments. Rob was an amazing leader.

Things went well. I developed strong personal relationships with all decision makers in the coach associations, motoring organisations and the inbound tourism executives.

Records will probably show my greatest idea was to establish a 'Coach Captains Club' at Thredbo. I had come to understand that it was the Coach Captains who made the decision where to ski and we were way behind Perisher and Smiggins.

The 'club' (an old clothes drying room), was fitted with comfortable lounges, giant screen TV, hot and cold food, movies, a library and more. Looked great. What the records don't show is that we had a massive snow dump during the club opening week which saw a rare (in those days before snow making) 'top to bottom' skiing at Thredbo—which would have brought the extra coaches anyway! And, boy, did they come.

But when the figures came in, months later, I claimed the credit and the Coach Captains Club was a huge success. They loved it, and we did end up way in front over the next few seasons. At the same time, we were successful in getting both APT and AAT, Australia's big two tour operators, from our competitors to Country Comfort everywhere and this was a massive revenue increase. The addition of new properties in Canberra, Dubbo, Port Macquarie, Brisbane, Cairns and Rockhampton helped here as well.

One of the greatest things working at Thredbo: Warren, Melinda and Ashley became great young skiers and won many a downhill challenge. That is, until Warren had a spiral fracture of the leg. Melinda got caught in a white out blizzard skiing with Grant Kenny and Lisa Curry and Ashley flattened a cameraman at the end of his race.

One morning, our terrific front office receptionist, Caroline Fenech, confided that McGarry was on the war path, and I was the target. Success, it seems, is not always welcome.

Our group revenues had quickly risen and I was fast becoming the white-haired boy, until the bonuses were worked out. McGarry called me into his office and declared that my bonus—which was more than my annual salary!—could not be paid 'because it was not in the budget'. I pointed out to him that neither was the unexpected $800,000 extra revenue over targets in the budgets—but he dismissed that.

In the end, they gave me two family overseas holidays for two weeks, a $5k clothing voucher and a $10k furniture voucher, plus cash—but he hated me for it, and for every year after.

Two things I remember about McGarry. One was when his wife rang with the good news that their 15-year-old son had been accepted to work at McDonald's. The screaming down the phone, the language and the observation that only peasants and the disabled worked at McDonald's was sad. The kid did not start.

The second was worse. Aids was the new big national threat. That dreadful Eva Van Graphorst case with the little five-year-old on the central coast banned from kindergarten, and all the hysteria. We were all ignorant (like the Corona Virus toilet rolls).

We had a young gay guy—Kevin Powyer—on our conference sales staff. A good bloke and a great team member. He was diagnosed with full blown Aids and given little time. Really sad. He had to confide in McGarry, as he needed to resign and there were benefits for any Lend Lease employee with a terminal illness, and McGarry was the one in charge of that. Not one of us had any inkling.

Within seconds of Kevin leaving McGarry's office, McGarry was out telling everyone. The reaction was horrible. There were some who refused to come back into the office until Kevin was dismissed and everything sprayed, and that happened instantly.

I sat with him a few times before he passed. The happenings in our office shattered him. Very sad.

Part of that year's 'bonus' was an eight-day family holiday to Club Med Bali—fabulous. We were going into Kuta, and I told the kids to beware of the hundreds of watch-sales people and fakes. Warren, then fourteen, came running up to us with a 'Rolex' watch. He assured us the salesman said, "It was a genuine replica". Some mothers do have 'em.

Eventually, I was promoted to 'National Sales and Marketing Manager', a great opportunity. This meant we had to uproot in Queensland and relocate to Sydney. A few years down the track, Lend Lease decided to sell our section and split into two parcels:

- Thredbo and
- The Hotel / Motel and Resorts Australia wide

THE BRIGHTER SIDE OF A DEATH THREAT

Thredbo went quickly to 'Greater Union', and Wayne Kirkpatrick stayed on and was made General Manager. He was a terrific choice and did very well. He went on to manage Ayers Rock Village and later a very successful CEO of Hamilton Island for many years. A class act. Wayne and Lesley are now retired and back in the Snowy Mountains.

Then we were informed that my original General Manager, Darryl Courtney O'Connor, had put together a syndicate of major investment organisations and had purchased the rest of the group lock, stock and barrel, and some of us were offered roles in the new team.

We hit the ground running in our new head office in Help Street Chatswood.

Country Comfort Management had four centralised divisions:

- Management / operations
- Sales and Marketing
- Finance
- Development

D.C.O.C. was Managing Director over all.

Management/operations came under the control of Rob Annis-Brown with Eric Sward as Operations Manager, Wayne Abrahams (Bubbles) as Food and Beverage Manager, Mark Harris as Purchasing Manager,

Sales and Marketing came under my control and we had a team of winners, including Mary-Anne Cahalan, Jenny Watson, Gayle Pryke and Graham Bull.

Finance was under the capable control of Peter Glenn, later replaced with Doug Meredith and a team of number crunchers.

Development was in the hands of Tony Leong—and there was no-one better. Tony is still a star. And all of us had been trained by our original dynamic receptionist, one Katrina Teakle. KT ruled!

Rob had put together a wealth of management talent and we quickly worked out we had a potential gold mine—client/guest wise—within our investors. The likes of the major super schemes, the Shell super fund, the Gas and Fuel Corp super fund (Vic), the South Australian local Government super fund, the M.B.F. super fund and others. We had access to nearly one million 'shareholders', so we quickly set about making many of them discount card carrying members—and it worked, especially in the corporate

/conference/ incentive area.

We became both the fastest growing and best bottom-line performers in our industry nationally, due to a lot of good ideas, terrific operations and some super promotions and events. But we had some almighty challenges along the way—and a lot of fun.

We needed a sense of humour as DCOC always said, "We will have some temporary setbacks." How right he was.

In three years, we went from twelve properties generating $10 million revenue to twenty-one properties generating over $30 million annually—and that was before Pennant Hills and Hobart and way before 'The Reef Casino' in Cairns.

We won 'gold' in many industry/tourism awards nights around the nation. We were on a roll. But behind the scenes there were many ups and downs. I will recap some of those moments in no chronological order.

Our special events and openings or re-openings were becoming legendary throughout the industry. We re-opened Tamworth after a major addition/refurbishment including the Smoky Dawson Club and conference facilities. We decided on a 'magic' theme and contracted Phil Cass—Australia's top illusionist/magician.

We had every dignitary from New England coming, and then Phil rolled the truck with all the props, crew, cast and set etc., about an hour out of town. We struggled on without a number of broken illusions and tricks and still put on a sensational night, complete with limping stars and dance troupe hurt in the accident.

The amazing Claire Hayes and her 'Pirates' did a fabulous job at our Singleton promotion. The town had never seen a musical like it. Our Singleton chef of some twenty-four years was Faith—a wonderful cook. Faith had a sister, Hope. There was not a third sister, but I know what her name would have been.

The best Singleton story I remember was when we had really dud Managers. Rob, Darryl and Co. lined up a 'strike'. We organised to meet a removalist van just around the corner at 9.30 a.m. on a Sunday—big secret. We would then move into the motel at 10 and evict the bad guys. Probably would have

THE BRIGHTER SIDE OF A DEATH THREAT

worked well if the removalist hadn't turned up a day early—waited an hour and then went into the motel to see what was happening.

He left empty. We waited on Sunday for the van and decided, at 10, we could wait no longer. So we moved in to find an empty flat, empty till etc. They had 'flown', and people were wandering around trying to pay their accounts.

By far our best 're-opening' was Canberra. A night never to be forgotten. Darryl had purchased the 'Park Royal' on Northbourne Ave and he and Tony carried out a major refurbishment and the re-branding to Country Comfort (later to our upmarket 'Chifley' brand).

Our Senior Management team were in control—George (top shelf) and Margaret Jones. I convinced D.C.O.C. that Canberra saw us as 'country cousins' and not up to Park Royal standard, so we should put on a 'Country Fair' as our theme. After a lot of convincing—he agreed.

George and Margaret loved the idea. I had good friends, Elwyn and Sandra Bell—Bells Carnival—who showed all over Australia. They brought the merry go round, laughing clowns, side show alley plus the famous Bells boxing tent and their wood-chop set up! We then organised the giant Oom Pa Pa electric organ from the Royal Easter Show and—to cap it off—Stafford Bullen from Bullen Brother Circus brought in a huge elephant. We set up in the 1000-delegate conference centre and left enough room for a 'grand parade' between all the fairy floss stalls, boxing tent and wood-chops.

What a night. Darryl wanted former P.M. Andrew Peacock, who had been a permanent hotel resident for fourteen years, to open the newly refurbished and upgraded hotel. He agreed.

George and Margaret did a fantastic job and the big day arrived. We had over four-hundred of Canberra's movers and shakers coming. Major General Alan Stretton (Cyclone Tracey, Darwin) warned me to be finished by 9.30 p.m. All Canberra functions finish by then.

Major General Stretton—who was seen doing the chicken dance at the giant organ—left after midnight, along with over three-hundred who had stayed on.

The grand parade was sensational—all inside the huge conference centre. Bands, lifesavers, the Raiders football team, marching girls, Canberra theatrical troupes, cheer leaders, Smoky and Dot Dawson in horse and buggy, world boxing champ 'Hit Man' Geoff Harding, and trainer Johnny Lewis in an open limo—and the 'Piece De Resistance', our Indian chef Youpali, riding the massive elephant.

Geoff Harding 'fought' a 'local' out of the crowd at the boxing tent. I was on the stand as a wrestler. The World Sawing champ, Dave Foster, strutted his stuff as did the woodchoppers. We had a ball.

Our kitchen staff had worked for days on a giant cake—Australia. Our food and beverage Manager, Bubbles, strolled through the kitchen, scooped up 'Tasmania' and scoffed the bloody lot. The chefs were beside themselves.

Outside in the dark, when forming up for the parade, the Bullen elephant put his trunk over the fence and pulled out a massive Palm tree from our competition next door, and proceeded to knock over boy scouts and footballers. (He damaged the Raiders green Viking van).

In his re-opening speech, Andrew Peacock said he had, in twenty-seven years of politics, never seen such a brilliant night. He said, "When I saw all the animals, I thought I had walked into a Labor Party caucus meeting."

At the time, Country Comfort was hosting a series of annual cancer kids tours (more later) and George wanted to raise $1,000 on the night. We raised $8,000. It was a huge success.

The opening of our flagship, Pennant Hill, by Kay Cottee, came close to this. Organised by Mary-Anne and Janet, and with another 100% effort from George and Margaret, we turned the new hotel into a ship. It was another wonderful success. The underground carpark was the engine room and dining area.

Also our promotions at the famous 'Old Melbourne Hotel' after refurbishment were great successes and great fun—still being talked about.

I do remember upgrading Glenn T. and his family into the new wing at the Old Melbourne and Mrs. Turner being trapped in the bathroom when the door locks fell out, and later trapped on the balcony. Locks fell out again!

I think the funniest thing I remember about the Old Melbourne was when my good mate, John Selfe, Sales Manager for Quality Inns, was staying there

THE BRIGHTER SIDE OF A DEATH THREAT

for a conference. He tells the story best.

He arrived at the reception desk and gave his name. The lass gave him a strange look and disappeared. Next thing he saw faces appearing and knew something was wrong. As the receptionist handed him his key, she advised, "Bruce, from Gay Escorts, rang. He will be thirty minutes late."

He did forgive me—eventually.

Whilst at Lend Lease, I was advised from Canberra that I had been awarded the 1988 Bicentennial Advance Australia Award. Groups of people and organisations from Batemans Bay and Eurobodalla had prepared the nomination. I trooped off to Government House and a very formal ceremony where the N.S.W. Governor, Sir James Roland, presented the award to me, heart recipient Fiona Coote, Normie Rowe and heart specialist Dr. Victor Chang. I felt very honoured.

Whilst working at Country Comfort, I did a number of overseas sales trips to the USA, U.K., NZ, Europe and Japan. I found Japan a fascinating, clean, safe place—nothing like I imagined. Tokyo Disneyland was an eye opener. Having been with Helen to Disneyland in America, I found the Japanese singing in 'It's A Small World' and the Japanese Mickey Mouse parade quite funny.

One trip, I was with a N.S.W. tourism delegation and we were in Osaka. My table was set up next to Tim Lloyd, MD of Matilda Cruises on Sydney Harbour. Tim had confided in me that his dad was very angry that he was dealing with the Japs. His dad had been in World War II and despised them.

This day, Tim was excited. He had the decision makers from Kintetsu at his table and had almost convinced them to leave Captain Cook Cruises and deal with him. His final commitment sealed the deal. "I will fly the Japanese flag every time we have a Kintetsu group on board," he said.

I leaned over and whispered, "And I'll tell your dad".

He went bright red.

One night, Tim and I were in Rappongi in Tokyo and we went down a side alley looking for an authentic Japanese diner—at the right price. We were sick of being ripped off in the touristy areas. Needless to say, we could not read the menu, so Tim pointed to three dishes and we waited.

One dish was really good and Tim was trying to find someone to tell us what it was. An old lady helped out. She spoke little English, but we both made out 'intestine of dog'. Hmmmmm

Tim loved Karaoke and there were thousands of bars to pick from in Tokyo. He loved singing 'Blue Moon'—badly.

A Thredbo story that should be told: Ski Instructor Heinz Gloor was one of the real characters in the Snowy Mountains. A Swiss—trapped in Australia because he had evaded compulsory military service back home, Heinz was always in strife. We all loved him—and still do.

One day, Wayne Kirkpatrick rang and said he wanted me to intro Heinz to a variety of Ski operators, as he was going to try him in sales. Our first call was to 'Snowy Express' at Parramatta, run by a bloke named John Timms—a small operator always promising loyalty and big numbers but never delivering. We sat in John's office. He produced his marketing/advertising plan, promised loyalty/exclusive Thredbo and guaranteed a minimum of five thousand skiers. All he wanted was a really good nett lift and lesson rate.

I gave him the best and both his and Heinz's mouths dropped. He was ecstatic and Heinz was horrified. Then I said, "John, you can pay full price up until you reach the guaranteed five thousand skiers—then we will refund $25 per person—$125,000."

The blood drained from his face. "What if I fall short of five thousand?" he asked.

I reminded him he had guaranteed that figure in his presentation. John started to get a bit angry and Heinz thumped the table. "Your business is chicken shit," he declared.

I immediately took him outside and pointed out that you do not say that to our clients. He still calls me 'chicken schmit', and Snowy Express delivered under one thousand, as expected.

Thredbo put on a 'super sales' guru, Barry Atkins. Barry only travelled first class, in limos and upgraded dining and accommodation. They sent him to the US ski fields like Aspen and Vail to pick up a few tricks. He skied for three weeks and came home. He put in a one page report recommending they put tissue boxes at the start/finish of all the chair lifts, pommers etc.

THE BRIGHTER SIDE OF A DEATH THREAT

Real value for money that trip.

The things that break the hearts of anyone in sales and marketing: Wayne Kirk had two major wins—for Thredbo. The first was he convinced top rating Sydney radio 'King' personality, 2UE's Gary O'Callaghan, to bring his family down for a weekend to try our exclusive new luxury apartments—a real coup!

Gary finished his night shift at 9 a.m., slept, then picked up the kids from school early and set out for Thredbo, arriving around midnight. On checking into the beautiful new luxury apartments, he discovered there was no tea or coffee in the unit. He rang reception and asked where he could go to get some, as he was hanging out for a coffee. He was told it would be brought over.

He waited till 1 a.m., then rang again. He was told, "The supervisor on duty (Tony Van de Niewenhoff—a goodun) was very busy and you will just have to wait."

At 2.30 a.m., Tony arrived at the empty unit. Gary had driven back to Cooma and booked into a motel with tea and coffee making facilities. He drove back to Sydney the next day.

The second was worse. Wayne had secured the world-wide launch of the brand new SAAB car; international TV, lots of film crew and supporters, big revenue and lots of invaluable media coverage. A huge win. Wayne convinced the Australian SAAB CEO to bring his family down for a weekend to familiarise themselves with the village. He made sure everything was in place and top shelf. The family, as requested, presented themselves to the staff at the Valley Terminal to organise ski hire/lifts and lessons. They asked for the Valley Terminal manager, Wayne Stinson, who came out and asked them for their letter of authority. When told it was in the apartment, Wayne stood back and, in front of everyone, raised his voice and said, "That's the trouble with you freeloaders. You want everything for nothing and don't bring the paperwork."

That's right—SAAB went elsewhere for their world wide launch.

One event that made us all laugh. Our then biggest client was APT. They rang in a panic. Rockhampton was booked out for 'Beef Week' and they needed to get a coach and 30 passengers dinner, bed and breakfast sorted. All we had was a small motel on Nebo Road in Mackay. Didn't usually get coach groups—too small—so I rang our Managers, Tom and Trudy Rutledge, and asked them to jump on the coach when it arrived.

I said, "Give them a cordial welcome, advise dinner arrangements and tell them to call you if they need anything. Make them feel special." was my closing remark. Tom rang next day to say all want very well.

Weeks later, APT General Manager John Burton called me and said, "Whatever you did on arrival at Mackay—can you do it chain wide. The passengers loved it!"

I didn't have a clue. I rang Tom and Trudy. They told me they did what I asked. 'A cordial welcome'. Blue cordial, pink cordial, yellow cordial etc. along with balloon glasses, ice and those little umbrellas, poolside. Some of our best ideas come from miscommunication.

Another classic: My good mate, Peter Colahan, and I organised to meet for breakfast on the Gold Coast—and I forgot. Three days later, K.T. called from reception. Come quick. A very smelly parcel had arrived addressed to me. It was my breakfast from three days ago—sent by Mr. Colahan.

Before that, I was scheduled for surgery to remove my gall bladder. Two days before, I rang the hospital and cancelled the surgery. (I am still President of the 'Australian Cowards Association'). I gave at least four great excuses. A few days later, K.T. called me to reception—a parcel had arrived by courier from Dr. Nigel Humphreys. It was a live chicken.

It would be remiss of me not to recall a couple of gooduns from Lane Cove Country Comfort. Lane Cove and Singleton were our two 'ugly ducklings' but they were, by far, our best bottom-line performers, percentage wise.

I used to stay at Lane Cove, commuting from the Gold Coast. One night, I was really worried. Sirens were common in that area as we were right next to the fire station—sometimes more than one. This night I swear there were upwards of fifty. They just kept coming . It was the night Detective Drury was shot—not far away!

Our Managers at Lane Cove were Pat and David Munro—great people. David was also a 'Regional Manager' and therefore spent time at other properties. This night, David was away and Pat had tradies in doing fire-extinguisher replacement. She had given them the whole bunch of motel keys and master keys and told the boss where they **must** be returned to.

THE BRIGHTER SIDE OF A DEATH THREAT

David had the second set with him in Muswellbrook.

Next morning, Pat rose at 5.30 a.m. to open the kitchen for the staff and 6.30 a.m. breakfasts. No keys.

She rang the fire extinguisher man. No answer. Staff were arriving. They put a ladder up to the windows. No joy. Locked solid. In desperation, Pat got an axe and smashed the glass door of the restaurant to gain access. What a mess.

In tears, she went back to reception to open and left the staff in to clean up and get breakfast. As she went to put the float in the till, there were all the keys. The guy had not put them back where he was asked. He just put them on the till and Pat had not seen them.

Another Lane Cove memory. Darryl had come up with the novel idea that every executive had to run a motel for twenty-four hours to understand what Managers actually went through.

He chose Lane Cove for himself—close to home and easy. At 2 a.m., the night bell went. It was me. I had a really bad ear infection and needed to go to RNS hospital. DCOC took me. There were four doctors on duty. One was Chinese, with very dirty hands and fingernails. The best humour I could come up with was, "I bet I end up with Tony Leong's cousin."

Sure enough, 'Meester Smiff'.

Darryl laughed his head off. I survived.

Lane Cove had an occupancy of 103% one month. You may think that is not possible. But a lot of 'very tired' couples just needed a room for 'a couple of hours' to 'have a rest'. We called them nooky bookings—great for the bottom line.

Pennant Hills—brand new—magnificent. The very first nooky booking. 'She' parked out front, checked in and slid a card with the room number under her windscreen wiper. 'He' casually strode past 'her' car and grabbed the card. 'She' was in 202 but had written '102' on the card. He wandered around knocking on the wrong door. Fortunately no one had checked into 102.

One night, Sydney experienced a massive windstorm. The N.S.W. Bus and Coach Association Annual Conference was at Pennant Hills, and the power went out in the district. George immediately sent staff in all directions begging and borrowing barbecues. He told the conference organisers to keep drinking by candlelight until it was sorted.

A barbecue dinner was served by candlelight at 9 p.m. to a very 'merry' 130 delegates and the Deputy Premier, Bruce Baird, had no microphone for his big speech.

A Dubbo couple booked into our old motel in Nyngan. (D.C.O.C. nearly lost his son Blair in our pool there.) It had been a Koala Motel years ago. They wrote to us expressing their happiness to be able to spend their 30th wedding anniversary in the same motel they had spent their first night of their honeymoon and their delight at being able to get the same room—No. 7. They also expressed their dismay to find the same Koala carpets and bedspreads!

Talking of Dubbo. Mike and Verna Stanton were managing when an Ansett Pioneer coach due at 5 p.m. arrived 4½ hours early. The team went into overdrive, as not all the rooms were ready. Mike welcomed everyone on the coach and advised those whose rooms were not ready to have a cuppa in the restaurant and we would be as quick as. It took an hour or so.

Later, Mike was apologising to two ladies for the delay and they were quite okay and thankful the Coach Captain had 'saved their lives'. The reason they were early was the Coach Captain advised all forty-four passengers that he was not taking them to Wellington Caves because 'a number of people had died from airborne bugs in the caves that they were keeping secret' and also he hadn't taken them to Western Plains Zoo because 'all the roads are a fine dust which goes through all your luggage—clothing and all'.

Mike was taken aback. There were no bugs in Wellington Caves and all roads in the Western Plains Zoo were sealed. He went up to have it out with the Coach Captain. Day/night cricket had just started and here he was with a fridge full of beer and hadn't missed a ball. Ansett Pioneer were not amused.

Another Ansett Pioneer story. They had come up with a special 'Red Carpet' deal which allowed their express service passengers to break their journey/stay overnight in one of our motels and catch the same service next day. Worked well for us in Armidale, Port Macquarie, Coffs Harbour and

THE BRIGHTER SIDE OF A DEATH THREAT

Batemans Bay in particular. Excellent restaurant revenue as well.

One night, in Armidale, the Coach Captain dropped fourteen people at the motel, and, unusually, waited. They all got back on the coach and went off after check in. Later, our receptionist had seen some of them returning and chatted. They told her the Coach Captain had warned them a lot of people were poisoned in our Squires Cottage Restaurant, but that he knew a Chinese restaurant in town which was 'fabulous'. Yep—we had never had food poisoning in the 'Squires Cottage' and the Coach Captain was on a kickback from the restaurant. Ansett Pioneer not impressed again.

Talking of food poisoning, our classy Port Macquarie Resort Style motel was on the riverfront, had its own beach and was magic—as was the Castaway Restaurant.

One of our chefs had had a 'lazy day' a week or so before a wedding and had not rotated the oyster boxes when the new ones arrived. Eighteen wedding guests ended up in hospital and we were in strife. Instant dismissal for the chef, and his replacement was our old air force chef from Sale, George Bell. George stayed for years—did a terrific job. We all went to Port for George's wedding. A great night.

George was also a gambler and lost his savings and his new wife's savings—then shot himself. Bloody hell. Why is this not an unusual event?

Back to Dubbo—the mice plague. Simply amazing. There were up to a hundred in every room. Try as we might to 'seal' them up it was impossible.

One of the best letters of complaint we ever received was from Dubbo—nine pages of woe. Briefly, the guest rang to check we had a spa pool before he booked his family and friends. We did. He booked. Two groups arrived for their Christmas holiday, only to find the spa was out of order—and closed! Guest annoyed—checked out to stay elsewhere (one family stayed).

He arrived back at the motel after spending an hour driving around Dubbo. The town was full, so he wanted his family room back. It had been let to another family. He was livid. Mike had one small room left with an 'uncertain' booking. He squeezed the family into the small room.

The families then decided to take advantage of our pool side barbecue—and the gas ran out after only two minutes. Angry all over again. Went to town, refuelled the gas, re-fired the barbecue and the quarter-cooked meat, finally sat on the grass with full plates—just as the automatic lawn sprinklers kicked in. Rob laughed for days—but he did give them a free week's holiday in Coffs Harbour.

We used 'Faulty Towers' as our training videos because it was so close to the actual.

I could go on for hours. Suffice to say we were and are still very thankful to Darryl, and all of us are still close today so we now have three families: 'Daydream Island', 'Batemans Bay' and 'Country Comfort' and were about to get our fourth ,'The Hills Centre'. More about that later.

Our only tragedy was losing the beautiful Mary Anne to cancer. It hurt.

Darryl must have seen Marilyn Monroe's *Gentlemen Prefer Blondes*, and he adopted their aims. It was time for me to move on… after nearly a decade of wonderful memories and successes. No more so than the 'Children's Hospital Express', which was 'born' out of the Canberra opening night's charity proceeds. That will be the next chapter.

Just like Daydream Island and Batemans Bay, we still also have many 'Country Comfort' reunions. Darryl just recently donated $5,000 to Brisbane's new Hummingbird House Children's Hospice to support my team. After the massive help he gave Bear Cottage, it was great to see.

CHAPTER 15

THE BRIGHTER SIDE OF A DEATH THREAT

The butterfly lives not months or years—but moments. Yet it still finds time enough to fly. Time is not marked by the years that one lives but by the deeds that one does and the joy that one gives.

…Author: anonymous

This chapter will be like a roller coaster of highs and lows. The twenty years Helen and I spent with the oncology kids at Camperdown, and later Westmead—leading into Bear Cottage Children's Hospice had a huge impact on our lives.

It all started at Country Comfort as I mentioned previously. I lost 23 kilos in twelve weeks and had been sponsored by lots of Lend Lease people on a per kilo basis. Our target was to raise $5,000 for the cancer kids. We raised $17,000 for Camperdown oncology unit.

We made an appointment to meet Dr. Michael Stevens—then Head of the oncology clinic. We offered either the cash or—because we owned Thredbo and the Country Comfort Motel chain—a series of holidays for patients and families, or, because we were Lend Lease with good buying power, e.g. equipment. Whatever they wanted.

Dr. Stevens came back to us. He would like to try a group holiday for the most seriously ill children—many about to undergo bone marrow transplants as a last chance.

Two things:
- Most had never experienced anything like it and may never get another opportunity and
- He wanted to measure the effects of such a trip on both the physical and mental state of the kids.

Our office team, particularly K.T. and Jenny W., got to work and developed a brilliant nine-day trip itinerary.

In February, 1985, twenty young cancer patients, a doctor, nurses and I met at Central Station and boarded the XPT bound for Wauchope. The rail staff were brilliant… for twenty years.

At Wauchope, we were met by police and driven in police vans to Port Macquarie Police Station where the kids were locked up and fingerprinted and later loaded into fire engines and driven under siren to the Country Comfort Motel on the Hastings River waterfront. A great start!

First up—change and onto the beach for a fishing competition. You should have seen the looks on their faces when they dragged in a few big ones. (They didn't notice they were already scaled and gutted). Then into the pool with life savers, and then into the beautiful restaurant where Clair Hayes and Co. entertained, and they ate a dinner fit for royalty.

Next day, exploring Fantasy Glades, a river cruise, Lighthouse Beach, cricket at Laurieton, Timbertown and the Big Bull, then another feast… all in their new Tajura Fashions exclusive team uniforms.

Day three on a Sonter's Coach bound for Coffs Harbour. At Kempsey, we stopped at the Akubra Factory—amazing. The staff put on a scrumptious smoko then measured each kid's head and offered their choice of any Akubra—including the European multi-coloured range. An hour later, every child had a brand new, personalised, Akubra hat.

Off to Trial Bay Gaol at South West Rocks, then lunch before the drive to the Coffs Porpoise Pool for a show, then to the army base for a run along the beach in an armoured personnel carrier, and finally to Coffs Harbour Country Comfort Motel and our pool-side barbecue dinner.

The staff had a bag of goodies for each child. I cannot forget the look

THE BRIGHTER SIDE OF A DEATH THREAT

on young Adam Palmer's face on the very first 'Children's Hospital Express'. Each kid had received a money box. Each kid had shaken it to hear any coins—nothing. Adam, at five, was the first to go back to the money box and open it—a crisp $100 note. He yelped, and then every kid raced to open theirs—everyone yelped! I don't think many had ever seen a $100 note. And this happened to every child on every Children's Hospital Express for the next eighteen years—362 children, and over $36,000 just on this one small thing!

Everyone got their own camera at Coffs, plus 3 x 24-frame Kodak films, plus lots more—another great night every year.

Day four we boarded the Atkinsons Byron Bay Coaches and headed north. First stop: Byron Bay High School. Mr. Jack Harper, proud Principal, and Mrs. Wilson's annual giant carrot cake. Every year, the students took our group on a wonderful school tour and sport classes.

Our kids were amazed at the fact that surfboard riding was on the curriculum. Mrs. Wilson and the home science students prepared a great lunch, then we were farewelled by the school committee and we headed farther north for the Gold Coast and our home for the next four nights—the Islander Resort in the heart of the city. No one then knew the resort owner Tom Tate. Nowadays, he is the famous Mayor Tom, and his team always organised an incredible welcome dinner party, every year, and a giant welcome cake; visits by Gold Coast's famous surfers and sporting heroes, face painting, animals and characters from theme parks and wonderful entertainment and all sorts of TV and film stars.

At this point, I should tell you we rarely paid for anything. XPT tickets, accommodation, meals, coaches, entry tickets, uniforms, Akubra hats, airline ticket. We had an incredible army of supporters—motel staff fund-raisers, travelling sales people, guests of County Comfort—organising industry fund-raisers for presents, gear etc. I remember, after five years, telling Tom Tate our ask of him was way too much. Fifteen rooms for four nights, a welcome dinner party, breakfasts etc.—and I would find somewhere else. He glared at me. "Don't you dare. This is the highlight of our staff's year."

He also reminded me he wanted no one told of his generosity—a pledge I kept until now.

I well remember that first year—taking about ten bald-headed kids across the road from the Islander to Surfers Photo Express, and a guy we have got to know well—the owner, Roger Brown. We handed in over fifty rolls of film to be developed. We turned up to pick them up next morning, prepared to pay some $800—no charge! "Plus, here is a photo album for every child. Plus more films, and keep 'em coming." For twenty years, we never paid a cent to Roger—a huge gift, and many great photo albums full.

For the next four days we experienced the very best of the Gold Coast. Stretch limos to the Sheraton Mirage, an annual treasure hunt on their beach, three huge pools, Seaworld and a helicopter flight, Dreamworld, Tiger Island, meals, the fabulous rides, Movieworld entertainment, and more, including best seats at Draculas Theatre Restaurant—plus lots of great photos.

Every child was told to spend their $100 from Coffs Harbour. It had to be split, "Something for you and something for those at home." Young Adam was from Blayney. At five years old, he bought a giant box of matches "because mum and dad both smoked". They cost $1, and the huge fluffy tiger he bought for himself was $99. Fair enough. Something for those at home and something for me—split 99 to 1!

We took stretch limos to McDonald's, Broadbeach, and Diane Smith. Then onto Jupiter's Casino, where the staff 'welcomed' the VIP kids all dressed in their best outfits and took them into the International Showroom and the best seats in the house. Tables full of goodies and ice cream sodas. At the end of every show, the other 1000 plus patrons were ushered out, and our kids went on stage with the cast and 're-did' some of the numbers with them. There was never a dry eye in the room, and photographer Regina King (the kids called her the 'yahoo lady') took brilliant photos for many years.

Every year, except one, we swam in the fish/reef pool at the beautiful Marriot Resort. Amazing.

A great day at Movieworld was followed by an amazing dinner and show at Draculas Theatre Restaurant. Again, I remember the first year. They apologised and said they could not afford to give away twenty-five tickets and meals, and so I paid. No problems. We were trying to give the kids a huge variety of experiences. That first night, at interval, we were told 'all drinks were on the house', and the kids were taken and made up as the show characters and then given T-shirts, frisbies etc., and we never paid one cent for anything, including tickets, for the next nineteen years.

THE BRIGHTER SIDE OF A DEATH THREAT

We realised, over the year, that the Draculas Theatre cast changed some bits of their show on that night to make it 'kid friendly'. The Newman family were wonderful supporters. The photos from Draculas were frightening, and I was always glad the kids were seen by their families before they saw the photo albums.

Then, on day nine, we headed to Brisbane airport and our Ansett flight back to Sydney, and every year a fabulous welcome home party in Ansett's private lounge—always with TV stars and theme park 'characters', and Ansett's Julie Steele.

It would be fair to say that for all those years we loaded twenty young cancer patients onto the XPT who all looked like they had 'flat batteries'. Eight days later, Ansett flew home twenty of the noisiest, bubbliest, happiest youngsters imaginable.

I remember that first year at the airport. Dr. Stevens said, "Forget the debrief and tests. I have never seen such an amazing positive change in kids. You must keep it going. And we did, until the politically correct and 'workplace health and safety' army moved in in 2004, and effectively stopped it. Don't get me started. An opportunity lost.

At this stage I should introduce the hospital 'characters'. Dr. Michael Stevens and his wife, Margaret, drove the Express and the Bear Cottage project with a 100% drive and support. Dr. Stevens was Head of the oncology clinic for years, ably supported by his Deputy Dr. Luciano 'Luce' Dallapoza, who is now O.I.C. since Michael's retirement, and another wonderful human, sadly a St. George tragic.

There was a fabulous team of doctors, nurses and staff who were amazing supporters of our efforts over the years. Sister Debbie Carter, Sister Lucy, who later married the talented 'Express' photographer, Grant Leslie (a school mate of our kids at Penno), Donna in reception, and some wonderful doctors. Westmead children are very fortunate. But—the standout—is, was and always will be Sister Chrissie Marrinan. Chrissie is an angel—seriously. I have never known anyone who got on so well with kids. She is amazing.

The kids would be 'glad' they were receiving painful chemo or lumbar punctures—whatever, just for the chance to 'sing with Sister Chrissie'. She was Queen of the castle. Sadly, this lead to a bit of envy from some sections of her colleagues and the odd parent—but that's a sad trait of life.

LANCE SMITH

Sister Chrissie ran the Children's Hospital Express for the whole eighteen years, and all the motel staff, coach drivers, pilots, theme park executives and others were in awe of her professionalism, talent and effectiveness—as Helen and I still are. We love her, and she still smokes like a chimney. Go figure. Chrissie is a real musical talent!!

Under her watch, we also organised and ran annual summer camps to Batemans Bay and winter camps to Thredbo—all amazing adventures, mainly supported by the Innes family, the Birss's, the Casbens at Farmer Johns, and the Thredbo staff. Thanks everyone—we did good and gave many hundreds of kids a sample of the good life.

Over the years, there was the odd challenge and stand out moments.

One year, a nine-year-old brain-cancer-sufferer was in tears one night at Port Macquarie. Not uncommon, as this was often the first time ever some of these kids had left there parents. As 'minister for good times', I went over to him and his mates to offer some encouragement. I asked "What's up, young fella?" and he said, "I'm going to be dead before Christmas and I won't get any presents." Gulp!

I am not allowed to either agree or say "No you won't be", so I blurted out something along the lines of, "Let's live for the present and have a brilliant eight days."

One of my little troops saw I was in strife and came over. She was my 'mate'. We were very close. Also nine, she had just come out of isolation and her bone marrow transplant. She said, "What's up?", and he had no choice but to say the same thing again. She put her hands on her hips and said—forcefully, "So am I—so deal with it". A nine year old. Sadly, neither made Christmas. Boy, another lesson learned. We all have to 'cope'.

Another time, we were at the Islander and it was the day before the stretch limos to Jupiters. Young Danielle, 13, a drop-dead gorgeous kid inside and out, marshalled a few of the older kids and explained that one of their group had been sent away with no money and no good clothes. She convinced eight kids to part with $50 from their $100 note, and they took Rebecca shopping. You should have seen the look on her face as she stepped from the limousine at Jupiters in her first ever designer outfit. It brought me, the Doctors, nurses and all who knew to tears.

THE BRIGHTER SIDE OF A DEATH THREAT

Beautiful Danielle passed away within three weeks of our return. It hurt. Sadly, we went to way too many youngsters funerals over the years. It is heartbreak territory.

On the very first Express, we had a very ill young girl from Glenhaven. There was a real risk she would not make it, but she was desperate to go. Great parents, wonderful and brave, they kissed her goodbye at Central believing they may never see her again. Twelve years later, I pulled up outside Katherine's home to go to her 21st birthday. As I was stopping, the radio announced the death of Princess Di. I sat, stunned, in the car for a while, then went in to enjoy a most unexpected birthday. Not only did Katherine survive our week, she went on to be college Captain and represented Australia under 18's in Netball overseas. Wow!

One funny thing. I had a message at the Islander, when we arrived one year, to ring the Marriott. I did and was told it was not possible to have our annual visit and swimming with the fish in their magic salt-water reef pool. I said "okay". Later in the week, curiosity got the better of me, so I called in to see Anne Maree to find out what we had done. Turns out they had the National Funeral Directors Conference on and were petrified the *Gold Coast Bulletin* would run a story of the cancer kids swimming in the pool with the Funeral Directors looking on. I didn't agree, but we went back every year after and the kids loved it.

One of the sad parts of this period was observing people's reactions to their kids challenges. One little girl would not take off her wig when we 'set sail' on the Express. It took Chrissy three days to coax her into the 'bald headed team'. She told us that for the past twelve months, since being diagnosed, her parents (they had two taxis) always had a Saturday night poolside barbecue at their house and they locked her up in her room every Saturday arvo—not to come out till Sunday. They told her it was a 'sin' to have cancer and they did not want their friends to know.

This will test you. A four-year-old from the Hills District—I won't say her name. Still too raw. I was with the family as she passed away at home (there was no Bear Cottage in those days).

The funeral was held and all were surprised one set of grandparent was missing. They were at the house burning every photo, plus toy, clothes, books, presents and all the kiddy's art creations and treasures. Grandad said,

"You have to forget the past and get on with life." The parents were beyond devastated. So was I. Every memory gone, forever.

Another kiddie, a beaut eleven-year-old girl with a huge stomach tumour and a great sense of humour. Her parents, nice people, could not cope. They kept changing her school so no one would realise she had cancer. I cannot figure it out. They asked me to look after the Australian people at the Greek Orthodox funeral service in Lindfield. Another awful day at the office. I still miss that smiling princess.

I had a good 'mate'. A chubby, fun twelve-year-old from Gulgong. I spent lots of time with his beaut mum and his step-dad, at Ronald McDonald House. He was motor bike mad. His classic response, when asked how many brothers and sisters he has, was 'counting steps—nine of 'em. His biological father had 'split' as soon as he was diagnosed (not uncommon). I found out the father had recently won a lottery, so I went to see him about buying his son a little 'Pee Wee 50' type motorbike—and make his dream come true. He didn't want to, but finally agreed. He turned up at Ronald McDonald House with the bike, but before he handed it over he got the boy and his mum to sign a letter saying they would give the bike back to him as soon as the boy died!

The hospital asked me to look into the fact that one little girl, from south of Wollongong, had a chemo treatment every Thursday, but they told me her parents would drop her at the hospital gate and wait for her that afternoon and would not come in. They knew I was close to her and wanted to find out why?

It took a few weeks. She finally told me. Dad was always in gaol. He continually re-offended and mum was always zonked out on drugs. At nine years old, every Thursday she left Albion Park by train in the dark at 4 a.m. for Central, and got a bus to the hospital—on her own! And then she repeated it every Thursday arvo, crook after a session on chemo. She got home in the dark. It was a twenty-minute walk from the station to her house.

That was one of the few times I got into strife. Helen and I enquired about adopting her and were severely rebuked. Stay out of it!

THE BRIGHTER SIDE OF A DEATH THREAT

Another strange one—at the time. Again no name. Chrissy and Co. all remember well, I was asked to enquire as to why a sixteen-year-old sister was often asleep on the floor of the hospital, where her thirteen-year-old sibling was in overnight, receiving treatment. Again it took a while to gain their trust, but we did it. Turns out the kids had a single mum always on drugs and spaced out. Wanting to stay together, the pair of girls knew they would be split and fostered out if the truth got out. So they ran away and were living in a shed on Canterbury race course. Showering and washing in the jockeys amenities there, going to school, and the older one, 'D', was working at Kentucky Fried Chicken. She paid all their bills, school fees etc. and had saved over $1,000 to buy a car as soon as she got a licence. They were terrified their mother would find out and take their savings.

I went and saw my mate at the NRMA. 'D' left school and started full time at NRMA Travel in 1993 and was the NRMA 'Employee Of The Year' about five years later. Her young sister survived and went into remission after two years. All that girl needed was a start. I am amazed at some of the challenges these kids overcame—way over and above the cancer death threat.

The biggest fright I ever had on the Express was in 1991. Dr. Stevens has always told me the real threat was something like chicken pox. With the kids having minimal immune system, it could wipe them out—the whole group! It is an ever present threat in their lives, at school, the hospital—everywhere.

One day, at the Sheraton Mirage, Chrissy came off the beach with Yasmin, a gorgeous kid from out west. Great parents. Chrissy was white. It could be chicken pox. Yikes. I froze. We grabbed one of our limos and straight to emergency at Southport. Every year Chrissy had set up a 'priority' system in every town in case we needed it (and we did on quite a few occasions) and it worked every time.

Turns out we had played cricket on a sandy oval at Dunbogan (near Laurieton) two days earlier and it was sand fly bites. I can't tell you of our relief.

In all 18 years, we never once lost a child on the Express itself. We did have to fly two kids to Sydney during the adventure over the years and some did not live long after our return, but we delivered an incredible lift to these young warriors and were very proud of our achievements. Take a bow, Chrissy.

I must leave this with one great story which typifies our results. We had a young thirteen-year-old girl in a wheelchair who had great difficulty walking a step. She also was fed through a tube and didn't eat normal tucker. However, she did want to go on all the fun things we were offered. So, hard-nosed Chrissy told her on the train that if she ate normally she could go on all outings. Port Macquarie, first night, was a problem. Breakfast Day 2 went much better and she ate everything on the plate with a knife and fork. By Day 4 Chrissy had the wheelchair stashed away and all the tubes out of her body and she walked with a stick. On the final day, Chrissy sent her off the plane in Sydney first and she walked—no stick, no tubes, up the aero bridge tunnel. Her parents looked straight past her looking for a wheelchair.

They did not see her until she stopped in front of them and said, "It's me". She never went back to the tubes and wheelchair, and later went into full remission. Chrissy, you really are an Angel. You should read the letter I got from that girl's dad!

Dr. Stevens rang in 1992 and asked me to come into Camperdown for a meeting with C.E.O. Dr. John Yu—an amazing, talented, great man who later became Australian of the Year. We had met on a number of occasions and I well remember him appointing me a Benefactor of the Children's Hospital in 1989.

The meeting was to tell me that he supported a bold new dream of Dr. Stevens, to build Australia's first ever Children's Hospice in Sydney, and what a challenge it was. I was privileged to be asked to be part of the team and this is our next chapter.

My last 'event' at Camperdown took some getting over. Samantha was five, fabulous and a bundle of fun. Her Grandma was with her everyday in hospital. One day, Grandma had to go the hospital pharmacy to get a script filled. As I held Sam's hand, she passed away. I will never forget that instant smile... all the pain was gone... forever.

Before I leave the Children's Hospital—in 1995 they moved from Camperdown, with all it's history and memories, to the new hospital at Westmead.

THE BRIGHTER SIDE OF A DEATH THREAT

Dr. Yu decided to invite every family who had lost a child there to come in for a special farewell. Over the decades, there had been many a tree planted, paver carved with initials and much more. They released a purple helium-filled balloon with a hand written letter to every child attached, up into the blue skies…

Can you believe the wind was perfect and they all headed south as they rose into the atmosphere? It was a very moving day and a brilliant 'release' for all the families.

In summing up, over the years these youngsters showed us their unbelievable resilience, their will to fight, their optimism and incredible sense of humour and their zest for life—certainly the brighter side of their death threats. I worked out that looking on the bright side never gave me eye strain.

And finally, probably the proudest moment of my life was the receiving of the Order of Australia—AM, in 2009. I was nominated by the Children's Hospital and Bear Cottage staff. It was a huge team effort by many over many years. I was lucky enough to receive the accolades on their behalf.

CHAPTER 16

BEAR COTTAGE AND THE CELEBRITY CAVALCADES

Optimism is the faith that leads to achievements. Nothing can be achieved without optimism, hope and confidence.
...Helen Keller. Writer, lecturer.

Dr. Stevens was confident they could oversee the design and construction of Australia's first Children's Hospice. He had been to Canada and the U.K. studying other like establishments. There were already fifteen in the U.K. and growing in number. There are now fifty-three, and we have only three.

Basically the hospice had two primary functions:
- A place to say goodbye when the time comes—the world's hardest word where children are concerned and
- A place where the families on this tragic journey can go as often as needed to have family respite, fun, build great memories and recharge their batteries—all whilst the youngster is in world-class medical care.

Many families had not been out together for ages, sometimes for years. Someone always had to remain home to look after 'junior'. At Bear Cottage, the whole family can go out shopping, to the movies, the beach, anywhere—safe in the knowledge 'junior' was in good hands. Plus they could sing around the hospice piano, play with the hospice Labrador (incredibly trained), and build beautiful memories of their time together.

I had the honour of naming 'Bear Cottage'. It was a no brainer. The bandaged bear was the mascot of the Children's Hospital and I suggested to Dr. Stevens it was a natural extension. He agreed, and the rest is history.

Turned out there was a 'Bear Cottage' teddy bear shop registered on Pennant Hills Road, and it took a while to get approval from them—but we did.

Finding a site was a real challenge for Dr. Michael and Margaret, and they had a number of false starts over many years before finally settling on the current site at Manly, in the grounds of St. Patrick's College. Perfect.

Next up, how do we raise millions of dollars to design and build Bear Cottage and then raise an annual two million dollars plus to operate.

First up—my idea to 'launch' the news of Australia's first Children's Hospice project and also raise funds.

A 'Celebrity Cavalcade'—multi-coach-loads of paying passengers and celebrities on a four-week adventure around Australia. I teamed up with a fellow who had been an Event Manager with the Commonwealth Bank and had worked with us on the George Bass Surfboat Marathon—Alan Turnbull.

The idea was good. The choice of Turnbull was bad. He was a dud in every way. Fortunately, in life I did not make many 'bad people' decisions, but he sure was.

The first Cavalcade was a great success. Ten coaches loaded up at Darling Harbour, lots of media, lots of characters, ten wonderful team leaders, lots of celebrities and teams from as far away as Alice Springs—led by their Mayor. It was 1993. John Selfe and Ross Arblaster did a brilliant job producing the brochure. The NRMA team was led by their General Manager, Richard Cox.

We staged some terrific events and had a lot of fun and raised the profile of the new 'Bear Cottage' project through the roof. We had T.V. crews on board, national newspapers, journalists and photographers plus raised well over $100,000 even before we started.

There are many memories. The excitement of our Darling Harbour departure; the co-ordinated 'green lights' to get us quickly out of the city

THE BRIGHTER SIDE OF A DEATH THREAT

heading north. All the coaches were decorated in their sponsor and team themes, once again Tajura Fashions supplying first-class coloured team uniforms and event jackets. Night one, Tamworth and a terrific Country Music concert. Night two, Coffs Harbour, the beach sand modelling competition won by the Batemans Bay coach team.

Night three, Gold Coast, a day at the races and a night at a huge Twin Towns show. Huge, because when I found out months before that their major show that night was Martin Lass on the violin and an eight-piece orchestra, and a Russian pianist named Igor Gavdaski, I rang Inge Lass and asked her if we could gate crash, adding Julie Anthony, Normie Rowe, Barry Crocker and others to the show for free. And we would buy 400 tickets.

Inge loved the idea, especially the 'free' extra celebrities and 400 ticket sales, and we combined the shows. Top night.

Bumping out after the show, I found myself in the huge goods lift with only the Russian pianist. I don't speak Russian, so I asked in my slowest, clearest English, "**Do you like Australia**."

He answered quickly, "I ought to. I was born in Brisbane and still live there."

Derrrrrr.

I remember sitting around a big campfire in Rockhampton listening to old Smoky Dawson, Tony Taunton and Normie Rowe working the crowd, along with a powerhouse Afro-American singer with a huge smile, Beau Smith. The Emerald Show—what a day and night, with Bells Carnival from the Country Comfort Canberra opening. We set a new Emerald Show crowd attendance record.

I remember Longreach and a fabulous concert crammed into the Stockman's Hall Of Fame theatrette.

Then the start of an amazing story. We were pulled up at the remote Barkley Roadhouse in the Northern Territory. Every day it was a different team's duty to entertain at smoko, and this day was the Tamworth team. Out strode one of our passengers, a tough looking, solid, older lady—Rhona Houlton. (Turns out she was a retired, strict, headmistress). She was to perform 'children's poetry', and she was sensational—a real Susan Boyle moment. Afterwards, I thought I would pay a compliment and started by saying, "That was great—where did you learn it?"

She hissed back, "Learn it! Learn it! I wrote it!"

LANCE SMITH

Oops!

We staged a great rodeo in Tennant Creek, then a huge concert in Alice Springs—titled 'Alice' and in honour of a beautiful eight year old 'angel', Alice Schollemar, from Griffith, who had recently passed away, breaking everyone's heart. Her parents were flown in by the RAAF, along with the girl band of the decade 'Girlfriend'.

The Territory's Ted Egan performed, along with a fabulous bush band, 'The Blood Brothers' and all our celebrities. We sold over 4,000 tickets. A big night.

We spent a fantastic two days at the Ayers Rock precinct. My old Thredbo colleague, Wayne Kirkpatrick was village C.E.O. and organised a great itinerary of tours and entertainment.

It was freezing. Minus two degrees, and I remember David Ivins counting our money, sitting in a tent, lamp on, and gloves!

We had negotiated directly with the Pitjantjatjattjara tribe elders—Whisky and his team were a delight. We met them at Curtain Springs and organised Uluru and a fantastic concert in the hills outside Marla Bore in South Australia. They did the corroborees and indigenous dancing around a huge bonfire. Brilliant. And we supplied all our celebrities. They loved it. There were many other campfires all over the hills. What a night!

Three quick stories here:

Leaving Curtain Springs, I saw one of the Cavalcade four-wheel-drives vacant and thought it was John Selfe's, and he had gone ahead on a coach. I jumped in and away went the convoy. I did not know it was Normie Rowe's four-wheel-drive and he was inside the roadhouse signing autographs. He was very unimpressed.

The second was bloody Terry Clark, our leading Coach Captain. We had an American professor on board. She had flown out just to come on the Cavalcade. Clarkey had purchased a normal box of washing powder and decantered it into a plastic bag. He then put circles of white powder around his coach wheels and tent entry. The professor asked why, and he told her it was a special powder to keep the dingoes out and him safe. She would not go into her tent until we produced some of the magic white powder—at 10 p.m. in Ayers Rock village. Bloody Clarkey.

The third was a classic. It happened at the Marla Bore gathering.

Whisky and the elders had told us they were sick and tired of being ripped off by their own people who came to their camps and offered a pittance for hand-made didgeridoos, aboriginal art, musical sticks, boomerangs and the like. They then took the craft work to Alice Springs and Darwin, where it was sold to tourists for a massive profit.

The elders were tickled pink we were bringing 400 potential buyers. One of our 'first time passengers' was a delightful retired widow from Mosman in Sydney—'Flirty Florence' (everyone had a nickname on their badge).

Florence, over the years, went on many of our cavalcades to places like New Zealand, Longreach, Tasssie and Tamworth Country Music Festival. Anyway, this night she was looking at aboriginal art works and talking to the artist. She suddenly saw a painting and immediately fell in love with it. She made the fatal mistake of saying, "Wow, I **must** have that," and asked the price.

The artist must have thought all his Christmas's had come at once, and said "$400 ma'am".

Florence baulked. She had not expected it to be that high. She said, "How much for a pensioner?" and he must have thought he was going to lose a sale.

He said, "$20."

Yep, he had gone from $400 to $20 in one move.

Florence ended paying him $100 and he was over the moon.

Years later, Florence rang out of the blue to ask Helen and I to lunch at the Southport Yacht Club. We had a great time going over the old memories. Florence died the next week. It was her farewell gesture.

Thanks to a brilliant and wonderful bunch of team leaders from all over the globe, we gave a lot of towns and people an amazing lift.

One footnote. Upon our return to Sydney we were in the Parramatta office one day and Melinda was talking to 'Kelly from the Tele'—one of the cavalcade journalists. She suddenly asked me "Dad, you were a hippy once weren't you?"

Knowing Kelly is a character, I said, "Lived in Nimbin, sex, pot and rock and roll—also went to Hait Ashbury in San Francisco to smoke, sing and dance."

LANCE SMITH

I then found out it was not Kelly, but another journo, doing a story on the righteous new generation. One hour later, a photographer arrived and we were a full page on next day's Daily Telegraph on my past sex and drug life.

My first call at 6.30 a.m. was from Alan Jones on 2UE. I didn't know where Nimbin was!

Leaving Marla Bore for the Celebrity stock car race in Coober Pedy. The local car club lent us all their stock cars for the feature race—very generous.

I knew I would win—I came 17th out of 20. Just in front of the NRMA General Manager, Richard Cox and Tony Taunton. Normie Rowe had snuck around and asked which car was the fastest. He was desperate to win. He came 3rd. On the last lap, he was passed by our favourite Coach Captain Terry Clarke, a former champion motor bike rider who came in 2nd. And the winner was—Melissa!—the tiniest coach driver I have ever met, but boy can she drive. She whipped us all.

Then the Kangaroo Court case in Port Augusta where David Ivins was struck by a flying toilet roll thrown by our Daydream Island mate, Patsy, and the judge, TV weatherman Tony Murphy, discharged the jury because he didn't like their verdict—one of many classic Kangaroo Courts run by Glenn T. all over Australia during our many and varied events.

A quick visit to Broken Hill and Smoky Dawson's good mate, Pro Hart, took us all to Silverton and also the famous living desert sculptures.

Then Dubbo—our huge concert at the R.S.L. A big night, with an even bigger announcement. Sister Chrissy came on stage to announce that Rhona Houlton, the retired headmistress on the Tamworth Coach, was going to publish a book of children's poems, *Poems For Bear Cottage*, and that the book would be illustrated by one of the young cancer kids travelling with us—the very talented Monique Noble.

The package was the book plus a CD of Rhona voicing the poems. The royalties all went to Bear Cottage—printed free by Double Day Books and then reprinted. A huge success. The very talented and beautiful Monique passed away as she was near completion of the very last illustration—and her dad, David, finished it. Another heartbreaking day at the office.

THE BRIGHTER SIDE OF A DEATH THREAT

Digressing, years later Helen and I were on an elephant ride in the jungles of Northern Thailand with brother Barry and June. Barry assured me no white man had ever been in this remote and dangerous jungle. We suddenly came across a herd of wild elephants. Panic. Until an Aussie voice yelled, "Isn't that Lance?" On top of one of the 'wild' elephants was Monique's dad, David Noble, and his family.

After a beaut 'spin' around Mt. Panorama race track, organised by our great mates, Fran and Warren Bremner (The oncology kids went as pillions or in a sidecar on motorbikes in the days before W H & S. They loved it), we ended up at the finishing line—Harvey Norman's Auburn store. Gerry Harvey, his wife Katie Page, and 2UE organised a great welcome and an on-air promotion. Both John Laws and Alan Jones were broadcasting from the store and they raised over $300,000 worth of cash and kind on the day for Bear Cottage. What a finish.

While we were galavanting around having fun on subsequent cavalcades, raising much needed funds and the profile of Bear Cottage, our committee— Chairman Dennis Merchant, Gary Pemberton then Chairman of Qantas, and also the successful Australian Olympic bid committee, Mel Gotleib (Qantas's number one frequent flyer), myself, Dr. Stevens and Manly Mayor, the hardworking achiever Jean Hay—were putting the jigsaw together and finally the cottage started coming out of the ground in the shadow of the magnificent St. Patrick's College on North Head, Manly.

Dr. Stevens was honoured with the Order Of Australia for the many years and tremendous effort he put into Bear Cottage—his heart and soul.

One major donation from our cavalcade mates estate was $400,000 cash from Smoky and Dot Dawson—plus other things they gave.

We celebrated Dot's 100th birthday shortly after they donated a beaut piano to Bear Cottage and led the first sing song. The Dawsons' also fully funded our music therapists.

Dotty passed away at 104 and Smoky at 96. I well remember Smoky's first major promotion for Bear Cottage—he was turning 80 and his good mate Ray Martin invited him onto the 'Midday' Show to talk about the proposed Children's Hospice… a new 'dream'.

The Midday producers rang me on Wednesday to ask if Smoky could come over tomorrow, Thursday, for a run through for Fridays show. They were planning a few special things, like Ray saying, "We've heard enough about the cowboys. Now here comes the Indians", as Kamahl came on set singing 'Happy Birthday' with a giant cake and 80 candles.

I rang Dot—she apologised and said tomorrow was not possible—how about Friday around 9 a.m. I thought that was understandable for an older couple. A day's notice was too quick and a 9 a.m. start was early enough. Channel 9 said, "No worries".

Turns out, on Thursday Smoky had an 11 a.m. show at Westfield Burwood, a 2 p.m. show at Westfield Parramatta, recording with Gina Jeffrey's from 6 p.m. to 10 p.m., then doing the midnight show at Kirrabilli RSL. Plus the 9 a.m. start Friday was because Smoky was on Doug Mullray's 6 a.m. Radio show at Bondi and not home till after 8 a.m. Wow! How wrong could I be. I reckon that's why they had such a great innings. They were far too busy to die.

Smoky and Dot were such strong supporters of Bear Cottage. Smoky bought out an album of duets for the cottage with the 'expected' ones like Slim Dusty, Col Joye and Lee Kernaghan, but also some unexpected ones like Jimmy Barnes and John Farnham. The launch was at 'Sheraton On The Park', with Ray Martin as compere and Smoky's close mates like R.M. Williams, on the main table.

We had auctions and raffles, and I told Ray we had made an amazing $19,000 on the night. He immediately got on the mic and told the world, "Thanks to your generosity, particularly Jim Bosnjak and Alan Pearce from the N.S.W. Coach Association, we have raised over $25,000 tonight for Bear Cottage, even before one album is sold."

I froze. I knew we only had a bit over $19,000.

Ray came straight up to me and gave me his personal cheque for $6,000 and said, "Say nothing."

The album itself made over $30,000 in royalties for the cottage—another terrific and successful project.

Finally, eleven years after our first meeting at Camperdown, Bear Cottage opened its doors on St. Patrick's Day (Dr. Stevens favourite) 2003, and they have done an amazing job keeping families together and some over many tragic journeys.

Well done, Dr. Stevens, Dennis Merchant, Gary Pemberton, Mel

THE BRIGHTER SIDE OF A DEATH THREAT

Gotlieb and the team.

On the second celebrity cavalcade, we did the Victorian Mt. Buffalo and Bright autumn/Anzac Day festivities. Brilliant. Plus we took Smoky back to Khancoban and the Khancoban Country Club, where he wrote the famous song some fifty years before.

Tony Taunton and the Howie Brothers will never forget the Khancoban townspeople. We squeezed over 400 into a club which said 200 maximum. All cheered and yelled. A special concert!

There was one event on the New Zealand cavalcade that cannot be left unsaid. Forty-six of us on a forty-eight-seater coach… including Smoky and Dot on their only ever visit to the land of the long white cloud. We were on the south island, approaching Mt. Cook, when Helen went through the coach collecting for that afternoon's helicopter joy flight. She had nearly three thousand dollars in the bag. We stopped for lunch at the hotel and Helen picked up the scraps and later threw them in the bin and we drove off to the airport. At the airport, Helen pulled out the bag with the three thousand dollars in it and opened it. Yikes! It was the lunch scraps. The three thousand dollars was in a bin back at the Mt. Cook Hotel. We fairly flew back and it was still there! Helen was a mess.

Footnote: I lent my only copy of *Riding All Over Again*—Smoky's album of duets, and I cannot remember to whom. If it is you, please return it!

CHAPTER 17

THE MAGICAL HILLS AND CENTRE STAGE, CAROLS AT JENOLAN CAVES AND LEADER

*There is one real measure of success—to be able to spend life in your own way, doing what you love.
Those who wish to sing always find a song.*

Leaving Country Comfort, which by then also included the Chifley and Sovereign Australis brands, was a tough decision, but I knew it was time.

First up, I answered a call for help from the President of the Australian Bus and Coach Association, Jim Bosnjak. I really liked and respected Jim. Still do. His primary interest was Westbus, a major bus company with a number of depots throughout western Sydney. They took many thousands of kids to school each day, and also had a coach arm based in Alexandria. Jim asked me to come on board to help develop a large travel club for his coach touring. He offered to match my CC salary and supply a new company car.

I took up the offer, provided they signed a two-year contract. They did. But the wheels fell off rather quickly.

I started in the Alexandria office; met a couple of champion blokes— Operations chief Rod Mortison and his deputy, Vince Morgan, who were the best in the business. Their GM was a guy named Greg Balkin. Somewhere along the line, Greg saw my 'entry' as a real threat. After just a few weeks he and I had a big blow up. I have no idea what about, and Greg left. Shame though because he, too, was a good guy, and good at the job. He has never spoken to me since.

Jim B. then made the decision Greg would not be replaced and that I would also take over as General Manager of the Coach division.

Now, there are some things I do pretty well, but running a coach company was not one of them. Fortunately, with Rod and Vince leading the way, we were doing okay but, unfortunately, Jim's older brother, Bob, was a pain in the butt. As a senior partner, under the Croatian family tradition, Bob was the company head and trusted no one—not even his family.

As I understand it, Bob and brother John were both born in Yugoslavia. Dad escaped during the war and made Australia. Mum followed—an incredible journey with two little boys. Jim was then born here. Dad bought a small Parramatta bus company and worked really hard. I am told Dad and John were tireless workers, determined to provide for their family. Jim later joined them. Dad passed, then, sadly, so did John, who had married a wonderful Aussie girl. So John's wife, Carol, Jim and Bob were the three Directors of Westbus when I came on board.

Bob hated Carol and just tolerated Jim. Sad times. Bob was often on the grog early in the day and would start making abusive phone calls to all the depots, including us in the coach division. I remember the financial controller changing his phone number. It was bizarre. Everyone just accepted it.

When Bob was overseas checking on their many assets in the U.K. and Europe, he insisted all mail, including those addressed as 'personal' to staff, be kept in bags so that he could open and read them all before they were distributed on his return. Caused nightmares in operations and finance departments.

Years later, after their mum's will was read, I read a double-page story in the Sydney papers outlining Bob's court case where he disputed mum's will. After spending massive dollars on legal teams, they still had not sorted anything out. I don't know what happened. Westbus was sold. I think Jim and Carol went on in other projects and did well. Hope so.

Anyway, one day I was summoned to a board meeting at head office Northmead—a rare event. Bob was waiting for me. He had me 'trapped'. His daughter was the accountant at the coach division and had seen a report

THE BRIGHTER SIDE OF A DEATH THREAT

from me re a staff weekend we had in the Hunter Valley. My report said we had done 562 klms in the new Mercedes coach. Her hub reading had 1820 klms.

Bob yelled at me for falsifying the reading and sacked me on the spot. Trouble was, two things:
- Bob was unaware I had a signed two-year contract, and
- Turns out the previous four-day-trip driver had forgotten to read the hub… and I had done only 562 klms.

I ended up a winner in the financial exchange, but it was the first time I had been 'fired' and, no, Bob never apologised or admitted his mistake. A year of turmoil—but I still enjoyed it and have kept up a number of the friendships.

On a funny note, one day Jim advised me he was hoping to be the 'Director of Transport' for the 2000 Sydney Olympics. He said that the four Japanese voting delegates were coming to Australia and had accepted his invitation to lunch at Darling Harbour. Knowing I had worked in Japan in my Country Comfort days, he asked me to organise the lunch. I did, and there were eight of us at the lunch. I had organised the sushi train, but no one started to eat, so I started with a piece of raw fish. Ten seconds later, I realised the fish was coming back up my throat so, in panic, I saw an avocado dip and ate a full tablespoon! I had never heard of Wasabi, and went close to death.

During this time, I had been enjoying my passion for musical theatre and toying with the idea of staging a big show at the 1500 seat, 5-level Hills Entertainment Centre at Castle Hill. Leaving Westbus seemed like the omen we needed.

We decided to do it—plus set up a touring/theatre special events company—Cockatours P/Ltd and Cockatours Productions. That way we could continue our Children's Hospital Express trips.

We were very fortunate to be given a beaut office in the Hills Centre Production office by Managing Director, Chris Rix, and General Manager, Jack Frost—two terrific blokes—to kick us off, and this started a fantastic decade.

To set the scene, we had met Glenn T. in 1985 when he was directing and staging *Annie* for the Sydney Youth Musical Theatre.

LANCE SMITH

GT was then Art Director on the hit TV series *Home and Away*, and a really creative talent. Melinda auditioned and won the lead understudy, 'Annie', plus one of the orphans. Glenn told me they needed two old people, so I ended up in the production as 'Daddy Warbucks'. Earlier, I had auditioned for the lead role, 'Captain Andy', in the Hills Musical Society's production of *Showboat*, and got it. I was on a roll.

During these shows and others, we met many truly talented and inspirational people. It all started when I organised a super Lend Lease 'Black and White' night at the historic Curzon Hall, Marsfield. A work mate, Di Crockford, told us the talented amateur group, The Hills Musical Society, should be the entertainment, with excerpts from their recent *Black and White Minstrel Show*. They were super. We got chatting and they told me of their forthcoming musical, *Showboat*, at the Don Moore Community Centre and suggested I should audition. The rest, as they say, is history. I won the lead role of 'Captain Andy', skipper of the Showboat.

David and Bev Ivins, Shane Caddaye, Lana Nesnas, Madeleine Johns, Annette Emerton and the lovely Margaret, Bruce and Jenny Rixon, Jan Mahoney, Max Court, Mark Pigot, Carole Barry and Moira Hooker were just some of those original Hills Musical Society members that became part of our extraordinary journey—and shared their abundant talents with us over the many years as we set the bar higher and higher.

After *Showboat*, I snared the lead 'Tevye' in the Hills Musical Society's *Fiddler On The Roof*. It was a turning point—and a great show.

One scene I will never forget from that production. We were doing the 'dark' dream scene. Betty Tougher (currently the little old lady in many of today's TV commercials) was playing 'Grandma Tzietel' and screamed 'Tevye' at me. Trouble was, she delivered it with such gusto her teeth came out and flew straight at me. Somehow I caught them, sidled over and palmed them to Betty, who 'reinstated' them and carried on!

Fiddler was such a strong and successful show. We chose it to be the first 'Pro-Am' show we could stage at the Hills Entertainment Centre. Our budget had gone from $6,000 at the Don Moore Community Centre to over $140,000 at The Hills—yikes! But it worked a treat. World renowned violinist Martin Lass was contracted to play 'The Fiddler'. I was back as Tevye; GT came back on with brilliant sets; veteran 2UE radio announcer, John Kerr was in. All were part of a very talented group.

THE BRIGHTER SIDE OF A DEATH THREAT

Even Sister Chrissy had a role as 'Motel's' mum. We also had an Anglican minister, Rev Max Court, playing the Rabbi. Max passed away recently. A top fella.

Our production team was Ian Court, Director, Bruce Rixon MD, Margaret Emerton Choreographer. With Glenn T's set creativity, they were the best you could get. It was a huge success in every way and got us off to a terrific start in our new venture, with many a 'house full' sign on Cheryl's Ticketek box office. The show ran for four weeks.

Because of my long association with the coach touring industry, we were very successful in that market. It was not uncommon to see ten to twelve coaches lined up outside the theatre and our cast members used to get on board after the show to personally farewell the groups. It worked, and we developed a healthy regular group following at every show over the years.

The Hills Centre then contracted us to produce all their musicals. Heaven.

Our decision to stick with well known musicals played out well with our growing regulars. *42nd Street, The Sound Of Music, Anything Goes, Oklahoma, Jesus Christ Superstar* and the like were all winners.

Our production of *Joseph and the Amazing Technicolour Dream Coat* used multiple choirs over the four weeks, and this generated thousands of parents, grandparents, friends and families of the kids. We also bravely used live animals on stage in many shows—camels, goats, cows were in Joseph and a magnificent stallion opened *Oklahoma*, with Curly on board singing 'Oh What A Beautiful Morning'.

Our animal trainer, Australia wide, was Tony Jablonski—a great friend of Smoky Dawson. Tony also choreographed and directed the horse opening of the Sydney 2000 Olympics, ran the 'Man From Snowy River' national tour and was the head of all animals at Movieworld and the Australian Outback Spectacular until his untimely death a few years ago. A fabulous fella and we miss him.

We had two near disasters with *Oklahoma*. In Sydney, Australian Opera Tenor, David Lewis, was playing Curly and was on horseback singing 'Oh What A Beautiful Morning' when the stallion got a wiff of a mare on heat nearby and bolted for the exit.

Somehow David held on and completed the song—albeit offstage. He came back on... on foot.

Clair Hayes was 'Aunt Ella'—sensational!

In Queensland, the brilliant John Nicholson, another Australian Opera tenor, was playing Curly. Our trainer, Tony Jablonski, had drummed into us that **nothing** on the set must change once we brought the horse on stage at rehearsals. **Everything** had to be *exactly* the same so as to avoid spooking the stallion.

One day, a bored stage hand thought he would 'add' something to the opening scene with Curly on horseback. He switched on the windmill—a scene-five action, with the light behind showing the blades shadow moving on the floor. The horse freaked out and reared up. Johno did an incredible job just to hang on and not fall twelve feet onto Sue Roberts in the orchestra pit, horse and all. Some mothers do have 'em.

Our success saw us branch out, thanks to the incredible support of The Hills Centre—Chris Rix and Jack Frost, Deslie Sutton, Lilliana and Lana, Mr Audio Andrew Crawford, the amazing Dennis Jones, Kath Connor plus Cheryl, the box office team, and the lovely Carley Borman.

After successful seasons in Sydney, we took *Superstar* to His Majesty's Theatre in Perth, *42nd Street* to the Theatre Royal in Hobart and *Fiddler* and *Oklahoma* to Queensland— all went well and all made money.

We also teamed up with the RAAF band and began staging annual ANZAC week commemorative concerts. Four concerts over two days—over 1,000 at every concert. We did this for years and had a Hills Centre record of twenty-eight coaches at one performance in 1997.

Part of our success was using well-known professionals in our shows—the likes of Martin Lass, John Paul Young, Normie Rowe, Sandy Scott, Pixie Jenkins, Dieter Brummer, Prinnie Stevens, Mark Williams, Ric Herbert, Angry Anderson, Bernard King, Jack Webster, Jan Adele, Ron Blanchard, Sean Kramer, Claire Hayes and others.

One of our greatest successes was the Hills Centre staging of *Annie*. It was directed by David Ivins with Maria Venuti in the role of Miss Hannigan, and I was again in the role of 'Daddy Warbucks', plus Glenn T. was back on stage as Gangster 'Rooster Hannigan'.

Little orphan Annie was played by Melissa Boniface, a scrawny nine-

THE BRIGHTER SIDE OF A DEATH THREAT

year-old student of St. Patrick's Campbelltown. In the programme she says her ambition is to one day be accepted into a ballet company.

Today the absolutely gorgeous Melissa (now McCabe) is the Principal Dancer in the Western Australian Ballet and winner of multiple national industry awards.

Two of our other 'orphans' were Jessica and Penny McNamee, both currently starring in major international movies, national stage musicals and TV series like *Home and Away*, *Wicked* and *Meg*. A very pregnant Penny starred in last year's *Carols In The Domain*.

In fact, Glenn T, Helen and I were in Melbourne winding up *Leader Of The Pack* at Crown Casino when another of our Hills regulars, Lana Nesnas, rang and invited us to the national touring production of *Dirty Dancing*—at that time in Melbourne. We were amazed to see seven of our Hills Centre 'juniors' in lead roles. Lana and Luke Jocelyn took us out after the show. A terrific catch up.

We are very proud of this era and also the careers that were launched.

Young Liz Scott, a friend of Melinda's from Penno High, and her Co-star in Barnum, also a talented young flautist, is today the head of the combined mass choir in the hugely successful Australian School Spectacular.

And so it goes… including our backstage/production students.

The crowning glory goes to Glenn T. and his *Leader Of The Pack* production.

Sarah Henderson once said, "Don't wait for the light to appear at the end of the tunnel; stride into the darkness and light the bloody thing yourself."

GT sure did this.

Somebody told us that the Laycock Theatre Group on the central coast were staging a musical, *Leader Of The Pack*, the Ellie Greenwich musical, and they had sold out every night for weeks. Glenn T., Melinda and I drove up, and our mates at Laycock let us sit at the sound desk. Amazing music, amazing show and an unbelievably amazing audience reaction.

Ellie Greenwich had written a stunning catalogue of '60s musical hits in the Brill Building in New York, including 'Do Wah Diddy Diddy', 'Chapel of Love', 'Be My Baby', 'Da Do Run Run', 'I Can hear Music', 'River Deep Mountain High', the world's best Christmas song, 'Christmas Baby Won't

You Please Come Home', and many others, including 'Leader Of The Pack'.

First up, we tried it at The Hills Centre; an enormous hit. Again, the crowds reacted amazingly—dancing in the isles every night. Next thing, Glenn was on a plane to New York and a meeting with Ellie and her Manager/brother-in-law, Bob Weiner.

Somehow he convinced them to give him the Australian rights—and 'Leader Entertainment' was born.

We negotiated dates with Star City Casino in Sydney, signed up John Paul Young to play Ellie's Producer (in real life it was Phil Spectre, a famous producer currently in gaol for murder) and Trisha Noble to play Ellie's mum. The role of Ellie was played by the super-talented Hayley Law. Glenn T. was the Narrator and Kath Connor 'ruled the roost'.

The contracts allowed for eight weeks with two possible four-week extensions. We used all 16 weeks. Star City Entertainment guru Ross Cunningham and his two off-siders, Steve Williams and Biccy Henderson, were great mentors and supporters. Charlie Hull as M.D., Beccy Blake was contracted for the PR/promotions, Bruce Pollack as publicity, Playbill to do the programme and the fantastic Lesley Shaw, who eats barbed wire sandwiches for brekky, as a very valuable consulting producer. Katherine Connor, Andrew Crawford, Greg Yates, Brad Law, Bonnie Charles and I made up the team.

We needed to raise a budget of over $3 million. **Gulp.**

Our chief sponsor, Bruce McHugh, bought hundreds of happy people to the show. He once said to me, "A victory without risk is like a triumph without glory." A great man.

We had come a long way since the $6,000 days. It was a humungous risk, and we had some massive challenges and unexpected twists along the way.

First up, Chris Rix was our original Executive Producer with me assisting. On January 2nd, 2003 he hung a sign on his office door 'Gone fishing' and passed away next morning. His funeral was the day before my 60th birthday bash at Thredbo... seventeen years ago. His biggest fan, Melinda, was actually in Australia the day of Chris's funeral but was the 'surprise' guest at my 60th birthday at Thredbo next day, so could not show her face. 'Leader' was three months from opening. I took over Chris's role.

THE BRIGHTER SIDE OF A DEATH THREAT

Then we needed a real pro to be our 'Production Manager'. This is the very important role of supervising the full bump in, dress rehearsals and the very important preview shows. The Production Manager hands the show back to us after opening night. We were lucky. We got the best.

Our Production Consultant, the very talented Lesley Shaw, knew Wane 'Swampy' Jarvis, world renowned Production Manager, who had just returned to Australia after taking *Riverdance* around the world.

Swampy was a real pro and we were totally comfortable with his planning and guidance. Two days before the start of the bump in, I took Ashley with me and we had dinner with Swampy at the North Sydney Travelodge to go through the run sheets and challenges. All was in order. We were ready to go.

Next morning, Swampy's wife, Kerrie, rang distraught. He had just collapsed and died at home, getting ready to go into Star City. I literally froze.

I rang GT, drove into our production office at Star City and advised the receptionist, "No phone calls until after our meeting".

During the meeting, the phone rang. The receptionist said, "I know you said no phone calls, but you need to take this one from New Zealand." It was Marc Anderson, Swampy's Assistant production chief on the *Riverdance* tour (Swampy's wife Kerry had rung him).

Marc was the only person in the world capable of deciphering Swampy's massive book full of notes. He was in Australia within eight hours and saved our bacon. A brilliant professional and great bloke. We are still very close to Marc and his gorgeous and talented wife, 'Cookie' (one of the *Riverdance* leads). Helen and I stayed with them in Ireland and keen to catch up again now that they are back in Kiwiland.

Ellie Greenwich, (who had never been to Oz) her sister Laura, and Manager Bob Weiner flew out from the States for the opening and the audience went wild when she came on stage at the end of the show during the encore and sang 'Da Do Run Run'.

A very very special and lovely lady, Ellie adopted GT., Kath, Helen, JPY and I. We were family. She came back out for the Melbourne opening at Crown Casino. Both Kath and GT spent time with her in New York before her untimely death. GT and Kath flew over for the sad funeral. Ellie will surely light up heaven.

LANCE SMITH

During this fabulous fifteen years doing serious theatre, there were many humorous and remarkable moments—way too many. I will pick out a few.

Pennant Hills Community Centre, *Sentimental Bloke,* the show opened with Ashley, the burglar, climbing up to the first floor balcony. At every performance, the audience were amazed with Glenn's set, and clapped like mad as the curtain opened

Carols, *In Jenolan Caves*, our huge success for fourteen years. I was in the Caves office discussing proceedings with the GM Andrew Fletcher when a guide burst in bewildered. "Boss, they are carrying a huge grand piano over the rocks in the Grand Arch!"

Glenn's 'piano' weighed about four kilos but looked very real. We used it again for *Inge Lass* on the cliff face at Alpha in outback Queensland—during our outback Trailblazer series.

David Ivins had bought a new car. Its first trip was to Jenolan. Coming down the treacherous and steep last five klms, his brakes and power steering failed—a computer glitch. He did an incredible job to save everyone, but was white when he got down to us (on an NRMA repair). He performed that night, but did not come to the always sensational after show party.

I saw him next day—still very pale. Migraines. He said, "At 2.30 a.m., I thought I was going to die. At 4 a.m. I was scared I wouldn't die." You could see the pain.

We were set limits of twelve coaches and seven hundred people at any Grand Arch concert. Our 'protector' was senior ranger John Callagham. What an angel! (He now is!)

One day, he took me aside and told me, "This can't happen again. I have coaches up behind Caves House, on the Oberon Road, in car parks one and two, plus all through the village and also on the eastern side of the Grand Arch. There are thirty-one of them, and I stopped counting at 1200 concert goers."

John, Andrew Fletcher and Co. were unbelievably supportive and the 'singing guide', Domino Cove, was always the hit of the show—singing from way up in the 'Organ Loft' in the roof of the massive arch. The lighting, the angels on all the rocks up high, the choirs all became part of that magical annual concert. Domino also sang at my 75th birthday, in the Cathedral

THE BRIGHTER SIDE OF A DEATH THREAT

Cave.

Ah—'Mrs Jones'. We had a huge challenge with the 'Leader' set at The Hills Centre. Glenn had designed a massive three-tier 'wedding cake'. It started as a single tier cake and had a scissor lift inside to take it up to three tiers, with the bride groom and celebrant on top under the arch. Brilliant concept. Trouble was, we had to somehow attach material to the three levels to make it look like a cake. We tried everything and everyone. Glenn threatened us, "Do not ask mum. She has already spent hundreds of hours on the pross arch, the giant juke box and lighting and the orchestra pit dressing blacks—absolutely no more!"

In desperation, Melinda went up to 'Lincraft' for help—no joy. She was coming out of the store in tears—just as Glenn's mum was coming in. She asked Mel what was wrong and Mel said she was under strict instructions from GT not to involve Mrs. T.

"Don't worry about him. Let's fix it," and, miraculously, she did. Glenn was amazed when he saw it all come together at the first dress rehearsal.

"How did you do it."

We told him, "Mrs Jones from Lincraft had solved it."

He insisted we give Mrs. Jones two opening night VIP tickets. We did. What we didn't know was GT bought her a beautiful bunch of flowers and knew where she was sitting. Imagine his surprise when he realised it was his mum. He did forgive us.

Every show had an exclusive cast, crew, orchestra and production team T-shirt always handed out just before the curtains went up on opening night. Some of them told a great story.

In *Sound Of Music*, at The Hills, Glenn designed and built massive Abbey Gates—very impressive. Looked like thirty tons. Probably 100 kgs. The trouble was The Hills Centre had not one fly tower and they had to disappear at the end of the scene. Way too big to go out sideways. It had to be in the air—and safe. For the first time ever, GT was stumped. The boys and the crew said, "Go away—leave it to us." We did. They succeeded and the T-shirts said—on the back, "He designed it. He built it. We made it fly."

Hobart was a classic T-shirt. Chris Rix had put $4,000 in the budget to get the *42nd Street* sets to and from Hobart in our container. The cheapest price we could get was $12,000. Yikes.

LANCE SMITH

Door knocking transport companies in Hobart, I met the GM of United Transport, George Hurst. His ambition in life was to be on stage, in a professional show, and have one line. If I did that, he would transport the sets both ways for $4,000. Done deal.

We had a 'one line' role. A waiter in the gypsy tea-kettle scene change, Maggie Jones, played by Jan Adele, and five dancers tapped their way across stage during the scene change, ending up at a café table, then, in time with the music, the five girls sat One-Two-Three-Four-Five, and again, in time with the music, and as number five hit her seat the waiter is there and says, "What'll you have."

Not too difficult! Wrong!

George just couldn't get it. His timing was way out. Jan and the girls tried their best to bring him in on time—and if he even got close, he would fluff the line.

Director Jack Webster was getting furious with this and, at the final dress rehearsal, yelled at me, "I don't care if it costs a million to transport the bloody sets—if he doesn't get it right—he's out!"

There was tension. I took George outside; we clicked fingers in time with the music. We worked on five clicks—'What'll you have' and he was ready—very nervous and sweaty but ready.

The scene came—the girls danced and 1-2-3-4-5. 'What'll you have' boomed out—right on cue. Trouble was—George forgot to step forward and the black curtain came down in front of him. No one will ever forget Jan's impromptu line, "Well, a waiter would be a good start."

Jack Webster was lying in the aisle, his fist pumping the ground and crying tears of laughter.

Somehow next day, just before opening, the T-shirts arrived and on the back was, "One-Two-Three-Four-Five. What'll you have."

We ran for seven weeks, full-night shows and matinees.

Bumping in to the Theatre Royal in Hobart was well underway—around 2 a.m., a hungry Andrew Crawford asked a local crew member, "Where is the nearest 24-hour supermarket?"

Quick as a flash the local came back, "Melbourne." Also, GT and Andrew were told to make sure they shifted their cars and did not get booked. They didn't. Turned out the fine was $5.

THE BRIGHTER SIDE OF A DEATH THREAT

Went to the big Hobart hardware store with GT on Friday to get some gear. Went back for some more on Saturday and went to pay. Shock, horror. Credit card missing. Yikes.

The check out lass said, "Are you Lance Smith?" I'd left it there the day before. Phew. Only in Hobart.

Talking of supermarkets. We were in Perth bumping in *Jesus Christ Superstar* into His Majesty's Theatre—best I have ever been in. Angry Anderson was playing King Herod and was there a day early, so came with me to the supermarket.

We loaded up five full trolleys of 'hampers' to put into all the cast and crew rooms for next day. As we approached the checkout, Angry saw a young guy with 'trainee' on his badge. At the top of his voice, with lots looking at him, Angry declared, "Here is the best person to check us out."

He was trying to give the youngster a lift. He did not realise he had Downs Syndrome, and we spent a very painful hour encouraging this young fella. "You can do it." Oh boy.

It was a great success. Perth loved us.

Back to Hobart. Brad Law (hubby of our Leader star Hayley) was our audio guru. Every Saturday afternoon matinee—and only that show each week—we crossed channels with a taxi company. Poor Brad was mortified. He couldn't get them out of our system. He ended up collapsing with Bells Palsy. Took weeks to come good.

During preproduction, Chris Rix suggested we take a few key Hobart people out for dinner to say 'thanks'. We chose the fabulous Ball and Chain, a renowned Hobart landmark. Two memorable things. The first: Theatre C.E.O. and Hobart Councillor, Anne Warwick, insisted on tasting the wine. "You must be joking," she spat. "Bring me something decent."

The shell shocked waiter went away and came back with another bottle. Same result. "That is awful—haven't you got something palatable."

The waiter froze. Chris Rix went purple. It was a B.Y.O. and she was sending back the wine *we* brought!

The second was even better. One of our other guests was our gay Hobart

Choreographer—nice fellow. Glenn took a shine to him and was being very 'loud', very funny, very Glenn! He got up to go to the toot and—as he passed the end of our table did the old TV spectacular—clicked his heels loudly, yelped and fell flat on his face. It always brings a laugh. Not so to the young waitress coming out of the kitchen with six precariously balanced hot meals. She screamed. The six meals went all over Glenn, the floor and the diners at the next table. Absolute pandemonium.

A few more classics:

Practical jokes, in my book, have no place in theatre. Patrons have paid good money to see a good show. However, in my early days in Batemans Bay, they seemed funny. Putting cayenne pepper and soap in Wako's pancakes, putting photos of nude men in the newspaper centrefold in foxy lady's big Oscar Wilde scene, Liz Doll hiding her false teeth in Lesley Wiles sugar bowl when we had a Sydney Director in Agatha Christie's *Murder At The Vicarage*, all seemed like fun. Sure made us laugh.

Even in Sydney, in *Showboat*, when I was on the deck of the Cotton Blossom having a long monologue with FIG Jam—Australian Opera Tenor David Lewis. David had locked his keys in his car pre show—and I threw it in mid sentence. Wrong. He forgot his next lines. Bad move, Lance.

But, as we grew into Pro Am and professional shows and the ticket prices sky rocketed, I changed my mind and let everyone know.

We were staging *Oklahoma* on the Gold Coast. Glenn always hid a duck on the set and we had to find it. That's fine. But Pixie Jenkins was playing Ali Hakim—the Persian peddler. Normie Rowe was playing Jud Fry—the smelly farmhand. The scene was in Jud's smokehouse, where Ali was trying to peddle nude pictures to Jud. He suddenly saw Glenn's duck and added it into his next line. Super bad.

Normie totally lost the plot and 1100 patrons paying $55 to $80 a ticket saw the scene implode. Glenn had the foresight to have security man the doors after the show—to stop me getting in.

They gave me the message from Glenn. "He knows what he did. He is devastated. He is suffering."

It's just as well they stopped me.

THE BRIGHTER SIDE OF A DEATH THREAT

Poor Pixie. Some low life stole all his show gear from the van at the Gold Coast Arts Centre. Thousands of dollars worth.

This is a classic. It also happened in Queensland. The second half opens when two same-sized small circular spots appear on the curtain before it goes up to pick up the two actors. For some unexplained reason, one circle was the right size, the other huge. Lighting guru, Ian Anderson, went off on the comms. Glenn had a deputy Stage Manager who was taken aback by the sudden yelling from Ian, so Glenn decided to put him at ease and lighten the mood. He told his offsider, "No worries. It just reminds me I have one testicle much larger than the other."

Only trouble was, Glenn had just before broadcast a standby call on the backstage PA and had forgotten to turn the speaker off. Hilarious scenes backstage listening to his 'confession'. The ladies in costumes were madly fanning themselves.

One early story. We did *Annie* at the Hills Centre with me in the role of Daddy Warbucks. Our Lend Lease receptionist, the one and only KT, or Katrina as her mum, 'Chook', calls her, bought along her little sister BJ (Belinda). BJ was super-impressed.

The following week, at school, the class were discussing the movie *Annie* and BJ told the class, "My sister works with Daddy Warbucks."

She was duly admonished and a note sent home that Belinda was lying in class. KT sorted it out.

Thirty years later, KT and Nick gave me a magnificent miniature 'Dussenburg' fully operational car—as featured in the *Annie* Musical. It has pride of place in our trophy cabinet.

There were many lines dropped over the years, but the funniest award goes to David Craig, a chemist from Batemans Bay. The Bay Theatre Players were staging *Ten Little Niggers* (probably banned today by the bloody politically correct). Act One, Scene One set the plot of everyone arriving on an Island for the weekend—long before the series of nine murders. David came on stage and totally forgot his opening line to the foxy lady....

He could only remember one line from Scene Six so he delivered it.

"So—Who do you suspect Miss Claythorne?" Trouble was no one had been murdered yet. Where do you go from there?

I should mention that during our Hills Centre shows, we teamed up with Baulkham Hills Lions, who ran a raffle for our favourite project, Bear Cottage, in the foyer. They raised nearly forty-thousand dollars. Full credit to their former President and still our good mate, Max Lockhart, and his District Governor, Geoff Cossart.

They later pledged $1 million to Bear Cottage and put in a huge effort over the years. Wonderful stuff.

Another story. Strict backstage rules. The key crew members are all on 'comms' to take direction from the Stage Manager—they are very confidential and often sensitive communications.

Rule number One: **Never** let anyone else wear your cans.

We were staging *Fiddler* in Sydney and, in the closing, very dramatic scene the final sight is Tevye leaving the stage—cart loaded, bound for 'who knows'—dispossessed. Very sad. The sunset lights then show up on the huge screen backstage as the smoke stops coming out of Tevye's house.

I was supposed to exit stage on the curtain side of the ground lights but tripped, ending up on the screen side of the ground lights and casting huge moving shadow over the screen. GT went off on the comms and said some very nasty things about me and my weight.

"Glenn Turner, how dare you? That is my father you are talking about."

Melinda had driven up from Canberra and sat at the sound desk—putting on Andrew's Crawford's comms.

Probably the funniest, unintentional thing I witnessed was in 'Leader' at Star City. We had an amazingly talented dance captain/swing, Marcia Tastidis. She was normally dancing in the chorus but covered about six of the leading female roles—and brilliantly. Sometimes two covers in one show. I don't know how she did it. The opening of Act Two was a showstopper.

As the lights came up, there were three girls hidden behind a small cover and they started 'Be My Baby' and came out on stage singing and dancing—a real show highlight. This night, when the lights came up, we all saw a shoulder sticking out from each side of the cover. Turns out Marcia

THE BRIGHTER SIDE OF A DEATH THREAT

had covered so many roles that night she thought she was covering 'Jasmine' in 'Be My Baby'. She dressed into that costume during interval.

Trouble was, Yolanda was there to play her normal role, so when the three girls hid behind the stage cover in the dark—there were four of them, including two Jasmines. Hence the shoulder out each side. It looked and was a really funny scene—but only to those in the 'family'.

Those years have many more stories. They were a wonderful segment in our lives and we are so grateful to have been given that opportunity.

Here at Hastings Point, we have memorabilia from Jenolan Caves, The Hills Centre, Bear Cottage, the Children's Hospital Express and the outback on all the walls and cabinets. It sure makes us thankful. What an amazing group of people and events we have experienced and how lucky we are. It made me realise you don't build a reputation on what you are going to do. It is what you have done that counts.

CHAPTER 18

TAMWORTH COUNTRY MUSIC FESTIVAL

Making a decision does not define you. It is how you face up to the consequences of that decision.
...Smoky Dawson. 1993.

When I left Country Comfort, and because we were hoping to start a touring events company, I discussed with Darryl the fact that the first five nights of the Tamworth Country Music Festival were 'soft', and a coach with dinner, bed and breakfast nightly would ensure we fill and they would eat dinner early, therefore the Cutty Sark restaurant could fill with a second sitting.

We negotiated a ten-year commitment. Then one of our former Country Comfort staff, Nola, and hubby, Greg, had leased the Almond Inn Motel and she loved the idea of coaches for the whole festival—so we booked the whole motel for the ten days and ran two lots of five-night tours every year, filling every coach for fifteen years.

We chartered coaches from Clarkes Coaches in Sydney. Terry was a long time supporter of the Celebrity Cavalcades, and he and brother Greg loved the festival, and we also chartered Stonestreets from Toowoomba to bring down the Queensland visitors. The Tour Manager, Rob Brown, was a country music tragic. He and Nick Peters were their first two drivers every year. We had four to five coaches every year, depending on how many beds we could muster.

LANCE SMITH

Our itinerary was always the same—and was sensational.

The first Friday, the coaches departed Sydney and Brisbane. Friday evening, we attended Bicentennial Park—the official opening concert. Ten thousand people B.Y.O. chairs. Great show.

Saturday, an official welcome at the Tamworth Tourist Info Centre, a town tour showing the main venues and then four hours in Peel Street—absolute magic. Buskers, line dancers, street artists, whip crackers, bands—all sorts of entertainment wall to wall.

Saturday night, the huge Starmaker Grand Final concert. Sunday out to Moombi and the Lindsay Butler annual L.B.S. Moombi Gully Show, with Shazza & Co—and it just kept going. The Kernaghan Family Show in the Town Hall, the Topp Twins at Blazers—part of the West Leagues complex—the Pixie Jenkins Tribute Show, Andrew Clermont and the Fiddlers Festival, the Gunbarrel Highwaymen and the Naked Poets.

The second group arriving on the Wednesday had a similar type itinerary, with the highlight being the Golden Guitar Awards concert on the final Saturday night, followed by the huge wind-up concert at TREC (Tamworth Regional Entertainment Centre). They, too, had a brilliant night in Moombi Gully at Rex Dallas's show.

Every year there are over two thousand shows during the festival. 70% are free.

Between Tamworth and the Carols At Jenolan Caves, we had a very busy December/January every year, then the first musical theatre rehearsals got underway early February.

We usually staged major musical theatre in April, July and October with smaller themed productions such as the Anzac Concerts in between. The years flew by—we were having a ball.

Back to Tamworth. Tamworth produced a wealth of wonderful people. In 1985, Country Comfort did a major upgrade and we decided to theme the convention complex into Country Music. I spoke to my old mate, Nick Erby, the country music radio guru, and asked him who was the crowd favourite with no bad side. He told us, "Smoky Dawson is the world-renowned singing cowboy, and they love him."

Turns out Smoky and his wife Dot lived about five minutes away from our Country Comfort Chatswood HQ, in Lane Cove. They said, "Yes, please."

We named the complex after them.

THE BRIGHTER SIDE OF A DEATH THREAT

And so the Smoky Dawson Conference Room and the Smoky Dawson Supper Club were themed and launched in 1988.

Smoky and the Howie Brothers and, more often than not, Tony Taunton, performed every year on the first festival Tuesday in the Smoky Dawson Supper Club for our groups. We would squeeze 140 of them into the club. Great night, plus Smoky and Dot always stayed on to do a private concert for our second week coach patrons in the Almond Inn restaurant on the Friday night, with a hilarious kangaroo court. Again, great times.

We were always lucky enough to have the Tamworth 'Elder Statesman', Rex Dallas, on our side and took many groups and also cavalcades out to the Dallas ranch at Moombi Gully for some wonderful concerts. There were three generations of Dallas's on stage. Now baby 'Ashleigh'—the then seven-year-old fiddle player—is a very well known and talented country music performer in her own right, and Rex is still reaching the finals of the coveted Golden Guitar. He's a champion as he passes eighty years young.

At the end of each Tamworth tour we were always buggered. One year we headed north to the Gold Coast with Helen, myself and the Hills Centre lighting guru, Ian Anderson, fully loaded with all sorts of tour left overs.

Midway between Tenterfield and Casino, as we were doing 100 klms per hour along the picturesque and winding Summerland Way, all three of us woke up at the same time as we careered through the bush—only trouble was—I was driving! Let me assure you, we stayed well and truly awake for the rest of the journey. In fact, it took two days for me to close my eyes again.

One year I will never forget, we had three coaches in the first week. On the Saturday morning, I jumped on the Country Comfort team coach to welcome everyone. I knew I had two birthdays on board. One was my sister, Franny (no one knew she was my sister), and the other our good mate, Lee Marks, from Longreach (again, no one knew we were known to Lee and she and Fran had never met.)

So—I embarrassed both by asking them to stand up—and we all sang a rousing rendition of 'Happy Birthday' and three loud cheers. An hour later, we started the Peel Street Walk at the southern end—near the snakes display and Australia's best whip cracker—Gail Nessmith. I then saw an old mate, the former CEO of Barcaldine Regional Council, there and we stopped to chat. I knew he was from Orange and our birthday girl, Lee, was also from Orange originally. So I introduced them and we talked 'Orange' for a while.

He asked Lee was she born there. She said, "No. I was born in Broken Hill." My heart skipped a beat. That's where my sister, Fran, was born.

So I called Fran over and asked, "Guess where Lee was born?"

Fran replied, "Not Broken Hill?"

Lee nodded.

"Not 1949?"

Again, Lee nodded.

I clearly remembered, as a 5-year-old, seeing a wide-eyed baby Franny for the first time in a crib behind a window, alongside another baby which must have been Lee. Small world.

The highlight for us was producing *Kitty's Music Hall*, two brilliant country music shows written and directed by the very talented Clair Hayes with Clair, Aldo Fabian, Linda Hale, Tony Taunton and myself on stage. The first all Aussie show, I was Blue the shearer. And the second, an American show based on 'Ghost Riders In The Sky' and 'High Noon'. They really were super shows but sadly, up against too many freebies, e.g. you could see Lee Kernaghan and his full band and friends for free in Bicentennial Park or pay $15 to see Lance and Co. Go figure.

Linda, Aldo, Clair and Tony were as good as you get anywhere.

I still have no regrets about 'Kittys' and our losses. Clair and Terry made it all worthwhile. A terrific show and experience—but when does 'Old enough to know better' kick in?

Another funny thing. One year, our long time great tour leader, Dennis Hennessy, checked his group into the Almond Inn. Hot day and cricket on, he found Room 24, the only spa room at the Almond Inn. Air con on, stripped naked, he lay on the bed watching cricket—and fell asleep. All would have been fine—if room 24 had been Dennis's. But it wasn't. The couple booked into 24 opened their door to find a naked man asleep on their bed!

It is fair to say our annual Kangaroo Courts were a real highlight. Most of them were scripted and staged by Glenn T and I. Dennis made it an easy choice that year.

Everyone knew we ran a tight ship. We always asked, "What is the difference between a luxury coach passenger and a hitchhiker?"

Answer: "30 seconds."

We did wait a little longer sometimes—but not often. One year, night one, I told everyone to be back on board all coaches fifteen minutes after the Bicentennial concert finished. I waited twenty minutes and told Brownie to head off. 'Pixie' Paul and Qantas's Phil then had to push 'Charlie', our wheelchair passenger, three kilometres up hill. I had forgotten he was on that coach. Bad Lance.

Tamworth 2005 is my 'forgotten year'. In December 2004, I was diagnosed with a large malignant melanoma. Surgery at Alamanda Hospital left me with 43 stitches in the shape of an H. Helen was amused, but not for long. A bad result came back 48 hours later. More surgery, this time with skin grafts. I now have a stubby holder in my chest. Discharged New Year's Eve and told, "No work for a least two months". But I went to Tamworth two weeks later. I cannot remember *one* thing about the tour or events… except the daily visits to Tamworth Hospital to have the skin-graft dressings changed because of Golden Staph. The following year I had all these people I thought I had never met telling me what a terrific time we had the year before. Ah…doctors' drugs!

Tamworth was fifteen years of fabulous tours and over two thousand very happy clients and Tamworth box office—the clubs, Golden Guitar shop and people like the Kernaghans, Pixie Jenkins, the Butlers and Dallas families all loved our spending.

Special thanks must go to Nola and Greg, Jodie McKenna, Nick Erby, Ivan and Mary Chapman, Shazza and Lindsay, Max Ellis, Rex Dallas, Jam drop Judy at the ACMF, Terry Hill, Barry Harley and the Tourist Centre team for their fantastic support over those fifteen years.

The Tamworth story must finish with our two biggest supporters—Smoky & Dot Dawson. Smoky's ashes were spread on top of Mt. Oxley Lookout and Dot lived to 104. Both these beautiful people are sadly missed by Tamworth, Bear Cottage and many many others.

CHAPTER 19

QUEENSLAND HERE WE COME AGAIN, PLUS OUR OUTBACK ADVENTURES, AND GRANDCHILDREN

You can be as happy or as miserable as you like —it's up to you.

…Billie—Bupa Aged Care, Pottsville, 2018

The move from a very hectic Sydney—it's crowds, it's traffic snarls—to Carrara, behind the Gold Coast, was the start of another very different and wonderful chapter of our journey. Queensland's Gold Coast and the outback.

In 1989, Country Comfort bonuses had supplied a $10,000 deposit on a beautiful house—37 palm trees, pool and backing onto a reserve at Boonooroo Park, Carrara. We let it to tenants for nearly ten years and paid it off! During our time in Sydney, The Hills, Tamworth, Jenolan Caves and the Celebrity Cavalcades, Warren, Melinda and Ashley all left the nest. Warren joined the RAAF in 1989. Mel headed south to the Australian Institute of Sport in Canberra and Ashley headed north to begin life as a white-water-rafting instructor in Cairns, with Raging Thunder, after leaving school in 1993.

LANCE SMITH

I cannot forget the last one to leave home was Ashley, very early one morning, in his prized little car, on a four day drive to Cairns. We waved him goodbye from our home in Francis Greenway Drive, Cherrybrook—and then Helen didn't stop crying for two days and didn't speak to me once. The last one gone. We were 'empty nesters'.

It was time to go north as we had always planned, out of the big smoke.

As we had previously lived on the Gold Coast when I first joined Country Comfort, and having had the house at Carrara for ten years, we knew all about the 1150 seat Gold Coast Arts Centre theatre complex and decided we would take our Sydney leads and use local talent for chorus/minor roles to do F*iddler On the Roof* while Sydney staged the Olympics.

Helen was a tad sceptical. We needed $170,000 to stage the season and I had had many dreams, schemes and losses during our time together that were uppermost in her mind. But we had survived all these and had lived a fabulous life, and Helen ended up all right with the *Fiddler* risk.

And it worked a treat. All Sydney leads—except the brilliant Martin Lass as the Fiddler—were available, and we were lucky enough to get Country Music 'The Fiddling Firecracker', Pixie Jenkins, in that role. Glenn T, andMargaret E. were available.

We then met the Arts Centre General Manager, Kelvin Cordell, who agreed, somewhat reluctantly, to our proposal, provided we teamed up with the local 'Gold Coast Musical Society'—thorn in his side.

We then met the Gold Coast Musical Society's heads, Wayne and Kris Matheson, and offered their group $10,000 to join forces with us, and away we went.

The upside was two key people at The Arts Centre, Sharon Doer, Deputy G.M. and marketing guru, and Phil Reid, head of the box office—two gems. Plus a great local talent pool including Marilyn and Frank Culell, and our great Sydney mate, Shane Caddaye to direct.

The downside: We had not realised Kelvin and his mate Robert Young had their own 'group', who staged musicals 'subsidised' by council and the 'Friends Of The Art Centre' with cheap theatre rental and grants, and we were a threat to their future funding. We were paying over $75,000 in theatre rental and no subsidies. Kelvin and Robert did everything to 'not help'—yet we still succeeded with both *Fiddler* and *Oklahoma* over two years.

THE BRIGHTER SIDE OF A DEATH THREAT

In fact, the then Chairman of the board asked me how much sponsorship dollars we were able to generate to cover the losses. He was amazed when I told him no cash sponsors and no losses. At this stage, I should point out all Kelvin and Robert shows were first class productions.

The Surfers Paradise Bowls Club became our rehearsal venue (great people) and we were lucky enough to entice our long time friend, Shane Caddaye, to direct the show. We also found two incredibly talented and wonderful people. Sue Roberts, Head of Music at Somerset College, agreed to be Musical Director and Marie Nicholson agreed to be our répétiteur. We had the best team imaginable.

While we were doing all the *Fiddler* preproduction tasks, we shifted lock stock and barrel from Cherrybrook to our Carrara home—in the quiet cul de sac.

I must say I was intrigued by the fact that our neighbours always walked around with cricket bats or big sticks. When I asked why, I was advised it was to protect us from the panther—now that was a big call.

I needed to go back to Sydney to finalise my departure from The Hills Centre offices. When I returned, Helen said, "Sit down. I have something to tell you."

I knew it could not be good news.

Now, Helen never argues. She always explains why she is right! Remember the lady from Batemans Bay and her affinity with emus, wombats, snakes and foxes. Helen had done it again. She explained that 'the panther' was in fact a huge black feral tomcat who lived in the reserve. She had adopted it and was feeding it with a view to saving the local wild life.

'Wild Thing' as we called him, had fangs—huge teeth that could not fit inside the mouth. He was very big, with huge paws. I could understand people thinking they had a panther in their midst.

Wild Thing bought us many half dead conquests—like cockatoos, rabbits, bush rats, once even an eagle that he had caught. He would come to the back wire door, knock and growl (he didn't meow) until we acknowledged his capture. So much for protecting the local wild life.

Wild Thing put Helen in hospital twice. We coped okay with that, but when he killed the next door neighbour's dog we were not too popular in the neighbourhood.

The strange thing was that three days before we were shifting to our newly-purchased townhouse at Clear Island Waters, after selling the house, Wild Thing went back into the bush. Somehow he knew.

I received a call from an old mate, Jeff Weigh. Jeffo and his business partner, Sir Frank Moore, owned Fortland Hotels, Motels and Resorts in Queensland and the Northern Territory and they needed a 'marketing audit' to measure the effectiveness of their advertising and promotion spend—something Jeffo knew we had pioneered at Lend Lease/Country Comfort thanks to Sue Hunt & DCOC.

Having previously known both Jeffo and Sir Frank, I readily agreed. I spent a couple of months at their office and properties in Brisbane, as well as their properties at places like Rockhampton, Carnarvon Gorge, Toowoomba and Alice Springs.

After a thorough feasibility study, the boys decided to accept a good offer from Accor and sold out. A great decision. Sir Frank had lived and worked in Longreach before buying a network of radio stations and shifting to the city. He became Chairman of just about everything in tourism in Australia, including the Q.T.C.C. (Queensland Tourism and Travel Corporation) and the A.T.C. (the Australian Tourism Industry Council) in Canberra, a position he was offered, ironically, in the Lend Lease boardroom in Sydney.

One of Sir Frank's Longreach Associates, Parry Smith, had offered him a 25-year lease on the two largest hotels/motels/resorts businesses in western Queensland: The Albert Park Motor Inn and the Longreach Motor Inn, both in Longreach. Sir Frank asked me to do a feasibility study, so I spent a great week in the outback... back to the memories of the 1993 Celebrity Cavalcade for Bear Cottage.

Realising he would be 102 when the lease ran out, Sir Frank decided not to go for it, but Jeffo was keen and asked me if we were interested in a partnership with he and Heather. We accepted.

It is neither the best nor worst financial decision we made—but it was the start of a wonderful seventeen years in our lives and we do love outback Queensland and, again, met and worked with many great characters and decent people—meeting a few duds along the way as per normal.

First up, the two motor inns were first class, great rooms, really well maintained, terrific restaurants, pools, conference facilities and commercial laundries. What was a challenge was the huge difference between the really slow hot months and the busy cooler months. 2000 and 2001 was slow, then

THE BRIGHTER SIDE OF A DEATH THREAT

2002 was the designated 'Year of The Outback' and very busy. We needed it. Thereafter it slowly picked up.

We took over in a January—not a good decision. At the end of February two long-time local tour operators, Norm Salsbury, Longreach Outback Travel, and Alan Smith, Outback Aussie Tours, both had sizeable accounts unpaid.

By mid March, neither had paid. Being new, I called into both with a gentle reminder. Smithy promised payment within a week and honoured it. Salsbury said he would pay when the Queensland Rail cheque was paid for the January travellers. I had connections in QR and rang them. I was informed he had been paid for January passengers in December and February passengers in January. I drove into town and the Longreach Outback Travel office and fronted Salsbury and his partner, Chris Rumsey, the local SES chief. I told them I couldn't cop liars. Salsbury threatened to sue me for prying into their personal affairs—basically for catching him out.

I discussed this with Jeffo, who immediately instituted bankruptcy proceedings—and won a court order. They paid us in full, with interest and court costs, but never stayed with us again.

Suffice to say, when we sold out in 2008 they were out of the business and Rumsey was in gaol. How Salsbury didn't go to gaol, I will never know. An absolutely despicable excuse for a human being—rare in the outback. I remember thinking the first time I met him, "I wonder who ties your shoelaces for you."

A guy named John Dollinger, 'big John' from Aramac, hated Longreach—as did most of his townsfolk. In an angry response, he once said to me, "But we got even with you bastards—we gave you Norm Salsbury." Turns out Salsbury had come from Aramac and J.D. was dead right—they got way more than even. I was told 'big John' passed away last year. They will miss him in Aramac.

A classic story of the bush: In years past there was a weekly Friday night two-up and gambling night in Whyton's Transport sheds. In fact, the two tables were still in the rafters there in our day. At the time, local entrepreneur Brian Stokes owned 'Spikes Pies' and was playing and winning one night. Two locals, Fred 'Diddy' Naylor (who worked for us), and his mate, Col Searles, were losing and left early. They returned a few hours later all cashed up and their luck changed.

Later that night, Spike turned on his pie-cart ovens to set up in Eagle Street for the late night drinkers. When he opened the first draw, everything was gone, and the same happened with every drawer. Two sausage rolls were left. Diddy and Searles had fired them up earlier, when they left the game, drove the pie cart into town, set up shop and sold almost the lot and went back cashed up.

Everyone in Longreach seemed to have a nickname and some were well thought up. 'Diddy' Naylor was given his in his young courting days—'Fred'. Son John was given the same name. Our builder/carpenter was a father and son team, Paul Wake and his dad. Their names were 'Ima' Wake and 'Wida' Wake.

Our refrigeration mechanic was 'Chicken' Ravenscroft and the cheques were made out to that name. Chicken's opposition was 'Big Bird' Stephen Smith. Our local fire officer was 'Cracka' Barr. 'Scotty', whose real name was Quentin, was our local talented bush poet, Lawn Mower (if they grew) and dog walker. There were many.

But the one that got me was 'Cep John', John Secombe. John was a National Party stalwart, Chairman of national organisations and a grazier from 'Kenya'—a station near Muttaburra. He was also with me on the Qantas Museum board. Normally, all bushies were called by their nickname at all times. This was not the case with John. In Muttaburra one day, I asked a local why they gave him that nickname. I was asked if I had ever drunk with him, "Because everybody shouts—Cep John."

Killed me.

John's wife, Pam, was a sensational lady and died very young. I was pleased that around ten times the population attended the funeral in Muttaburra, the geographical centre of Queensland and a terrific little town.

The bushies were a resilient lot—salt of the earth. I was really saddened to see the recent end of many dry years and suffering was devastating floods and the loss of millions of cattle and sheep. I know that they will bounce back. That's what they do—but it will be a long, painful journey for many.

Around 2005, we purchased the Longreach maxi taxi and, soon after, Queensland Rail advised they were considering abandoning 'The Spirit of The Outback'—our twice-weekly train to the end of the line: Longreach, a

THE BRIGHTER SIDE OF A DEATH THREAT

24-hour trip from Brisbane. Every tourist that disembarked stayed either four nights or five, depending which train it was, and we had ten crew rooms every Wednesday and Sunday, our biggest client by far. Ouch! I hot-footed it to Brisbane and was told that they were losing huge amounts on the service as well as getting lots of complaints from the 'Summertime service', as Longreach virtually 'shut down' for the off-season, November to February, and they were sick of the continual complaints.

I held a meeting with those involved. Council wouldn't budge. The Powerhouse Museum was closed November to March. The Pastoral College gave us permission to run their normal tours, even when school was not there. GM Peter Scott was a top guy and did what he could to help. He even gave us the twelve-month tour rights—even through the lucrative peak times.

The School of The Air agreed to limit the closure of their tours to the actual holidays—a small win. Salsbury had the boats and refused to cruise in the slow months, and they were the main cause for complaint.

The Stockmans Hall of Fame and the Qantas Museum agreed to stay open as normal.

So, with the help of Parry and Paul, and a new mortgage on our Gold Coast townhouse, we outlayed well over $300,000 and purchased the beautiful MV *Longreach Explorer*—a two-deck, 51-passenger catamaran, plus a 48-seater Greyhound coach, and promised QR we would cruise year-round and also combine with the Stockmans Hall of Fame and the Qantas Museum, plus offer town and district coach tours at a discount over the off-peak.

They were very grateful and pledged support.

Four things happened:

- Norm Salsbury was very, very pissed off—and that was good
- QR committed to a major off-peak promotional campaign for the next three years and we broke all previous summer records every year—very welcome news.
- The M.V. *Longreach Explorer* was a real hit. Captain Kimbo at the helm and Coach Captain doing all the pick ups etc., with myself as cook/waitress/entertainer/deckie and dishwasher. We had a ball and made good money!

We successfully brought other businesses on board and within two years

Longreach was 'open for business' year-round.

You know, they say we only live once. That is not true. We only die once. We get the chance to live every day, and I saw every sunset over the magnificent Thomson River Coolibah trees for years. Life was great. Loved it.

There were lots of highs. Around 2006, there was a South African kids choir who were going to sing at dawn in Bladensburg National Park, near Winton, with our own Kate Miller-Heidke. I still have goose bumps. They will never fade. As the sun came up, those magnificent African kids' powerful voices pumped out a rhythm I will never forget.

The generosity of outback people was amazing. A local rural family were in real trouble. Their young fella was driving the station ute and rolled it, killing his mum. Dad took the kids away for Christmas to the coast, and their homestead burnt to the ground. Every photo, every memory of mum gone.

Damien Curr, who owned the Wellshot Hotel at Ilfracombe, decided to do something for the family. He rang to ask for seven rooms, as he had convinced country musicians, Adam Brand and his band, to come out and do a fund raiser. He was happy to pay, but we insisted they were on us, and I also said our 50-plus staff wanted to do more. We asked him who was looking after the fund raising dollars?

"Isisford Shire—a bloke named Trevor Latta."

I froze. I knew Trevor Latta from Batemans Bay—a real dud. I did not know where he went after he got out of gaol, but Isisford is the ideal place to hide.

I did something rare for me. I rang the local head of detectives, Steve Butler—a top man. An hour later he rang me. "How old would your Trevor Latta be?"

I said around 60, and he told me this Trevor Latta was 23. Ouch! I met him, later, when he was working at Barcaldine Council—a really nice young bloke, and I had nearly got him hung, drawn and quartered and run of the west. Helen says the only exercise I get is jumping to conclusions. Right again.

Anyway, back to Ilfracombe and the Wellshot Hotel. Damien and his gorgeous bride, Bridgette Adams, were top people who knew how to put on

THE BRIGHTER SIDE OF A DEATH THREAT

a great night. The town with a population of 72 raised well over $50,000 on the night. Brilliant.

Sadly, the Currs sold the pub and it wasn't the same. Nice people… but…

There was a Charleville band, 'Ned and the Kellys.' Brilliant. The town's Mayor Mark O'Brien, Charleville legendary Doctor Chester Wilson, bus proprietor Trevor Ekkles, master I.T. drummer Bill Grant, famous bush pilot 'Cracker' McDonald, and National Parks ranger Chris Everson. They were simply the best, and they were coming to Longreach to play at a huge night at the Qantas Museum.

Mark rang me and offered to play F.O.C. in return for board and lodgings the night before. He suggested the Wellshot Hotel and asked me for Damien's number. I told Mark there were new owners who would be delighted with their good fortune, and that I would organise it.

The new owners were Jo Scott, sister of legendary Queensland forward Matt Scott. I was staggered when Jo said, "No thanks, we don't do those things anymore."

The end result—Ned and The Kellys played for board and lodgings. They had never had such a small crowd. The MV *Longreach Explorer* had their best fun night ever, and we all woke up a little dusty next day—but smiling.

The people make the bush.

Stan and Val Emslie had made their yard in Cassowary Street into an oasis—using materials scavenged from the local tip over five decades. In my early days, I was showing this 'treasure' to some visitors and got talking to Valles (nee Schneider, and a cousin of our very own yodelling queen, Mary Schneider.)

I asked Valles had she always lived here, meaning Longreach.

She said, "No, we have lived here for the last fifty-eight years," and pointed at the house over the road and said, "I lived there till I was eighteen." The Emslies are now well into their 80's and Stan is leader of the town band and Choirmaster of the Longreach Community Choir and a Church elder. Pillars of society who had only ventured away from Longreach about six times in eighty years—and not for long. Love em!

Talking of the town choir—in 2002, 'The Year Of The Outback', I had an idea—again. I rang the owner of the *Yellowbelly*—Alan Smith. The *Yellowbelly* was then doing evening dinner river cruises and I wanted to impress our fifty staff for a Christmas treat.

Smithy agreed with me, so fifty of us headed into the twilight up the outback Thomson River. After a magic sunset and dinner on board, we began cruising back to Longreach when we broke down, in the dark, in the middle of nowhere. I suggested we sing a Christmas carol and we sang 'Away in a Manger'. At the end, I said, "That was pretty ordinary—what we need is a choir."

They were not aware that, in the dark, Smithy had steered us towards the bank and the Coolibah trees, and suddenly lights came on and the town choir was right there in amongst the bush setting. They sang 'Away In A Manger' and there were tears all through our boat. Wow. Another goose bump moment, and the photo was the front cover of the next *Australian Heritage* magazine. Amazing.

Another high was the night the Qantas Australian Girls Choir flew into town to sing 'I Still Call Australia Home' under the wing of their new exhibit—the magnificent 747 jet donated to the museum by Qantas. It was sunset, and a black sky with lightning in the background. Truly amazing.

John Travolta 'flew in' one day. He is a Qantas International Ambassador. It was about 47 degrees Celsius and the crowd waited under the outback sun. John could have gone out a side door, as he was running late, but told his minders, "They have waited in the sun, lets go talk to them," and he did. Thoroughly good guy.

It was not uncommon to see kangaroos, emus, dancing brolgas and rare bustards (the world's heaviest flying bird) in yards and lawns all over Longreach. Every street in the town was named after a bird.

Melinda flew in from London to run the Longreach Motor Inn. Patsy, from Daydream Island reception and Gold Coast mate, Lynne Thornton, came up to give us a hand. Our old Daydream skipper, Graham Mee, came out every time Captain Kimbo went on holidays, to skipper the *Explorer*.

THE BRIGHTER SIDE OF A DEATH THREAT

Batemans Bay mates, builder Derek Campbell and Geoff Lassau, kept coming out to help, and it was very much appreciated… and, of course, Glenn T.

Some of our old Country Comfort Managers also came out to help at various times over the years. Lex and Colleen Kettlewell were super.

There was a hilarious night. Glenn T. had come up to do some refurbishing of the Longreach Motor Inn restaurant. Very hot weather. He decided to take a late night dip. Melinda had already come back from the pub with a bunch of locals.

Picture this: A few burly bushies and Glenn swans in wrapped in a beach towel. One of the boys asked GT could he share his towel. GT said 'fine', and gave it to him. I think they were expecting Glenn to be wearing togs—but no!

Bev Ivins rang one day. Son, Nathan, was looking for a fresh start. We know young Nath and readily agreed to put him on. He was, as expected, a great team member and thankfully stayed well over a year. A few years later, Nath decided to fly to Darwin and drive back through Longreach to catch up with friends.

A few hours south of Darwin, he pulled off the road to drive up a hill to an 'historic site' and found a guy with a bicycle towing a small trailer. He had ridden from Cairns. It had taken two months. He was on his way to Darwin to pick up a car he had bought on line and paid a 50% deposit. He told Nath his mobile battery was flat and he asked could he use Nathan's phone just to let the vendor know he was only two days away. All Nathan heard was, "What, do you mean you've sold it?"

The vendor had taken a higher offer. The poor bugger was devastated.

Helen and I ran into Nathan recently when he had a coach group on tour in Exmouth WA, when we were visiting Warren and Lou at Learmonth Air Force Base. He is thriving and going great guns in Tassie.

Longreach had a unique 'mother nature' event seemingly after every drop of rain. Either a moth plague, dung beetles, shocking flies, bugs—I remember the Qantas Museum had a band playing outside all wearing fly veils.

I also remember well that we had prominent signs in every unit

LANCE SMITH

'*Warning—You are in the Outback. Never leave the unit door open.*'

We often heard the screams. It would either be a huge goanna on the bed, a snake in the bathroom or a kangaroo, emu or brolga who had just wandered in.

We became very close to many great people. The Millars, Grant and Lee and three youngsters were managing the Children's Hostel in Ibis Street when we met them in 2000. What talents. Singers, songwriters, musos and a fabulous family. Lee had always dreamt of going to Paris and had been saving for years. Grant saw a house he loved in Galah Street, along from the Longreach Motor Inn. He 'borrowed' Lee's savings for the deposit… .and called the new home 'Paris'. They shifted in when they left the Hostel. A year or so later, I had been away for about a month and flew back into Longreach with a high ranking executive from Tourism Queensland. To show him just how friendly bush people are, we rocked up to Millars, knocked, but went straight in and—with no sign of Grant or Lee—I put the kettle on.

Imagine my surprise when an unknown person walked out from the main bedroom and asked, "Can I help you?" or even imagine her surprise when, as the new tenant, she walked out of her bedroom and found two strange men in her kitchen making themselves a cuppa! The Millars had moved. Why wasn't I told?

Grant, Lee and colleague Michael, with all their kids as backup singers, made two hugely successful CD's. They began an outback dinner/musical show and entertained thousands of happy customers over the years. Like all of us, their kids 'growed up'. The Millars are now grandparents with two more children marrying this year. We love 'em all. Lee had a major car accident, broke sixty-one bones, went to hell and back. Brave girl.

During our time in Longreach, we certainly needed lots of good local assistance—and got it. The BP Service Station owners, the Longreach Fire Brigade Chief, the local Laundromat owner, the local Scout Master—'Wolf', the car wash owners, the town's athletic coach, the bicycle shop owners and, certainly the Mayor. The most remarkable thing— they are all just one person. John Palmer has also been Citizen of the Year and been awarded the Order of Australia—well deserved. None of it would have been possible if it weren't for his equally dynamic wife, Sue.

THE BRIGHTER SIDE OF A DEATH THREAT

The Palmers have been round the world with us twice and are still very close. In fact, the Barcaldine Chandlers—Rob and Deb—the Longreach Palmers and Millars are the best mates one could ever dream of having. And then there is the beautiful, delightful, intelligent, hard working Kim Anderson.

When Melinda returned to Oz to run the Longreach Motor Inn for us, she struck up a great friendship with this remarkable girl. We all became great mates. Kim then met a rugged, redheaded roustabout—obviously nicknamed 'Blue'—and they produced a lively lad, 'Rusty'. Kim's training business really took off. She bought a second house in Eagle Street and turned it into a variety of training rooms for herself and visiting professionals. She was conducting courses right around the bush in about twenty towns. She was a real goer. Mel then left and flew to Dubai to work once again for Showtime Arabia (TV).

Kim had been feeling off and had been a regular at the doctors for over a year, until a visiting locum pressed alarm bells. Stage Four Cervical Cancer. It was all downhill from there.

Melinda and Lyth flew out from the U.K. with a young Angus and Isla and met Rusty and Kim for a great week at Seaworld Resort. But, sadly, the end was drawing nigh.

Kim's last wish was to marry Blue. She rang and asked me to MC their reception—just fifteen to twenty 'best friends', including Melinda, who had agreed to fly home for the wedding.

What can I say? Well over two hundred 'besties' were at the wedding at the Australian Stockmans Hall of Fame. Blue and his brother, plus a now seven-year-old Rusty flew in by helicopter to a specially constructed chapel. The band, answering a call from the Longreach community, flew in from Melbourne (no charge). We had one of the all time sensational bush weddings, thanks to an incredible team of locals headed by Sue Palmer and the Stockmans Hall of Fame staff. The chapel and the reception setting was amazing.

Kim made her 'farewell' performance one of the best events any of us have ever attended—certainly my most memorable MC job. The speeches, the presentations—all very moving and excellent.

They had a caravan 'hidden' about ten feet from the bridal table and Kim had to lie down a few times. She danced bare feet and had a wonderful night.

As expected, her funeral a few weeks later was a very sad occasion and I was then asked to host her special memorial service held on the Gold Coast.

In the five years since, Rusty has thrived. He has done really well at scouts under Wolf John Palmer. Blue and his mum, Mary, (who shifted to Longreach) have done a super job. Sue Palmer and many locals have certainly been 100% in Rusty's corner. Rusty was Longreach's Primary School Captain and this year headed to 'Downlands', a prestigious boarding school at Toowoomba.

Kim would be so proud of them all. RIP beautiful girl.

Thankfully, at the same time, there were some *great* things happening in our world—grandchildren.

Without doubt the arrival of grandchildren on the scene completely overshadowed all the great things happening in Longreach.

Yes, I had been told to expect 'change', but totally unprepared for the wonderful gift and enrichment our grandkids have bestowed on Helen and I. We were in Longreach, and over 2,000 klms from Tiah's arrival in 2005, but they could hear us cheering in Sydney.

Then, we were nearly 20,000 klms away when Angus graced our world at York, U.K., shortly after. **Wow**! Grandma and Pa soon became our new family names.

We have been blessed with seven fabulous grandkids—all individuals, all different and all unique.

Ash and Marney with Tiah and Boston have been in Cairns and Sydney. Melinda and Lyth, Angus and Isla have lived in and around Yorkshire at Newton On Derwent, Pocklington, Spittall and now Barmby Moor (and you can throw in their farm in the rolling hills near Whitby). Wazz and Lou with Evelyn, Bridget and Andrea have been all over Oz from Wagga Wagga to Learmonth, up the top end of Western Australia and Amberley, Queensland to Williamtown. They are now back at Medowie… forever, we think… in their new home.

As I pen these pages, all three families are building/renovating their dream homes.

THE BRIGHTER SIDE OF A DEATH THREAT

To me, the most amazing thing—all seven of our grandkids each have four grandparents who love 'em to bits. I had only one grandparent, so to see all of these kids with four is wonderful.

Even better—we all get on.

I am well aware the grandkids will all have their wins and losses, strengths and weaknesses, good times and tuff times, just like the rest of us. However, all seven are off to a great start. Mums and dads and grandparents who love them to bits plus an extended family of uncles, aunties and cousins living all over the globe who **all** get on. How rare is that.

Both Helen and I thrive on the constant reports on the kids many achievements in all areas.

Whatever the future holds, they have a great base to launch from.

Like any other ageing Pa, I would love to stick around and watch them all grow up and kick goals—but, whatever happens, I will be watching!

I reckon we've travelled a million miles to grandparents days, school concerts and sporting fixtures, carnivals, grand finals, holiday visits, family get-togethers and more. We've loved every minute of it. Another brilliant piece in the jigsaw of life.

Back to the MV *Longreach Explorer*. I had come a long way since MV *Merinda* in Batemans Bay, and we made a real success with our outback sunset dinner cruises.

Captain Kimbo, downstairs controlling the vessel, and I was deckie, waiter, chef, barman, entertainer and washer-upperer. I had a remote microphone and Kimbo and I bantered between each other. We had a set script of stories and jokes at the various points on the outward journey in daylight. Because I had seen so much of Oz, I used to wander around the top deck asking the passengers where they came from and chatting. That was a real hoot.

One night, a couple said they were from Batemans Bay. I said I had heard it was a beautiful place and then asked if they were from Surfside, Batehaven or Malua Bay areas.

They were taken aback and said, "Well, actually, we are from a tiny town just north called East Lyn."

I said, "That's where they make the best apple pies in Australia." (I had seen that on the roadhouse sign for years). She nearly jumped overboard with excitement. "I cook them," she screamed. She was delighted.

Another night, a couple said 'Sydney'. I asked 'north, south, east or west'. He said 'Castle Hill—northern suburbs'. (Our hometown, and many miles from the northern suburbs.) I should tell you that by this time we had purchased the Longreach Maxi Taxi, which I had driven all day because our day driver hadn't turned up, and I had taken this couple on three trips. They were staggered when they arrived at the boat and there I was again... all decked out in uniform.

I said, "Oh—I heard Castle Hill is in the beautiful Hills district. Are you near Old Northern Road or Showground Road" (where our office was). They were taken aback.

He said, "Well, just off Old Northern Road." So I replied "The Bull and Bush end or the Oakhill College end?"

That really threw him and he said, "Halfway to the Bull and Bush."

I then delivered the killer blow, "Oh—somewhere near the old Church that is now a funeral chapel?"

They could not believe it. "That's our street—Francis Street!"

They were in shock.

On my next round he asked me how I knew. So I told him that he had been in my taxi all day and it was part of my studies to get a taxi drivers licence. I'll bet he is still dining out on that story today. I never told him we were from there.

There were many such stories. Another was a couple from the 'Gold Coast'.

"North, south or central," I asked.

"Central—a little area called Clear Island Waters."

You could have knocked me over with a feather because that's where Helen and I had our lakeside townhouse. There are only two streets that enter that canal area—so I said, "Do you come in on Fairways Drive or Santa Cruz Boulevarde?"

They were amazed. "We live on Fairways Drive."

And so on it went—great nights.

THE BRIGHTER SIDE OF A DEATH THREAT

Helen and I were in the U.K. when we got word that Smoky had passed and we agreed to come home early for the funeral. Just two days before we also heard that Parry Smith—our Longreach landlord—had passed away.

I rang Parry's son, Paul—a great guy—from Melindas. Paul and I have a commom hate—gossip! Very prevalent in the bush. I said, "I have heard a bit of gossip that Smoky and Parry are outside the pearly gates. Smoky is playing his guitar and singing and Parry is taking round the hat."

Now, Parry was known to be very careful with money. We all knew it well! Paul's reply to me was, "You better get a message to Smoky to get his share fast."

We do have to laugh, even in sad times.

I remember once, Parry, in his eighties, had flown to Brisbane for some tests. I heard he had had some sort of turn in Brisbane and was flying home Sunday night. I called around and he told me he had been at the Brisbane motel very late Saturday night, when bad pains started in his chest and left arm.

At around midnight, Natalie called a cab and took him to emergency. At 4 a.m., they told him he had had a mild turn but could return to Longreach and do tests there on Monday.

He told me he had experienced a long and very painful and uncomfortable day at Brisbane Airport. They had to check out by 10 a.m. and the flight wasn't until 4.30 p.m. "Six hours in a hard plastic seat," Parry said.

Now, Parry had many millions in the bank. He owned a string of outback motels, hotels, concrete plants, medical centres, Mitre 10 stores and more, even an ambulance station, so I asked him, "Why didn't you stay in bed and get a late checkout?"

His reply was, "They wanted an extra fifty dollars."

That was Parry McScrooge.

One of the highlights of Longreach was the visits from lots of people from our 'past life'. One day, I was summoned to reception—'some old friends from Batemans Bay'. It was John Stevenson and a mate. John had called in once before with Les Grimson, the baker from Batemans Bay. We chatted for nearly an hour before I realised Johns 'mate' was Theo Cassidy—a guy I thought the world of, and hadn't recognised. I felt such a goose.

Another day, Brud and Marg Baghurst called in—they were from the original 'Baghurst Motors' at Batemans Bay and we had taken their son to the USA on one of my many adventures. They told us they were heading for Isisford, and I remembered Derek Campbell and son Glynn were arriving that night and Derek said he wanted to take Glynn to Isisford. Population 91.

I immediately saw a chance to get one back on Derek, and I told Brud and Marg to walk into the Outer Barcoo Interpretive Centre (the only air conditioned building in Isisford) at exactly 10 a.m. next day—not a second before or after.

When Derek and Glynn arrived, I told them I needed to go to Isisford next day, so Derek was really happy. We set off at 7.30 a.m. It is only a 200 klm trip. As we drove into Isisford, there was a dilapidated old garage sign from years ago—now closed. I remarked, "Reminds me of Baghurst Motors" and we proceeded to talk about them.

We arrived at the OBI Centre at 9.45 a.m. and went into the air con and smoko. At exactly 10 a.m., I 'shook' and Derek said, "Are you okay?"

I replied, "I felt the Baghursts had just walked over my dead body." Derek had not seen them for 20 years. He then looked up and Brud and Marg Baghurst were walking towards us waving. Derek freaked!

The rest of the outback was full of 'treasures'. Towns like nearby Barcaldine and Winton were great places. Barcy, with its Tree of Knowledge, goat races, Australian Workers Heritage Centre, Rob and Deb's Ironbark Inn and Steakhouse were all gems. But Winton takes the cake. I reckon it may well outgrow Longreach in tourism in the years ahead.

Longreach is the regional airport and Government capital—health, education, law etc. and has the Australian Stockmans Hall of Fame, the QF Museum and the Thomson River—all sensational. But Winton has incredible potential. The Australian Age of Dinosaurs, Stage Four, will make it one of the world's biggest and best natural history museums. David Elliott and his team have done an unbelievable job.

They are backed up with things like Lark Quarry—the world's only recognised dinosaur stampede site, the brilliant Waltzing Matilda Centre—the only museum in the world dedicated to a song, the famous North Gregory Hotel where Banjo's first ever public performance of the song was

THE BRIGHTER SIDE OF A DEATH THREAT

staged, and the brilliant Rangelands and Bladensburg National Park.

Some of the nations best outback mesas have made Winton a real force in the international film making world. Throw in the Musical Fence, the Truck Museum and Willy Maher and they have a great story to tell... not to mention former American President, Lyndon B. Johnson, crashed his bomber on Winton's Carisbrooke Station... and survived. Great town.

Winton recently lost a fantastic Mayor, Butch Lenton, an incredible man.

So many characters, so many great experiences, but driving taxis and coaches, nightly dinner cruises and two motels to run were taking their toll on this ageing couple. We had bought Jeffo and Heather's share back in 2005, plus we had put together two great years, business wise. It was time to sell. We were not doing a good job.

In 2007, we put the Albert Park Motor Inn on the market first—a magnificent award winning resort-style motel. It sold to the first people to look—Mark and Jenny Gladman from Victoria. We are still good mates today and they have been on one of our European river cruises with us.

At the end of that year, we put the Longreach Motor Inn on the market. Again, the first in the door, Damien and Judy Kennedy and Judy's brother David Neal and his wife Tanya, bought it. They have been there over eleven years and we are very good mates. During the period before settlement, they came out on the 'Explorer' dinner cruise—realised the money it was making and that their kitchen could supply the food—so they bought the boat and coach. Brilliant.

Just prior to settlement, a local came in and made us a great offer on the taxi—so we took it. Our goal had been realised.

My memory of driving out of Longreach, in February 2008, was of very mixed emotions. That morning, we drove into both the Qantas Museum and the Stockmans Hall of Fame and paid each of them $9,100. That was our 910 January rail passengers @ $10 each from our special QR summer package promotion. Three years before, the figures were 226 passengers and we were over the moon at that. It was a huge increase on 2006 the year before, so 910 was unimaginable.

And we were leaving behind some fabulous friends and some great staff. Jodie Helder, receptionist at the Albert Park; Nicole Avery and Robyn Hughes, reception at the Longreach Motor Inn; Captain Kim Nichols on the boat; Espen in the Longreach Motor Inn kitchen had all saved our bacon on many occasions, and we really missed the Millars, the Palmers, the Emslies, Doug and Vickie, our beloved Kim Anderson—the gal who ruled Longreach—plus our close working mates, Al Smith, Lloyd Mills, Tony Martin, Danny Sheehan and Peter Homan. We had really met a top bunch in the bush. There were many others we really liked.

But the good news was we were going to stay in touch. During my years on the board of the Outback Queensland Tourism Association I came up with an idea—again. It was sort of a cross between a Tagalong four-wheel-drive tour and a Variety Club bash.

We gave it a name. 'Outback Trailblazer', and the idea was to get 30-50 cars, 60-100 people, and stage crazy events in small outback towns and regional centres.

When word got out Helen and I were leaving, I was approached by one of the all time great bush characters, Rob Chandler, Mayor of Barcaldine and Chairman of RAPAD, the seven outback councils. Rob said Barcaldine council would hire me to develop and stage a series of five outback trailblazers. Done deal. I will be at Barcy for the March 2008 council meeting and we would sign a contract.

That was the start of a sensational ten year's adventure covered in the next chapter.

When we left Longreach, we had a few dollars, so I dropped a hint to Helen that she might buy me something that goes from 0 to 140 in three seconds.

She bought me a set of scales!

CHAPTER 20

THE OUTBACK TRAILBLAZER AND ANGEL FLIGHT

The greatest danger for most of us is not setting the bar too high and falling short—but setting the bar too low and achieving our mark.

…Michelangelo

When Mayor Rob phoned and asked me to present the Outback Trailblazer concept to Barcy Council, there were some sceptical that it was a bit too ambitious. To their credit, they adopted and backed the project, and we chose to get behind a relatively new nationwide organisation, 'Angel Flight', founded by Brisbane promotions guru, Bill Bristow.

At the time there were over 1,000 aircraft owners and pilots who gave their aircraft and pilot services for nothing other than fuel to daily fly non-emergency rural and remote patients from the bush to their city treatments and back at no cost whatsoever. Angel Flight also had some 1500 'earth Angels' who gave their cars, four-wheel-drives and their driving services, for absolutely nothing, to ferry the patients from airports to hospitals etc., and they receive no Government funding.

LANCE SMITH

Our ambition was to have a tag-along type convoy of four-wheel-drives, cars and trucks with corporate and private teams staging fun special events in small and regional outback towns, raising funds for, and the profile of, Angel Flight, and also developing a wealth of positive media coverage of the bush and their characters, while spending valuable dollars in tiny communities. A big challenge, but as Rob says, "You can't win a race if you don't run."

The 'Outback Angels', as the team members were called, sure turned into great ambassadors for the bush and Angel Flight. They had an amazing and fun experience during the five events over nine years… and trebled in size!

Our first great achievement was to convince Country Music all Australian girl, Tania Kernaghan, to be our patron. They love her in the bush and so do we. She agreed.

Our next was to get our Marney on board as our creative graphic artist / brochure and manuals designer and the renowned Qld Coast photographer, Tom Anthony to record the antics.

We did an initial run around the nearby bush towns to look at possible special events and crazy activities. Muttaburra, Yaraka, Ilfracombe and Barcy were the keenest. Jericho, Jundah and Alpha were open to suggestions. Longreach expected it. Windorah 'needed it' and Aramac and Stonehenge couldn't care less. John Dollinger and his Aramac committee told me they had got Warwick Capper to a B & S ball in the '80's and we wouldn't top that.

In late 2008, we mapped out a 'plan', handed it to Marney to create a brilliant brochure and headed out to the market in early 2009.

We needed sponsors. Woollam Constructions, who had built the Australian Stockmans Hall of Fame, were first in, closely followed by local engineers, George Bourne and Associates. These two ensured we would press the go button.

We were excited. Qantaslink, Ballandean Estate Wines and the RACQ were next and then TPD Media, Dean Miller and the gorgeous Karen Hanna, and TEQ came on board. We were set—all underwritten by Barcy Council.

And so, on October 18th 2009, 27 vehicles and 74 team members had a fantastic welcome dinner/launch at the Australian Workers Heritage Centre in Barcaldine, hosted by Cricketer Len Pascoe… before heading to breakfast

THE BRIGHTER SIDE OF A DEATH THREAT

next day at Ilfracombe and into 'the unknown'.

Marney had done a brilliant job with the official manuals and John and Bev Ursem at Action Graphics had produced fabulous team uniforms, classy dress shirts, travel bags and themed costumes. We looked a pro show. The vehicles looked great.

You never forget the first of anything. Our first motel in Batemans Bay, our first big theatre, *Fiddler*, our first Children's Hospital Express, our first Bear Cottage Celebrity Safari were all never to be forgotten memories, and the first Trailblazer was right up there.

Driving in to Yaraka—population 19, to re-enact Banjo Patterson's famous 'Bush Christening', had a story behind it.

In 2008, Susan Glasson was President of the Yaraka State School P & C. She introduced me to the school principal, Tammy McClymont, who said, "Lance, I would like you to meet our student, Bella!"

Yep—that's right! The school had just one student, and they closed it down before we arrived. So we had to borrow twin ten-year-old sisters out of Blackall/Tambo Shire from the School of The Air to do the poem. There was not a dry eye in the town. Ten years later, and these two girls are now world class models strutting the catwalks in Paris and New York! Oh, from such humble beginnings.

We were all standing on top of Sandy Kidd's spectacular red-sand hills at Windorah, overlooking the channel country, sipping champagne and watching a glorious sunset when Tommy Hoad—a quiet (when sober) member of the Jundah team—sidled up to me to whisper, "It's my birthday today." So, out there in the middle of nowhere, we had a rousing 'Happy Birthday' rendition soaring aloft over the channel country, led by Channel 7's Dean Miller.

That night, we had an American singer-songwriter performing at the Western Star bush pub. All went well until the girls' nickers started flying. From there on—pear shaped.

The hard working team who had spent the afternoon erecting forty tents on solid rock were furious. Eighteen were not used. The 'guests' slept on the 'green beds'—the nature strip on the main road outside the pub.

Next morning, Tommy Hoad sidled up to me again—very apologetically. He mixed up the date. Today was his actual birthday, not yesterday. So—at the Jundah breakfast—another rendition of 'Happy Birthday' rang out.

LANCE SMITH

When he pulled the same story next night, in Longreach, I finally woke up. I was the idiot being duped. Tommy's birthday is January 10th—same as mine. But we celebrated his birthday every day for years on the Trailblazer. Legendary stuff, especially in Tambo.

I remember the official Angel Flight dinner at the Qantas Founders Museum. Angel Flight pilots had flown in from as far away as Brisbane and Cairns. The lovely Tania K. was at her first official Patrons function. We had V.I.P's from all over—and someone had stolen my only new XXXX dress shirt. The always creative Glenn T. cut right up the back of a 'large' shirt to the collar. Did up the front buttons and told me not to turn when making my speech. It worked. This dinner followed 'the great riverboat race' on the Thomson River. The three cruising vessels: The *Thomson Belle* paddle steamer, the *Yellow Belly* and the *Longreach Explorer* catamaran, with over 130 passengers on board with flour bombs, huge water pistols, tomatoes et al, crossed the line at four knots per hour in a photo finish—but the photographer, Mayor John Palmer, and his camera fell out of the dingy as the boats crossed the line. No official result was ever recorded. But John P. was bitten by a huge red-claw yabbie—justice. We vowed to come back again.

No one will ever forget our night in Muttaburra—population 98. First up, we made a last minute change to take the dinner venue from alongside the huge 'Muttaburrasaurus Langdoni' dinosaur sculpture into the enclosed yard at the rear of the Town Hall. The reason—it was so dry the kangaroos were in town in their hundreds and the roo poo and pee stink were too much in the open.

After a sensational dinner, prepared by Fiona and the locals, we auctioned 'Borat' to whoever wanted this 'olympic champion' swimmer on their team at tomorrow's aquatic festival. 'Borat' turned out to be Alan Smith—Smithy—in a mankini with sheep's wool hanging out in various places. It was hideous! People are still being counselled years later, and all photos have been destroyed, I hope. But, Woollams paid a few thousand for Borats 'help' and Muttaburra finally had their new cardiac unit funds—winners all round. Thanks Woollams. But the best was yet to come. Night Golf!!

Yep, little green glowing balls. What a fantastic time was had by all. A 'ute' motorised bar going around the pitch black course. Young Macca Chandler out driving two golf pros. Ben Southall (Best Job In The World)

THE BRIGHTER SIDE OF A DEATH THREAT

air swings. Top night. While all that was going on, JPY was singing his heart out in the bush pub bar, much to the delight of the Muttaburra locals in the geographical centre of Queensland.

Next day, the mud skippers aquatic festival, the dress up races and obstacle courses are still being talked about. Brilliant. As was the 2 a.m. skinny dipping/fence climbing. We know who you are!

How could we top that? But we did. Next day driving through the famous Bowen Downs, where the driveway from the front gate was 103 klms to the house. We ended up at Lake Dunn—wow. First up, our Trailblazer international cricket match, complete with two streakers, then the dinner and sports night at the 'Desert Recreation Club' on the banks of the lake. Then the canoe and kyack racing. What a night!

A local ringer had fallen from his horse a week or so earlier. A few broken bones and other injuries. Couldn't work. Kids to feed and many bills. Rob Chandler raffled a bottle of port and the young fella had a few thousand dollars he wasn't expecting. Can we top that. You betcha.

Next night's dinner and cliff face concert at the Alpha jump up is still being talked about today—ten years on. Sensational.

When 'Hark The Herald Angels' was sung by Tania K. from half way up the cliff face and suddenly the whole Alpha school, dressed as Angels, appeared on the cliff top, the crowd stopped breathing. G.T. had 'reincarnated' our big hit from the Carols in the Grand Arch at Jenolan Caves. Stunning.

By this time, we had been joined by Tony Edwards from Qantaslink, a delegation from Tourism Queensland under Leanne Coddington, and a host of more media. We were now around 90, and along with all the locals who had been at the concert, we lobbed at the golf club around 10 p.m.

The Directors had made an executive decision earlier because they thought we would be too tired and not come back, so they sent all the staff home except one. Mayhem! Over two hundred thirsty souls, a big band, and a crew of ten from the concert who had not eaten. Thank goodness for Angelo and Mary and Ballandean Estate Wines.

Three things I remember about this:
- The Directors had never worked so hard behind the bar and the club took record takings in three hours as the band pumped.

- Somehow, miraculously, the one staff member, also the local newsagent, cooked GT and the crew a magnificent dinner, and
- We met 'Darryl' for the first time. I heard a commotion and saw that Rob Chandler had taken off his coat and was being held back from this loudmouth with funny teeth who was giving him heaps. None of us knew that Channel 7 cameraman, 'Punk', had an alter ego—named 'Darryl'. He was hilarious—and a pain! Great night.

You cannot believe this—but we had saved the best till last: Our Governors V.I.P. Garden Party at the Oasis gardens of Kyneton Station. Nine planes flew in to the station homestead. The Gold Coast Somerset College Choir sang on the massive verandah. Glenn had done an amazing job with decorating, lighting the trees, dam and gardens. And our guest of honour arrived—in a real Cobb & Co coach. It was former Longreach Mayor, Joan Moloney. A class act.

I had to keep pinching myself to make sure I wasn't dreaming. Every single person was in a dinner suit—there in the middle of outback Queensland—it was so impressive.

On closer inspection you saw they were dinner suit T-shirts supplied by Action Graphics. Stunning. And we finished a very late night at the famous Iron Bark open air steak house where Mrs. Robert's Somerset kids sang 'Jersey Boys', and we saw the 'Abba' girls (TK and Monique) for the first of many times.

What a week it was. We had only raised just over $50,000 for Angel Flight, plus more for local issues, but had raised the Angel Flight profile with so many national TV, radio, newspaper and magazine positive stories. Over the five Trailblazers, we raised half a million dollars for Angel Flight and were very proud of all the results. Bill Bristow said the Angel Flight phones rang hot with offers of more aircraft and earth angels. We all knew we were on a winner… and I had signed up to do five!

I well remember walking into the Council chambers to deliver my first report. I was expecting rose petals, champagne and a standing ovation. I looked at the stony faces; Rob looking at the floor. What has gone wrong. Jenni Gray opened the discussion. "We took all the risk. We did all the work. So why did Longreach get all the f'ing publicity!"

Ah, parochialism is alive and well!

THE BRIGHTER SIDE OF A DEATH THREAT

Believe it or not, Jenni and I get on very well. I am one of her greatest fans. But—she calls a spade a... shovel!

But I did 'rue' the fact that Jenni did not ring me with congratulations when a superb Barcaldine Regional Trailblazer story and pictures were three pages of the next issue of the R.M. Williams' *Outback* magazine.

We all got over it and went immediately into planning mode for the 2010 Trailblazer. Council said it had to be bigger and better.

Stonestreet Coaches and Travel then came on board in a big way. Our twenty-seven vehicles became forty-four thanks mainly to Tony Edwards and the Marios in their Alpha Romeos, and this time 102 of us met at a fabulous QR dinner and show hosted by the CEO of QR, Paul Scarrah (current CEO of Virgin Airlines), under the Tree Of Knowledge at Barcy—our heartland. And off we headed for two of the biggest events ever staged in the outback. After a fishing comp and cricket at Isisford, we headed west to the 'Outback Oktoberfest' at Jundah. What a night.

When we first broached the idea to Monique that we use her bush pub as the hub of the Oktoberfest, she jumped at it. However, we knew we needed the town on side. The public meeting saw forty-three of the sixty-eight residents turn up. The towns sixteen kids and baby sitters made up the missing twenty-five. They went for it.

About two months out, Monique rang me. She was really worried because of media coverage. She was getting calls from everywhere about people who were coming from near and far, and Monique said, "If we run out of food or grog, the nearest suppliers are well over 200 klms away."

So I promised we would pull other publicity planned with TE, who were not happy. But I did point out to Mon that those coming in utes, campervans, trucks and caravans would all have some food, and we had ordered enough German beer, sauerkraut and sausage to feed and water a whole country!

The sixteen kids at Jundah School were all learning the two famous German Christmas carols, 'Stiller Nact' (Silent Night) and 'O Tannanbaum' ('Oh Christmas Tree') in German. Plus 'Bridgette' at the Brisbane German Club had found us a brilliant 'Oom Pa Pa Band'—'Rudi (Goldberg) and the Continentals'. They were the real McCoy!

John U. and the Action Graphics team had made 250 men's and women's 'lederhosen' costumes. We had purchased two $700 Cuckoo Clocks from the Mt. Tamborine German Cuckoo Clock Shop as fancy-dress prizes for locals. Jundah were organising sheep races and a Calcutta, plus an extra two hundred tents. Council were making three huge 'Wilcommen Au Jundah' green signs to go over the existing big road signs.

Air Lufthansa and the German Tourism team had sent heaps of decorations and lights. Qantaslink were flying in the band. All their gear—including huge German hats for a dance competition and the full set of musical bells. Monique had also secured the service of four German backpackers to come out and work. We were organised.

About three weeks out, on a Friday, I had a call from a very unhappy TE. publicity exec. "You asked us not to advertise your Oktoberfest. We have today received blunt messages from our Frankfurt, Berlin, Munich and London offices asking for more details on the major media story that had erupted in Europe. She told me—in no uncertain terms—I was to have 'images of Jundah being turned into a German Village' to her by lunchtime Monday, and they had to be 'very obviously Australia.'"

I was at a loss. Helen and I were going away for three days and there is no mobile reception in Jundah—hence rare mobile phones—therefore cameras.

I rang Monique at the pub to plead my case. Monique did something unusual. She burst into tears. "It's all my fault."

What had happened was we had 'fluked' our choice of dates. It was exactly 200 years to the day of King Ludwigs wedding, the horse races and the very first Oktoberfest in Germany.

Monique and the town decided to go 'all out' and had contacted a Bavarian manufacturer of authentic 'dirndl' and 'Lederhosen' and ordered forty costumes to be made. When she told them it was the 200-year anniversary and that a Queensland tiny outback town, Jundah, was putting on a special tribute etc., an enterprising PR team member from the manufacturers released the story in Europe—and it went viral.

What happened next was typical of my life. Monique was still a little teary as a couple walked into the pub for a cool drink on a hot day. They asked Monique what was wrong and she told them. They were professional photographers recording the outback—problem solved.

Knowing nothing of this, I was a tad surprised when I received an

THE BRIGHTER SIDE OF A DEATH THREAT

email from TEQ on Monday—"Congratulations, perfect. You are a true professional!"

Gad. What had I done?

Wednesday's half page photo in the Courier Mail—which then went National and International—showed the huge road signs being put up by some gorgeous girls in their German costumes with local characters looking on. Sensational.

What a night! What a turnout! What a huge win for the Trailblazer team. Around 1 a.m., I witnessed the State Member, Vaughan Johnson, and Longreach Motelier, Damien Kennedy, having a full-blown discussion in German and, somehow, they understood each other.

Ray Kernaghan stole my best long white socks. JPY had never before sung in German and a brawl broke out behind the pub—near where Woollams truck was bogged in a drain.

A perfect night in the outback, and Tommy's birthday—zum gerbastag lieber Tommy!

The next night in Longreach was by far the largest event and biggest risk we ever undertook on the Trailblazer series. I had gone to the Stockmans Hall of Fame the previous year to discuss possibilities. I was advised their biggest frustration was that the local communities within a 300 klm radius had no 'ownership' of the Hall—even those in Longreach.

They loved our idea of a huge multi-community Christmas concert involving fourteen towns and twenty one schools with a massive children's choir to sing Christmas carols and welcome 'Santa'—who would arrive on a dray being hauled by a full bullock team. The Jundah school would sing two carols in German. Wow!

We had a great promotional media story—the Kernaghan family—Lee, Tania and mum and dad were photographed boarding the QR Spirit of The Outback in Brisbane, with 'pop' Kernaghan's giant portrait. It was to be brought to Longreach and presented to the Hall of Fame as the family were singing at the concert. Made national TV and radio coverage. We sold well over three thousand tickets. But—it had presented many challenges. Ballard's Transport brought over two tonnes of lights and audio gear from Brisbane—at no charge. Local hire company Manager, Ian Harris, donated heaps of security fencing, scaffolding and gear. It was a massive team effort.

LANCE SMITH

All twenty-one schools came bringing over two-hundred-and-eighty children to town by bus, at no charge, a night early for a rehearsal, and the Longreach Agricultural College was feeding them and housing all who had not been billeted in town.

It was a stunning concert, which opened with local indigenous Elder Ron Beazley playing an eerie didgeridoo from way up on top of the Hall of Fame sails as the moon rose. Goose bumps again.

The choir was just great—unbelievable harmonies. A kid—I think named Hitson, from the School of the Air—sang 'True Blue' with a guitar, surrounded by his schoolmate, draped in Aussie flags. He stole the show. He was later flown to Sydney to perform it at an International Rotary conference.

A young girl, Holly, from Ilfracombe, brought the house down with a bush poem about a drunken grandma trying to kill a red-belly-black snake and protect the family. A teacher from Winton Catholic School brought gasps of delight when she sang 'Oh Holy Night', and so it went. The bands were fabulous, as were Tania and Ray Kernaghan.

The huge surprise was when compere Channel 7's Dean Miller introduced 'A smelly fisherman from N.S.W.' with a song about air pollution. The crowd screamed when JPY stepped out and sang 'Love Is In The Air'. Surprise!

Mayor John Palmer's speech was one of the most heartfelt we had ever heard.

It could have ended in disaster. Both Santa and I were nearly badly injured when the bullock team took off suddenly in fright. The less said the better.

But the most amazing thing happened after Santa did his thing. He was backstage hiding behind a temporary wall, out of sight. I began removing the sweaty gear when Glenn screamed at me 'stop' and pointed upwards. I looked up, straight into the five-hundred-and-fifty wide eyes of the children's choir upstairs. You see, in the bush there are no Department stores; no Christmas Santas. Most of these kids were seeing Santa for the very first time in their lives. I nearly blew it.

That 2010 Trailblazer had a fabulous finish. Jericho, a town of around one hundred, had a drive in theatre with space for around forty cars plus a grandstand. I drove to Canberra and the Film and Sound Archives to beg to

THE BRIGHTER SIDE OF A DEATH THREAT

be able to show the 1955 Aussie film classic, *Jedda,* at the Jericho drive-in, along with some silent old Qantas footage we were able to source.

The archivists told us that the *Jedda* star—Rosalie Kunoth-Monks, who played Jedda, was alive and well in the Northern Territory. Imagine how delighted we were when Rosalie and hubby Bill agreed to be there on the night... as a ***huge*** surprise.

When the film ended and the tooting and applause died down, Dean Miller announced our special guest and Rosalie took centre stage. Jericho will never forget it. Wonderful.

Alan Smith wrecked his back on a stock whip/rope dance with Tania Kernaghan.

On the final day we had the Teddy Bears Picnic at Tambo. What a top day. Blackall had the honour of hosting our final night—a '60's dinner and show in the cultural centre.

I have worked with lots of committees and local action groups, but the two girls from Blackall Tambo Shire were standouts. The decorations, the stage, the lights were stunning and the Gold Coast '60's band, headed up by Brenda Lee Heathcote and Scott Lloyd Shelley, were simply the best—not to mention an appearance by 'Stephie Graff' and the return of the ABBA girls, and everyone was dressed up. What a finish, and we sent over $100,000 to Angel Flight, with another truckload of positive media stories, including two half-hour specials shown by Channel 7 in every state—some twice.

This time Council were over the moon—and worried it could get too big. A pleasant challenge.

So—the decision was made to stage further Trailblazers every eighteen months to give us the time to organise all the exciting events. Anzac Week 2012 was chosen, and Rob C. called it the '12 River Run', with events to be organised with outback rivers front and centre. We were getting bolder and everyone wanted in... including new sponsors, Wagners from Toowoomba's proposed Wellcamp Airport, who have supported us ever since. Great people.

We even got our first flying team entered in the 2012 event—wow.

The big day arrived—Saturday 21st April. QR had put on a fantastic 'Jazz Train to the Outback' with members of the famous Galapagos Duck band members on board. Barcaldine was a hive of activity—all day arts and craft, buskers, bands, Ballandean wine tastings, school student performances, stalls, games and competitions and a great pub crawl. Then the special briefing in the old silent movie theatre and the launch of Tania K's new song, 'Believe In Angels'.

That night's 'Jazz On The Alice' dinner and jazz under the stars was amazing. All those on the QR jazz train, all sixty-one Trailblazer vehicles and one-hundred-and-forty-seven outback angels on the Trailblazer joined many locals on the banks of the Alice River and went wild. What a great start. The QR catering team were amazing.

Next morning's, Barcoo Gully Cup, on the Barcoo River at Blackall, was won by the Stonestreets team. Then we headed south-west for lunch and cattle branding on the seventy-thousand-acre Leopard Park Station and a fishing competition on the Bulloo River. Then the Adavale Pub and sports carnival dinner and show at the rodeo yards. Adavale—population seventeen. Locals, 'Mookaye' and his brother 'Meatant', did a great job.

Adavale loved us, money and rain. It doesn't get any better in the bush, although the poor buggers in Julia Creek, Winton and Cloncurry would challenge that after the recent devastating floods and stock losses.

It's sounding like a broken record, but our two nights in Charleville were sensational. An early dinner at the Cosmos Centre with the wonderful SOTO (Stay On Track Outback) police girls, and then the big one: 'Woollams Anzac Tribute Concert' at the RSL.

President Greg Field said a full house was one-hundred-and-eighty, but we could squeeze in fifty more if we had to. Four-hundred-and-four people crammed in and witnessed a brilliant show nationally: Normie Rowe, Tania and Ray Kernaghan, JPY, 'The Andrew Sisters', 'Dame Vera Lynne ', Ned and the Kellys, Grant and Lee Millar. ABC Radio recorded, and then broadcast the show. Superb promotion. What a line up. The reason we had to squeeze so many in is because QR had promoted a 'Troop Train to Charleville' to join the Trailblazer. We were getting bigger and braver.

Recently, Mayor Ann Liston said Charleville would really welcome us back anytime. I did receive a 'thank you' from RSL President Greg Field full of great praise, but ending with, "But—you bastards—what will we do next year!"

Next day's dawn service and march salute were taken by Trailblazer Brigadier Chris Hamilton and Vietnam veteran Normie Rowe, who made a special speech supporting the Aussie flag—and the colours of the cenotaph predawn were stunning. More goose bumps and more rain.

THE BRIGHTER SIDE OF A DEATH THREAT

Anzac Day afternoon is what the Trailblazer is all about. Two things happened that show the calibre of generous people. First up, 'The Fox Trap' at Cooladie—population nine.

Roxanne and her team at the Fox Trap roadhouse put on a typical beaut smoko. During our half hour stay, they presented us with $3,000 for Angel Flight—twelve months proceeds—100% of their courtesy bus weekly to Charleville, plus Mrs. Flemming donated a magnificent patchwork quilt. That is huge for people who need so much for themselves.

The second—equally humbling: The welcome rain caused us to cancel two activities because we could not get through due to gushing crossings, including night golf at Quilpie. So quick thinking locals transferred our dinner to under shelter at the Quilpie Race Track and set up a stage and a great mini golf course. The local seventeen students performed for us—their very first public performance.

Two things happened:
- The huge applause frightened some of the kids, who cried, and
- Because we knew they needed $2,000 to go on a trip to Canberra, Mayor Rob took the hat around during their encore and then turned it upside down on the stage. $3,800 Then everyone cried, including the teachers, the kids, the trailblazers and either Judy McDonald or Marney took a stunning photo of our tent city and the black/purple storm clouds—eerie!

The trailblazers could not believe breakfast next day. Toompine pub—population one human, two alpacas, two donkeys, seven ducks, nine chooks, two poddy calves, fifty nine pet goats and a seventeen year old miniature pony. The pub without a town is how they describe it, and Jonesy is the hostess with the mostess—a legend out here and her party trick is animal mating calls!

The Eulo fair was ten out of ten. As we drove into town from our mud baths and port, from the Palm Grove date farm across the Paroo River, there was an old-time London bobby waving as we drove into town and the fair. Trouble was it was the actual town policeman dressed up, and seat belts were required. Oops!

What a fabulous fair. The ghost stories were awesome, topped off by a speech from the Eulo queen. Again, tears all round. The outback sure has some great yarns. Like the next town, Cunnamulla, and the robbers tree, just out of town.

Joseph Wells was the last man hanged at Boggo Road Gaol. He had robbed a bank in Cunnamulla, ridden out of town, climbed off his horse and whipped the horse to keep going, then climbed a huge dense tree. As the police posse rode out of town, they saw Well's faithful dog sitting at the base of the tree looking up for his master—bingo!

There are great photos of the 'Village People', led by JPY performing Y.M.C.A. at the Kernaghan campfire sing along. We were the first-ever guests in Judy Roberts' beaut new Warrego River Tourist Park, and enjoyed great support from Mayor Jo Taylor.

And then it was on—the Culgoa flood plains, 235.5 klms of mud and challenges, crossing twice in and out of New South Wales, ending up at Dirrinbandi. Here we were to stage the biggest street parade ever seen in town, then the 'Dirrinbandi Dash'—a tribute foot race to local aboriginal, Tom Dancy, who won the Stawell Gift in 1910 and did not stay to get his winning one-thousand-pounds and green jacket. A renowned stockman and boundary rider, he was buried in 1957 in an unmarked grave in Dirra.

We capped that night at the famous Nindigully pub. One giant hamburger fed fifteen hungry people. It was to be Ned and The Kellys final professional performance—but they have had more comebacks than John Farnham and Dame Nellie Melba combined. Mayor Rob—in a green dress— and the square dancers were a big hit dancing in the park.

The most incredible thing at Nindigully Pub was the sight of Tony Edwards, Rob Chandler and the Marios selling their Subaru Brumby cars to locals in the bar. They sold seven and raised over $25,000. Great stuff.

More rain overnight and everyone soaked. Our final day/night in St. George became another Trailblazer legend. We kicked off at the Unique Egg (a must if you are ever in St. George) to see what an artist can do carving emu eggs. Amazing. Then we had the fun dragon-boat races on the Balonne River and prepared for 'Balissimo on the Balonne' Italian night at David Blackett's Riversands Winery. Wow! Wow. We squeezed over two hundred people out of the rain in a giant cool room, all dressed up. Tania K. had convinced Reno and Jade Morea to make the journey from Tassie. How good was that band... dancing on tables and singing 'Oh Dana'. What an amazing night, and everyone in Italian costumes!

THE BRIGHTER SIDE OF A DEATH THREAT

Just when we were on a real high—three incredibly successful Trailblazers, lots of money for Angel Flight and a wealth of national and international publicity for Queensland's outback and all those towns who had a ball—our world fell apart. Young Andrea, our wonderful backbone and Barcy council event guru, our biggest supporter, was diagnosed with Cancer and went very quickly, leaving behind a great hubby, Mike, and a young family. We were all heart broken, especially when Angel Flight flew her home from Brisbane to say goodbye. Barcy and the Lingard family lost a wonderful asset.

C'est La Vie—we all went to work on the 2013 Trailblazer 'Andrea's Dreams', and we sure turned her dream into a beautiful reality. The Trailblazers were getting bigger, brighter and better as we lifted the bar.

Mt. Tabor Station is a massive 190,000 acre high-country cattle station run by Bidjara Elder, Keelen Mailman, and her mob, and run well. The Lost City is the remnants of the majestic sandstone plateau worn away by thousands of years of rain and wind and is an area of awesome natural sculptures.

Keelen welcomed us with a traditional smoke ceremony and in Bidjara tongue, and the baked porcupines and witchetty grubs and kangaroo were delicious—an amazing adventure, capped off with a visit to the seldom seen Gumby Gumby, where Al Smith paid a moving tribute to the elders burial grounds and the legend of the tiny Junjudy people. That night was our 'grand final' screening in Possum Park Injune. Ashley and Tryg were out until midnight recovering broken down Alpha Romeo teams.

Another incredible experience: As the vehicles departed Lake Maraboon, they were each given a CD of Richard Fidler's ABC Conversations with Dr. Greg De Moore, author of *Tom Wills, Australia's First Wildman Of Sport*.

Tom Wills was born in New South Wales in 1835, shipped back to England for his education, and came home to Melbourne. He is still arguably Australia's finest cricketer, well before the Don. Plus he is the founder of Australian Rules Football. His family purchased 10,000 acres in the Minerva Hills, and all twenty-one of the extended family set out in January 1861, by steamer, for Moreton Bay, and then eight-months overland—droving 10,000 sheep they purchased on the Darling Downs. They arrived at their new property, 'Cullin La Ringo', in October 1861.

Tom and his young brother were immediately dispatched to collect some supplies left on route. When he returned, all nineteen of his relations had been massacred by the aboriginals. To compound the horror, local vigilantes then chased and killed some seventy aboriginals.

The book is a fascinating record of a talented, tortured soul who achieved so much for reconciliation yet committed suicide in Melbourne at the age of 43.

Ned and The Kellys wrote the 'Tom Wills –Howzat' song and the world premier was performed that morning at the massacre site. More goose bumps as Tom Wills grandson, also Tom Wills, was there! Tears all round, followed by breakfast and a book signing at Springsure Golf Club. In the shadows of the massive virgin rock, Gail Nixon and her team were sensational.

Another first—a buffalo rodeo! In Clermont. What a hoot. Then local buffalo jockeys, the Cooke sisters, who were the trainers of the 'Crocodile Dundee' buffalo. They rode the beast jumping through fire hoops—spectacular.

After the show, we all tasted barbecued buffalo at the sing along. All was okay until we were told we had just eaten the son of the lady buffalo we had all patted.

Next day, another great first. 70 klm. along the dirt track we found Mistake Creek. Population one, and that was the school teacher. There were eleven students. No one will forget the three eight-year-old stock whip officionardos—two boys and one girl.

Then the whole eleven sang 'I'd love to have a beer with Duncan' to Tania K., who promptly sang to them. A top breakfast and we were told the school had a Christmas project—a 2014 calendar with each kiddie given a page about them and December was a combined picture with the teacher.

They were hoping to sell the two-hundred ordered. Our Trailblazer members ordered and paid for three-hundred-and-twenty-six before we left. Helen and I sent them to every overseas person we knew. Exquisite Christmas presents!

Onwards across the Ballyando River to the Lake Degulla Station water ski club. Joanne Salmond and her team from the I.C.P.A. (Isolated Children's Parent Association) had prepared a fantastic luncheon spread. When we drove out, the raffle had raised enough funds to build their long dreamed of club extensions—the full amount.

THE BRIGHTER SIDE OF A DEATH THREAT

It is worth telling here that on the many outback route surveys and travel runs, every time Brandy and I were visiting remote stations—like Keelen Mailman on Mt. Tabor or Joanne Salmond here at Lake Degulla—we always went to a bakery around 6 a.m. and bought hot hi-top loaves.

These people only ever had fresh bread on their monthly trips 'to town' for supplies, so we were always very welcome. During the nine years, John Brand and I delivered over three hundred fresh loaves and, in return, ate—it seemed like—three-and-a-half tons of scones, freshly baked cakes and jam tarts!

It was here that Monique 'got us into strife' again. She reported to the RACQ service teams (they sent two patrol wagons on every Trailblazer), that she could hear a hissing coming from under her car bonnet.

The RACQ patrolman lifted the bonnet—screamed—and jumped, slicing his head open on the bonnet edge. Monique had run over and killed a huge king-brown snake, nearly three metres in length. She then coiled it on top of her air filter and reported the 'hissing' under the bonnet. Ouch! She thought it was funny!

We rarely repeated an event, but the 2013 Alpha Cliff Face Concert was an exception. The crowd of nearly four hundred were stunned when violin Maestro, Martin Lass, appeared next to a previously unseen grand piano on a rock halfway up the cliff face, and Martin and his concert pianist wife, Inge, put on a never-to-be-forgotten fabulous show. As it was a Christmas concert, Santa appeared.

Tania K. sang 'Believe In Angels', again, halfway up the cliff top, she got to a point where her arms and eyes pointed to the cliff top. The spotlights came on—nothing. The bus driver, with all the kids in their Angel costumes, was lost on the bush tracks—and didn't make it in time!

Thankfully, they were in place for the big finale—'Hark The Herald Angels Sing'.

But, as usual, only Glenn and his team could see the stuff ups. The crowd were blissfully unaware and had an amazing experience—still being talked about today, six years on.

Another time, we did something very unusual. We had been in rugged country for a few hours before we arrived at Arcacia Downs—a very beautiful, famous property. The magnificent homestead had been used by Qantas for board meetings in the early days. Now owned by David and Sarah Jane Fysh, I wanted everyone to experience the 'School of The Air' from the station, and they had a special nanny's flat and classroom adjacent to the homestead which was adjacent to the airstrip.

Everyone got to see the three kids doing an actual 'on air' lesson—which would make tomorrow's visit to the School of The Air in Longreach much easier to understand.

Smoko that afternoon was again the Morella CWA ladies, this time on Dariveen Station—another twenty klms driveway from the front gate to the homestead. What Tony and Jan Heatherington have achieved with their three-acre oasis, pools, lawns, gardens, shrubs, dams and trees is amazing and a credit to them in such a dry, arid landscape. The roos love them!

That night's campfire dinner at Smithy's, on the banks of the Thomson, with the Millars and Tania K. will be long remembered, when they closed the show with 'Mull O' Kintyre'. More tears.

The breakfast at the School of The Air—their seeing young Declan and Co. from that end was great—and later the Kangaroo Court at the Barcaldine Court house was a hoot. The police arrested me (on Glenn's instruction) and Helen was the main prosecution witness—dressed up as me. You had to see it. Not pretty.

So—after four world class Trailblazers, the last had to be a beauty. First up, it became too big for Barcy Council and was taken over by RAPAD—a combination of the seven central Queensland councils—with Chairman Rob Chandler.

I reported to C.E.O. David Arnold and his wife and Office Manager Kristine, who had both been on previous Trailblazers.

We set ourselves up for either a huge finale or an embarrassing flop. We pulled out all stops, asked huge favours and set about organising a memorable swan song.

We had already worked out that sixty-five teams in cars, trucks, buses, four-wheel-drives and planes was our limit, and we set out to make it an Anzac Week to remember.

Just over seventy teams and one-hundred-and-eighty-five outback angels, TV film crew, journalists, pilots, RACQ patrols, police from the

THE BRIGHTER SIDE OF A DEATH THREAT

SOTO unit, even a special RAPAD training team. Then it was south-west to Eromanga, the furtherest town in Australia from the sea in any direction. We drove through all the oil fields into town—years before Eromanga was gone. Businesses closed, school closes—even the pub closed and the population was down to twelve.

Then—oil. Eromanga is now a thriving community, but very remote. Shire President Stuart McKenzie and wife Robyn have really put the town on the map with their mega fauna discoveries.

The Barcoo Gully Cup at Coopers Creek was a hoot. Mayor Julie Groves, in car fifty-eight, tried very hard to win. China and JPY combined at the Windorah Pub dinner to give the locals and us a great night. Thankfully, no knickers thrown and no green beds used!

Then the stony desert track to Birdsville. We had our first major vehicle mishap about one-hundred-and fifty klms along the track—a van rollover, caught in the ruts. Another two-hundred-and-twenty klms, we turned and climbed up to Deon's Lookout. Spectacular. Even the one-hundred klm winds could not take away the magic.

The Lookout is on Mt. Leonard Station and dedicated to Deon Brook—son of our mates, David and Nell, from Birdsville. He was tragically killed in a chopper crash nearby. It is a fitting tribute to a fine young fella.

After the massive rainbow-serpent rock art and a team photo sipping champas at the soon-to-reopen Betoota Pub, we arrived at the Birdsville Bakery for a camel pie with Dusty.

Along the way, as usual, we had our very own mobile frothy-coffee van. Sergeant Bean and Constable Plod (Trevor and Belinda) were two Longreach police who volunteered every year. They served up in many remote settings—and donated the lot. Thousands of dollars every year. Thanks Merlot, Trevor and Belinda.

That night, we all ventured to the top of 'Big Red', the famous sand hills on Adria Station on the edge of the Simpson Desert, one-hundred-and-nine klms from the station homestead. We took fantastic pics of the whole team on top of 'Big Red' at sunset.

Then it was back to town and our dinner on the tarmac—at Birdsville Airport—sponsored by Wagners and the Wellcamp Airport team, car sixty-seven. Angel Flight pilots flew in from Sydney, Brisbane and the bush and we lit up their aircraft with coloured lights. A top but cold night.

Before heading to South Australia next morning, we had breakfast with State School Principal, Tiffany, and her five students, who kept us well and truly entertained.

At the border—by tradition, all motors were switched off and all vehicles had to be pushed up and over the border. Took sixty-three fit souls to get Smithy's coach over the line.

That night was another huge feather in the Trailblazer cap—our ABBA concert and 'drag' racing at the Birdsville Hotel. Wow! Malcolm Turnbull was our special guest. When he addressed the crowd—many in drag—he said it was just like a walk down Oxford Street in his electorate.

When 'Priscilla the bus' arrived with 'Sophia' and her entourage (Glenn T. at his sexiest), they thrilled the crowd and the 'drag' races would have been a brilliant success if Phil Stonestreet hadn't broken his foot. He shouldn't be wearing dresses anyway.

Then ABBA. What a show. Tania K., Brenda—Lee, Bill and Scotty were brilliant.

The media had a feast—great images. Problem was, *The Guardian* had an international front page scoop that went worldwide. The headlines screamed, "Malcolm Turnbull on stage with transvestite"—but the picture was of Malcolm on stage with me, not Glenn T. Poor Melinda had problems explaining it to her U.K. pals. The images of Sophia and Malcolm were priceless and made it into many national edition and TV news hours.

There were many, many great stories from the ABBA night. Just like Jundah's Oktoberfest and others.

Next day was truly a knockout. We started with breakfast in the haunting Dingo Caves on Roseberth Station, a two-million-acre property—think of that. Then past the rare 'waddie trees' via Sydney Kidman's 'Carcoory Homestead', we turned off at Glengyle Station and drove for thirty klms into the centre of the world's largest clay pan—'Bilpa Morea'.

Who will forget it? On arrival, Tania, Brenda-Lee, Scott and Bill were set up to host Australia's most remote 'Claypan Boogie' dance—two-hundred devotees stomping in the dirt. What was even more amazing was the real camels, arabs and tents set up for the International cricket match—with our two Captains, Mayor Rob and limping Phil (big chief broken foot).

THE BRIGHTER SIDE OF A DEATH THREAT

To hit a six, the closest boundary was thirty-two klms away. Amazing stuff and great TV.

But wait—there's more.

After driving through Cuttaburra wetlands and a huge variety of waterbirds, we arrived at Bedourie—the nerve centre of the Diamantina Shire—to meet 'Colgate' and Doug Coombs. What a pair!

Our adventure to the amazing 'Pippegetti Waterhole' and the crystal-clear waters was the start of our best ever aquatic festival. As we gobbled up the tasty kangaroo skewers, we all watched a series of races through huge blow-up plastic obstacles and floatation devices. The law enforcement handicap was the highlight! Six officers from Birdsville, Bedourie, Charleville and Longreach tackled the course—and the winner—the girls from S.O.T.O. at Charleville Police Station. Almost a Stephen Bradbury finish.

On that final Trailblazer, no one will forget the big Anzac weekend finish. We drove out of Boulia around 5 a.m. on the Friday into the most blood-red sunrise I have ever seen. Spellbinding.

After a journey through the awesome mesas and a peak at Corn Paw Lookout, the remote Middleton bush pub listening to Leicester's life story, we arrived in Winton for lunch with Robyn Stevens and her team of Winton Scouts.

Later, over three-hundred Trailblazers, the QR troop train passengers, the Defence Force delegation, plus the wonderful Mayor of Winton, Butch Lenton, and his delegation visiting from Winton New Zealand, all donned Anzac uniforms of the three services and headed over to Bladensburg National Park at sunset... over three hundred 'troops'.

I have goose bumps thinking about that blood-curdling light-horse brigade charge, and then Tania Kernaghan, Grant and Lee Millar and Twocan Twango with the light-horse tribute song—surrounded by uniforms, swords, horses and riders. Wow, wow, wow!

To cap it all off, all three-hundred of us were sitting in the exact spot where young Colin Morgan-Read lived and worked on the then Bladensburg Station before he packed up, left and was killed at Gallipoli one hundred years ago tomorrow. Colin's descendants, Jenny Milson and her family, were with us on the night. More tears.

Folks—if you have never been to Bladensburg National Park, Scrammys

Gorge, the Octopus trees in the tormented forest and the lookout—pack now and go there!

Tania's campfire singalong was sensational.

Saturday 25th April, 2015: Anzac Day—one hundred years on. The last day of the last Trailblazer. Winton will long remember the dawn services, wreath laying and parade march.

The Salute taken by Air Vice Marshall Bill Collins (Ret'd) and Wing Commander Bruce Graham. They were joined by twelve uniformed army, air force and navy personnel—what a morning. The QR troop train passengers and the Winton New Zealand delegation all joined in.

Later we crammed over three hundred into the historic North Gregory Hotel for a re-enactment of Banjo Patterson's 'Waltzing Matilda' that had it's first-ever public performance in that very room so long ago. Another goose bump moment.

And then the 'grand finale'—our final farewell dinner and Anzac concert in the Winton Shire Hall.

'The Glenn Miller Orchestra' tribute by BJ and the big band, the 'Andrew Sisters', Dame Vera Lynne and who will forget hundreds of Australian and New Zealand flags being waived in 'Auld Lang Syne' sing along.

Glenn T. masterminded a huge finish, and I was knocked out by the magnificent gift presented by Mayor Rob Chandler to Helen and I. Another great chapter of our fifty years together was over. We had set out nine years previously to showcase our wonderful outback environment and many treasures plus introduce hundreds of new outback Angels—new ambassadors to the people of the bush and our many great characters.

So many untold stories. Our next door neighbour at Clear Island Waters, Jim Knott, came in one day and asked if his two U.K. sisters could come on the week-long outback 'pre trail blazer' route survey. Those two girls had the most amazing week of their lives meeting these outback characters and seeing the wildlife and terrain. We saw them last month in Whitby Yorkshire, and they are still awestruck all these years later.

Another one. The day Mayor Rob told me I didn't need to check out the goat races prior to the next Trailblazer. "Nothing ever goes wrong."

I decided to check them out anyway and the first race saw a cart and goat and rider spear into the crowd and an ambulance needed to cart the

THE BRIGHTER SIDE OF A DEATH THREAT

injured to hospital. Rob's famous saying is, "No worries, she'll be right."

So many great yarns.

Along the way, we raised over half-a-million for Bill Bristow's Angel Flight team, spent heaps in small communities and created a wealth of national and international positive media stories for Queensland's bush. Way beyond our wildest dreams.

It is dangerous to start thanking individuals when so many gave so much—however. Tania K., Mayor Rob and the BRC team, all at RAPAD, Action Graphics, Marney, the TPD team, the invaluable John and Maureen Brand, Stonestreets, Woolums and GT—take a bow. You led us all through so many wonderful concerts, special events and experiences never to be forgotten. Thanks to our superb sponsors and longtime supporters.

There was definitely a tear in the eye as Helen and I drove east out of Winton after that huge final weekend and into the next chapter of our lives.

R.I.P. Andrea and Butch—two wonderful souls. We miss you dearly.

Meanwhile, life continued with us living in our beaut, waterside townhouse at Clear Island Waters. We loved it. Helen had more wildlife families than Noah had on the Ark. Cockatoos, lizards, swans, rainbow lorikeets, magpies—even a wild fox living under a balcony. She was one happy girl.

I had joined the gym—Fitness First—across the road. I had a fall on the treadmill which caused chaos but, overall, enjoyed both the gym and the heated pool year-round for many years.

On a sad/happy note, my father's brother, Harry, and his wife, Betty, had lived in the same house in Eastwood for over sixty years. They were a wonderful couple, married for over seventy years and very close to all of us. Harry finally turned up his toes in his mid nineties. His funeral at Eastwood was a real celebration and his beloved Parramatta league team colours were draped over the coffin, and their theme song played as he left the church. Betty passed away a few weeks after. Lovely people—we will miss them.

My old Daydream boss, Joy Collins, was 'losing it' and she had no family. The old staff took her to lunch regularly and every year on her birthday. When she was 80, we organised with her to pick her up at 12 noon for a 12.30 p.m. lunch.

Patsy came with Helen and I to pick her up, and the others went straight to the restaurant at Ashmore. Helen rang her apartment and Joy said, "You're early. I'll be straight down."

The receptionist told us she was very excited. We had a fabulous lunch. Around 3 p.m. we drove Joy home. The receptionist gasped, "What have you done?"

It turns out Joy, herself, had organised forty guests plus entertainment at the Marriott Hotel, plus Joy had also organised with Mayor Tom Tate a lunch with twenty-five people at Toms Islander Hotel. The only reason she went with us was that we turned up first. Joy had no idea.

Then she started having bad falls. After three very serious falls, we could not work out why the hospital were sending her home. The nurses said they were unable to talk to us—just the Power of Attorney, her former next door neighbour. Patsy then found out that he had wheeled Joy into his Solicitor and had her will changed, leaving her apartment and money to him.

We were all shattered. Now we knew why they kept sending her home. He wanted his inheritance. Every one of us knew that Joy had always wanted half her estate to go to the Surfers Paradise Lifesavers and half to Young Care.

To cut a long saga short, we ended up in a legal battle, but because nine of us told the same story and had not one cent to gain—we won and he was struck off. Trouble was, Patsy and I were then appointed Powers of Attorney and Sue Smith Executor of her will. This started a very sad three years watching her go downhill. All of us acknowledge the incredible job Helen did, almost single handedly, looking after Joy seven days a week. She is now doing that for her dad who is here in care at Bupa Pottsville Beach.

The end result, the lifesavers and Youngcare each got their fifty per cent share of the estate—a victory for the good guys. Joy would have been very happy.

There were many tears at the Surfers Paradise Surf Lifesaving Club as we all watched the surfboat crew out at sea with raised oars, as Joy's ashes went into her beloved Gold Coast ocean, as had her mum's some years ago. Every year in perpetuity, a young lifesaver will win the $5,000 Joy Collins' Scholarship. This week, Club President, world Ironman champion, Trevor Hendy and I were meeting to decide the 2020 winner, but the border-closing

THE BRIGHTER SIDE OF A DEATH THREAT

and Corona Virus have put that on hold for the moment.

Around this time, SKAL International—a world-wide tourism travel organisation who had been terrific to me at Country Comfort, were setting up a new club in Australia—Southern Gold Coast. They chartered at the National Congress in Brisbane in March 2014 with me as President and an American lass, Amery Burleigh, General Manager of Sofitel Gold Coast, as Vice President. The International SKAL President from Paris was there to personally hand us our charter as Club No. 717 around the world. Twenty three of these are in Australia.

And it was just last year when mum's sister, Sheila, passed away at ninety six. Great lady, fabulous artist.

Her memorial service was conducted by my brother, Barry, at North Sydney, and it was a terrific celebration—at the end of that generation. Very sad.

It was now time to slow down. That is until I read an article in the *Courier Mail* one day about plans to build a children's hospice in Brisbane.

CHAPTER 21

HUMMINGBIRD HOUSE CHILDREN'S HOSPICE—ANOTHER GREAT PROJECT

'Dream as if you'll live forever. Live as if you'll die today.'
...James Dean

After my fantastic 70th birthday on Daydream Island—where it all began when I was working there when I met Helen fifty years ago—I declared I would slow down... sort of... after the final Trailblazer. After all, I now possess a lengthening past and shortening future, (thanks Helen Garnor) and need to change pace, but not stop! They say we 'only live once'. That is not really true. To me, we only die once but we live everyday, and as I approach eighty, there are still a number of items on the bucket list and things I can achieve.

Our lives have been full of special people, special times, special events. Helen and I have been lucky enough to see our three kids blossom, achieve, breed and succeed—in many parts of the world.

Over the past few years, visiting Wazz & Lou and the three girls—Evy, Bridget and Andrea—in Exmouth WA, or, more precisely, Learmonth Airforce Base, and a number of trips to the U.K. to stay with Mel, Lyth, Angus and Isla in Yorkshire, plus many great stays with Ash, Marney, Tiah and

Boston in Sydney, we realised just how wonderful life is and how much we have been blessed with not only an extended family but an amazing circle of friends we have been privileged to meet along our journey. Our family and friends reunions are sensational.

Our own lifestyle—the years on the waters' edge at Clear Island Waters—could not have been any better.

One day at The Lakes, Helen pointed out a feature article in the *Courier Mail* written by Frances Whiting about Queensland families using Bear Cottage Children's Hospice in Sydney. It threw me a bit, as we had always thought of Bear Cottage only servicing N.S.W., but soon I realised that there was no children's hospice in Queensland. The U.K. had grown to fifty-three, but we only had two: 'Very Special Kids' in Melbourne and Bear Cottage.

The article told the story of a Brisbane couple, Paul and Gabrielle Quilliam, a former oncology nurse and her hubby, now fostering young babies with serious challenges, who had a dream to build Hummingbird House Children's Hospice in Brisbane. The story went on that a Queensland family using Bear Cottage insisted the Quilliams come down to Sydney to check it out. They were on the ferry nearing Manly when Paul's mobile rang. It was the family advising their little girl had just passed away, "…but keep coming".

So Paul and Gabrielle saw, first hand, the incredible services performed by a children's hospice. The whole article was a great read. It made Helen and I even prouder of the work we had put into Bear Cottage all those years ago, and the ongoing terrific results. I realised that two of our original committee, Gary Pemberton and Mel Gotleib, were now in Queensland, so I sent a copy of the article to them that day.

I then sent an email to Paul and Gabrielle wishing them well, telling them of our involvement with Bear Cottage, and offering to have a coffee with them if they were ever on the Gold Coast. Within two hours, Paul was on the phone. The week that followed was the start of another wonderful chapter in our lives.

Firstly, Helen and I met with Gabrielle and Paul and instantly recognised we were talking to a dynamic, talented, decent, enthusiastic duo. Wow. What we didn't know was that Gary P. and Mel Gotleib would also reach out to them that week.

THE BRIGHTER SIDE OF A DEATH THREAT

The results were instant and life changing. Marg and Gary asked the Quilliams to present their project. They were obviously as impressed as we were. Paul and Gabrielle walked away with over $3 million to match the promised Government funding, and their dream was underway. They were gobsmacked and a little tearful. Then Mel G. sat with them and, as usual, showered them with a prestige, vintage vehicle, memorabilia, valuable furnishings, a new golf buggy and more.

For our part, we also introduced the Quilliams to our great friends at Woollam Constructions and, along with our other corporate supporters, the Wagners and Phil Stonestreet, we developed a terrific 'flying Trailblazer'—an air safari convoy of light aircraft leaving Wellcamp Airport and a brilliant week in Queensland's outback and Daydream Island (where else!) to take place in October 2017.

We certainly had mixed results. First—the good news. Woollams were selected to construct Hummingbird House and it turned out to be a terrific decision in every way—a real win-win. The building and concept have already won many national and international awards and Woollam's brought many very generous industry colleagues on board during the construction phase. What a top job they did. Well done Craig, George and team. The whole Hummingbird House team are in awe of your building and ongoing support.

The not so good news was that in March 2017 cyclone Debbie wiped out the Whitsundays and Daydream Island was closed, causing us to postpone the air safari for twelve months. We then realised the $100 million rebuild was going to take all of 2018 as well, so we cancelled the event.

The good news is that between our good mates, Woollams, the Wagners, Phil Stonestreet, RAPAD and the Toowoomba community, we did contribute some $80,000 plus to the Hummingbird House Foundation during those two years, and we all celebrated with a fantastic 'thank you' and second birthday party at Toowoomba's 'Downs Steam' historic railway museum in October 2018. Some eighty supporters had sherry and aperitifs as they rode in the 1930 Gatsby Flyer train and later celebrated in the finest dining car in Queensland, serenaded by a brilliant barber shop choir—the High Altitude Singers—and sipping delicious Ballandean Estate wines. Some great things never change.

Hummingbird House Children's Hospice opened it's doors as part of the Wesley complex at Chermside in October 2016 under the guidance of

LANCE SMITH

Dr. Fiona Hawthorn and her team.

In less than three years, they have established a reputation as world leaders in children's palliative care, respite and after death support.

The Quilliams handed over the completed project and stepped away in late 2018. History will be very kind to them and the incredible strength and tenacity required to achieve such high success. Queensland will be forever grateful to Paul and Gabrielle. They are destined to great things, and we are privileged to be a small part of their dynamic team over the past five years. We had lucked in—again!

Paul was recently flown to London to receive world-wide recognition of their well deserved success. And to cap it all off, my old Country Comfort boss, D.C.O.C., who did so much for Bear Cottage, recently donated $5,000 to Hummingbird House on our behalf.

Back to our world. The dark clouds were gathering.

CHAPTER 22

IT'S FAREWELL FROM ME

At birth we bring nothing with us.
At death we take nothing away.
...An old Chinese proverb.

Let me say at the outset, my age isn't bothering me, it's the side effects!!!

We were organising an extended family week-long gathering down at Ulladulla/Batemans Bay for early 2017. Forty-three of the possible forty-four were coming. (Shane had a great excuse—he was competing in the Rotterdam Triathlon in Holland).

About a month before, I had been experiencing some strange aches, pains and haemorrhaging, so trotted off for tests. I was diagnosed with a high-grade, aggressive, muscle-invasive bladder cancer. The first surgery revealed it had penetrated various muscle layers, but had not reached the bladder outer wall. That was a plus. First time I carried 'a bag'.

I saw urologists, oncologists and specialists galore and signed up for a three-month radiation course at the John Flynn Private Hospital, and also enlisted the support of two excellent ladies—one a herbalist/naturopath and the other a great acupuncturist/holistic healer I had known for years. The team went to work.

LANCE SMITH

The family get together in Ulladulla immediately became much more important to me as the future was looking a tad uncertain. Mel, Lyth and the kids came from the U.K., Joel and Ange came from Austria, Karina, Simon and kiddies came from New Zealand, Waz, Lou and kids came from Western Australia and we had an absolutely wonderful week of fun and games and were visited by many of our Batemans Bay friends for barbecues and picnics. It doesn't get any better.

The radiation course was okay. There were many others knocked around far worse than I was. Anyway, the end result was a complete clearance. Much celebration.

My combined 75th birthday with Virginia in 2018, held at Mount Panorama Bathurst, was a fantastic weekend. Who will forget the magic voice of Domino in the Cathedral Cave at Jenolan Caves, and I definitely had a spring in my walking stick. Life was good.

That was until later in the year, and some seventeen months after my radiation treatment, when some tell tale signs resurfaced. I went back into hospital to discover the cancer was back.

I had run out of radiation options and Dr. Chabert recommended a trial called BCG, which had been proving very successful around the world It wasn't pretty—but it sure beat the alternative.

They set me up for a weekly admission to hospital every Monday for November/December, then a break of six weeks before more anaesthetic and a cystoscopy to check the results.

In layman's terms—because I don't understand the tech stuff—a catheter is inserted into the penis, down through the prostate and into the bladder—no anaesthetic. Then a chemist comes in dressed in a martian space suit. Then a toxic poison, a strain of TB, is prepared and the new suited-up ward sister comes in and injects the solution. The room is then sealed for two hours, and I had a series of exercises to do to ensure the mixture coated the full bladder.

The idea is that as soon as the brain gets a message about the poison, it signals every good immune cell in the body to head to the bladder and 'eat' the poison. At the same time they 'eat' the cancer… and over the next day you pee it out. Strict cleaning precautions were used in this process.

The next eight hours were bad news. Every Monday night. Probably worse for Helen than me. The Tuesday's were pretty ordinary, but I came

THE BRIGHTER SIDE OF A DEATH THREAT

good most Wednesdays. I was laid up with urinary infection twice, which delayed the process a bit.

But—in February last year—the answer. Another one hundred percent clearance. So we set off to the U.K. for three weeks, then followed up with a great week with fifty close friends and old staff on Daydream Island. And boy did it all go well.

The U.K. trip found us in Yorkshire at Barmby Moor to check out the amazing restoration work being carried out on 'The Manor House' by Lyth and Mel. A huge project, but they are well up for the challenge. We went for a week's family holiday in Cornwall. Lyth had rented a fabulous cottage on the waterfront at Fowey, just metres away from the marina and jetty where his boat was moored.

We went fishing, crabbing, barbecuing and more. Whilst there, we took Helen to the southern-most tip of the U.K.—Landsend—and also went to a show 'The Secret Garden' at the most unbelievable theatre I have ever seen. The Minack Theatre is open air and perched on a cliff top high above the sea. What a setting—Wow.

Then the mandatory trip to Whitby for fish and chips at Trenches with Gwyneth and Angus (Mel's inlaws) and Jim Knott's mum and sisters. Yummo!

No sooner back home and than packed off for our 'reunion' with many of our Daydream staff of fifty years ago and some long time mates.

Fifty years since I got down on bended knee at Whitehaven Beach to propose to the most beautiful person I still know. Surrounded by lifelong friends, we had the best reunion week imaginable. These two trips were originally planned as a 'farewell tour'. This now changed to a much looked forward to future.

And soon it is winter. Time has a way of moving quickly! I think Robin Stevenson got it right about how the winter of one's life catches you unaware.

It seems like yesterday that I was young, marrying my beautiful Helen, and was embarking on the new life full of hope. Yet, in a way, it seems eons ago, and I do wonder where all the years went. What I do know is that we have lived them all. I have glimpses of how it was back then and of all our hopes and dreams. But here we are in the winter of our lives, and it catches me by surprise. How did I get here so fast? Where did those seventy seven years go? Where did my youth go?

I well remember seeing older people through the years and thinking that was many years away from me—that my winter was so far off! But here it is my friends—retired and getting older and grumpier by the minute. I am moving slower and see lots of old people around me. Some are in better and some worse shape than me, but, like me, their age is showing and we are now those older folk that I used to see and never thought I would be.

And, even more ironic, our three wonderful little children are already wondering where their youth has gone. Well—get ready. Winter approaches.

Every day now, I find showering is just that much harder and taking a nap is not a treat any more. It is mandatory, because if I don't, I just fall asleep where I sit.

And so… now as I enter the final season of my life, unprepared for all the new aches and pains and the loss of strength and the ability to go and do things that I wish I had done but never did, I have to accept that winter has come and I am not sure how long it will last. Given my last three years, it is a roller coaster.

Yes—I have regrets. There are things I wish I had done better, things I wish I hadn't done, things I should have done, but, indeed, there are many many things I am happy I have done. It's all in a lifetime.

So, if you're not in your winter yet, let me remind you that it will be here faster than you think. So whatever you would like to accomplish in your life, please do it quickly. Don't put things off. Live for today and say all the things you want your loved ones to remember.

Life is a gift to you. The way you live your life is a gift to those who come after. I have tried to make it a fantastic one.

Live it well… enjoy today… do something fun… be happy… have a great day. Remember, it's health that is real wealth—and not pieces of gold and silver… oh I wish.

And the amazing part is—our kids are becoming just like us. But old is good in some things. Old songs, old movies, and best of all, old friends and old memories.

We have many to thank for such a wonderful journey. What a way to sign off… and hope there are more chapters to write. I've worked it out. I can't go back and have a brand new start… but I can start again now and

THE BRIGHTER SIDE OF A DEATH THREAT

have a brand new ending.

And, finally, can I pass on a few life long observations almost eighty years in the making? There is one thing you must do… look at the world in a positive fashion and through rose coloured glasses. For example, my stomach *is* flat—it's just that the 'L' is silent.

"There are only two days in a year when nothing is achievable—'yesterday' and 'tomorrow', so today is the right day to love, to achieve, to believe, to dream and… mostly….. .to live."

That comes from the Dalai Lama.

There are only four things you cannot get back.

- The stone after it is thrown
- The words… after you have said them
- The opportunity… after it has been missed and
- The time… after it has passed.

There is a song, 'I Was Born With A Smile On My Face….my whole life has been a pantomime'—great words and true of me. Despite the few assholes I have met and obstacles confronted in my pantomime, I have never wiped the smile off my face… and never will. We have had a great run.

I keep hearing the words 'age related'. Just recently I have realised how closely related I am.

There is a wonderful world out there. Enjoy it.

Finally—today is the first day of the rest of your life. Make the most of it.

Start where you are

Use what you've got

Do what you can… easy.

Thanks for such a wonderful innings.

We are too soon old…..and too late smart.

ABOUT THE AUTHOR

Lance assumes that the few people who brave his ramblings and pour through these pages will know him well. However, just in case you found a copy at the tip or in some giveaway lucky dip, Lance and Helen met in the Whitsunday Islands not long after his return from living and working in Europe and the UK in the 1960s. They married 50 years ago.

As far as his heart is concerned, 'Home' is still Batemans Bay, where they reared their three children. They now have seven grandchildren living all over the globe, whilst they are happily retired and living on the beach at beautiful Hastings Point in Northern NSW.

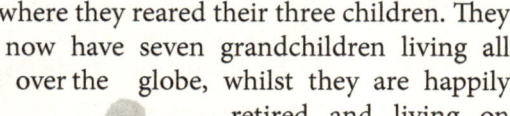

Lance and Helen still love life and their wealth of wonderful memories. And, yes, it is obvious, this is his first attempt at writing.

www.ingramcontent.com/pod-product-compliance
Lightning Source LLC
Chambersburg PA
CBHW020419010526
44118CB00010B/334